Roman Dirge's

LENORE
WEDGIES

Collecting "Lenore", issues 5-8

Written and Illustrated by
Roman Dirge
Publication Design by Christopher

Published by Slave Labor Graphics
848 The Alameda
San Jose, CA 95126

First Edition: October 2000
ISBN: 0-943151-31-7

LENORE: WEDGIES

Contents

WEDGIES

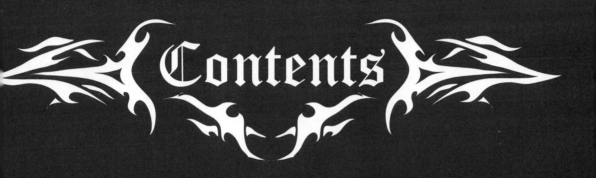

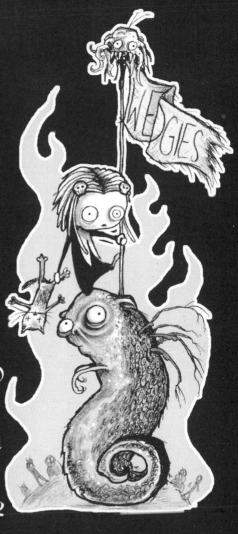

Introduction...

Did I tell you I 'ReaLLy' like LeNore? Hello HeLL OOOO...
click click click click... thhhwaap

Sometimes betrayal lunges, like a phantom knife, past the sick, abandoned shock of tickle hair growing undisturbed in the middle of the spleen. last minute last images lasting inside seeping out - the burned rat, the vivisected spiritboy, the subconscious leftovers. as the knifing task is finished, we are none so lucky as sweet Lenore - none so lucky as to have roman sew back together these body parts of emotion: his breathing of life, curiosity, and ambition flows into us vicariously through her.

Tale wagging and taxidermy of the barbie doll squirrel, the samurai sloth, supping on the intestine noodles inked all quietly disturb - in the deep down rolling wrenching manner: only a slight bobbing in your boat far out to see, but knowing some one laying lax on some shore is sure to be screwed. whether these optik messages take shape in full scale gnome slaughter or sublimely domesticating the kitty, Lenore's perverse and dark sides serve to wash and continually test an already disturbing and irritating 'reality'.

The world of Lenore dances brilliantly between the clearly insane and childish musings of never grown uppers. She is a walking dichotomy; in death she should be void of anything of substance of anything hidden and secret; in reanimation, she should at best be a mobile shell - vapid and plain. Twisted vexing on me, she is none of this - she pulses with more life and substance than most yet to deaders; with every passed adventure she sheds another dainty skin revealing more locked secrets to the reader. unmanaged and uncouth, the antithesis of sugar and spice and everything nice - perhaps this is the most endearing thing about her; past her death and with no care for etiquette she's set up shop a mile beyond the precocious city limits and straight into the downtown one avoids at night.

One's mind can't help ponder, one's eyes set to wander - what closure will be found in her days and nights of the undead adventures - what will assuage the anti-debutante leaving us with tooth rot spices, grieving for our four panel vices? i've no insight to set loose, no means with which to explain the levers and switches behind the curtain.

Through Lenore, roman reminds us that what lurks inside this reanimated ragamuffin is what lurks in the one true heart of us all - six-tenths good intentions driven on by three-tenths impish malevolence roughly spackled over by one-tenth sheepish faux naiveté. so turn the page with me and reveal what dreams of schemes LeRomaNoir has provided herein...

nivek ogre
(Skinny Puppy)

> "unmanaged and uncouth, the antithesis of sugar and spice and everything nice"

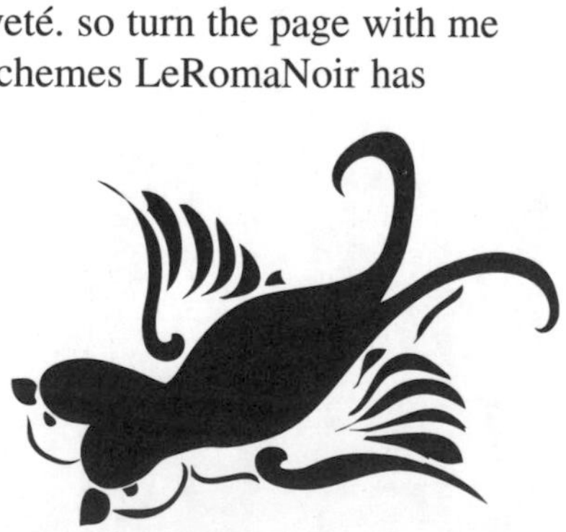

复

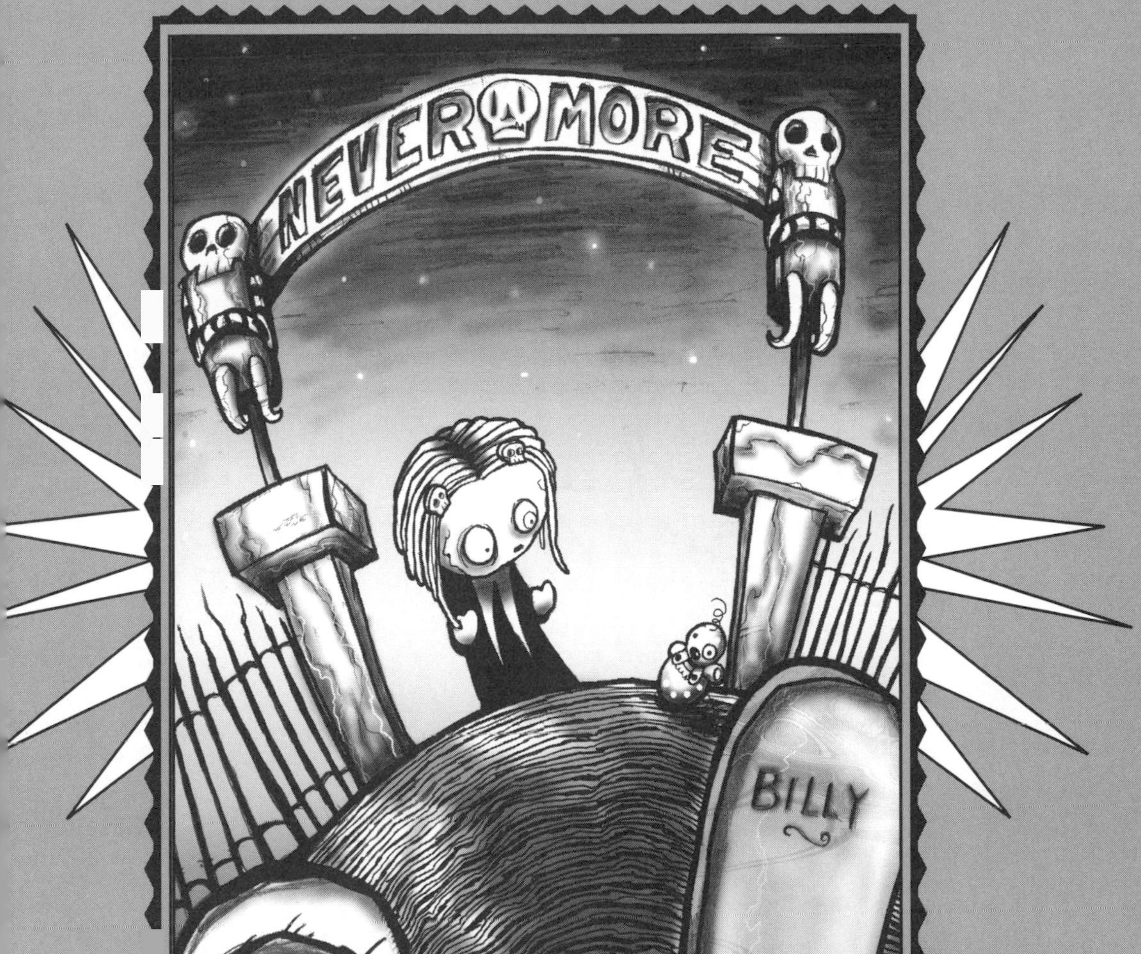
NEVERMORE
BILLY

issue five

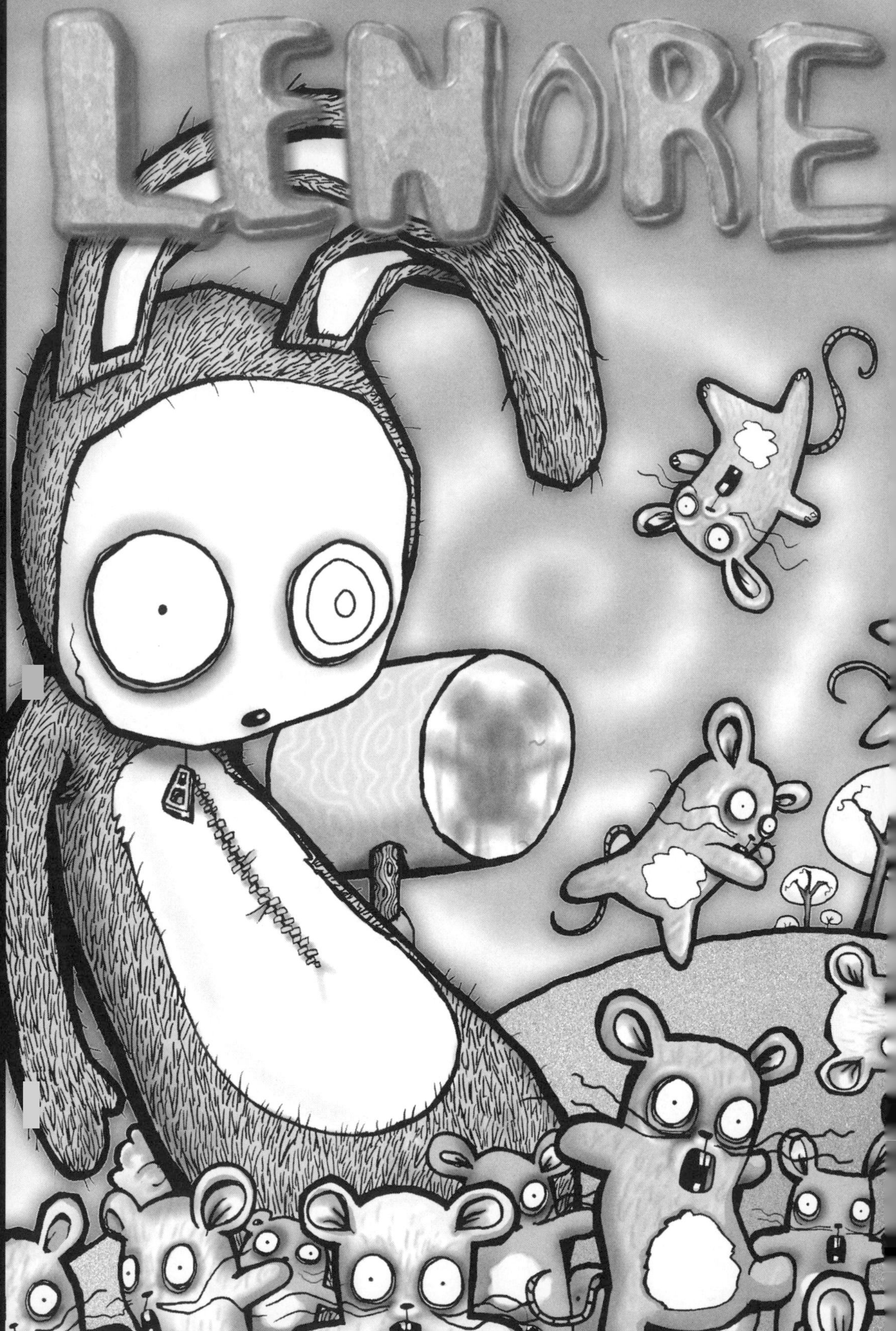
LENORE

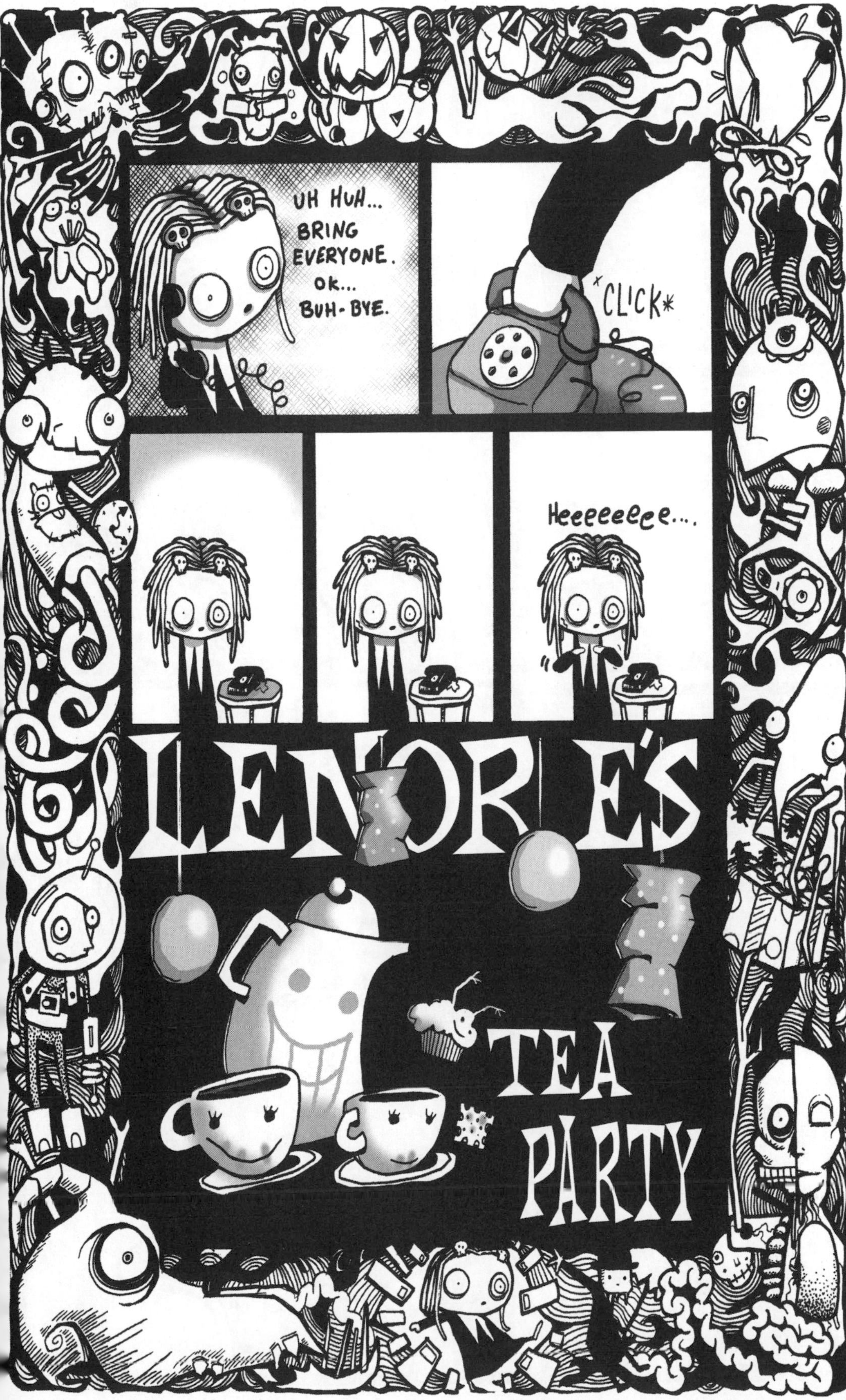
UH HUH...
BRING EVERYONE. OK... BUH-BYE.
CLICK
Heeeeeeee....
LENORE'S
TEA PARTY

♪♫ LUCK-BE A LADY TO-NITE! ♪♫

WE'RE HERE!

WOO-HOO!! HI EVERYBODY!

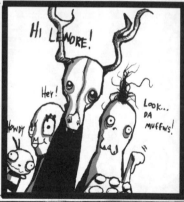

HI LENORE!

HER!

HOWDY

LOOK... DA MUFFINS!

I'M SOOO HAPPY. TAKE YOUR SEATS.

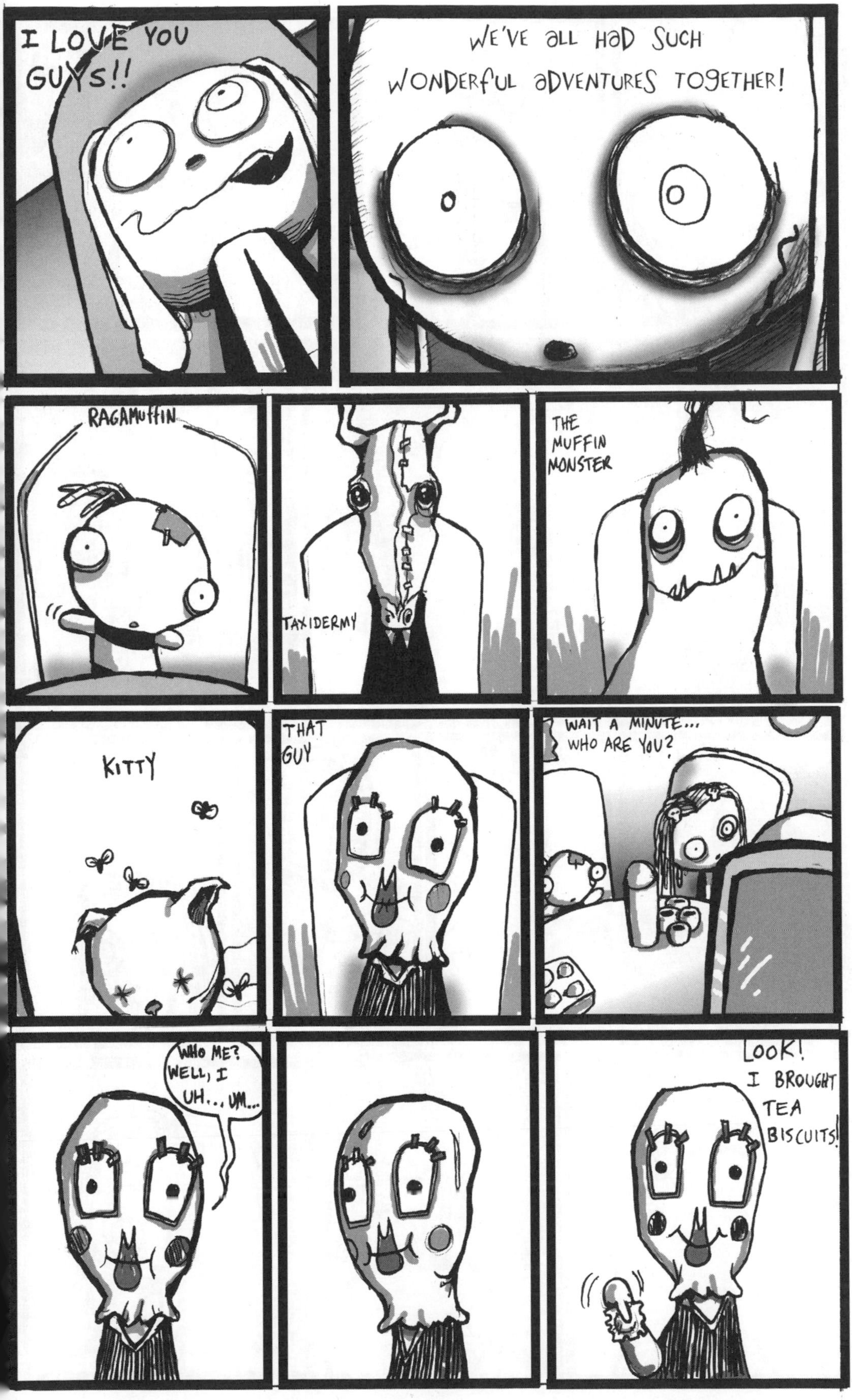
I LOVE YOU GUYS!!
WE'VE ALL HAD SUCH WONDERFUL ADVENTURES TOGETHER!
RAGAMUFFIN
TAXIDERMY
THE MUFFIN MONSTER
KITTY
THAT GUY
WAIT A MINUTE... WHO ARE YOU?
WHO ME? WELL, I UH... UM...
LOOK! I BROUGHT TEA BISCUITS!

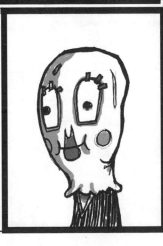

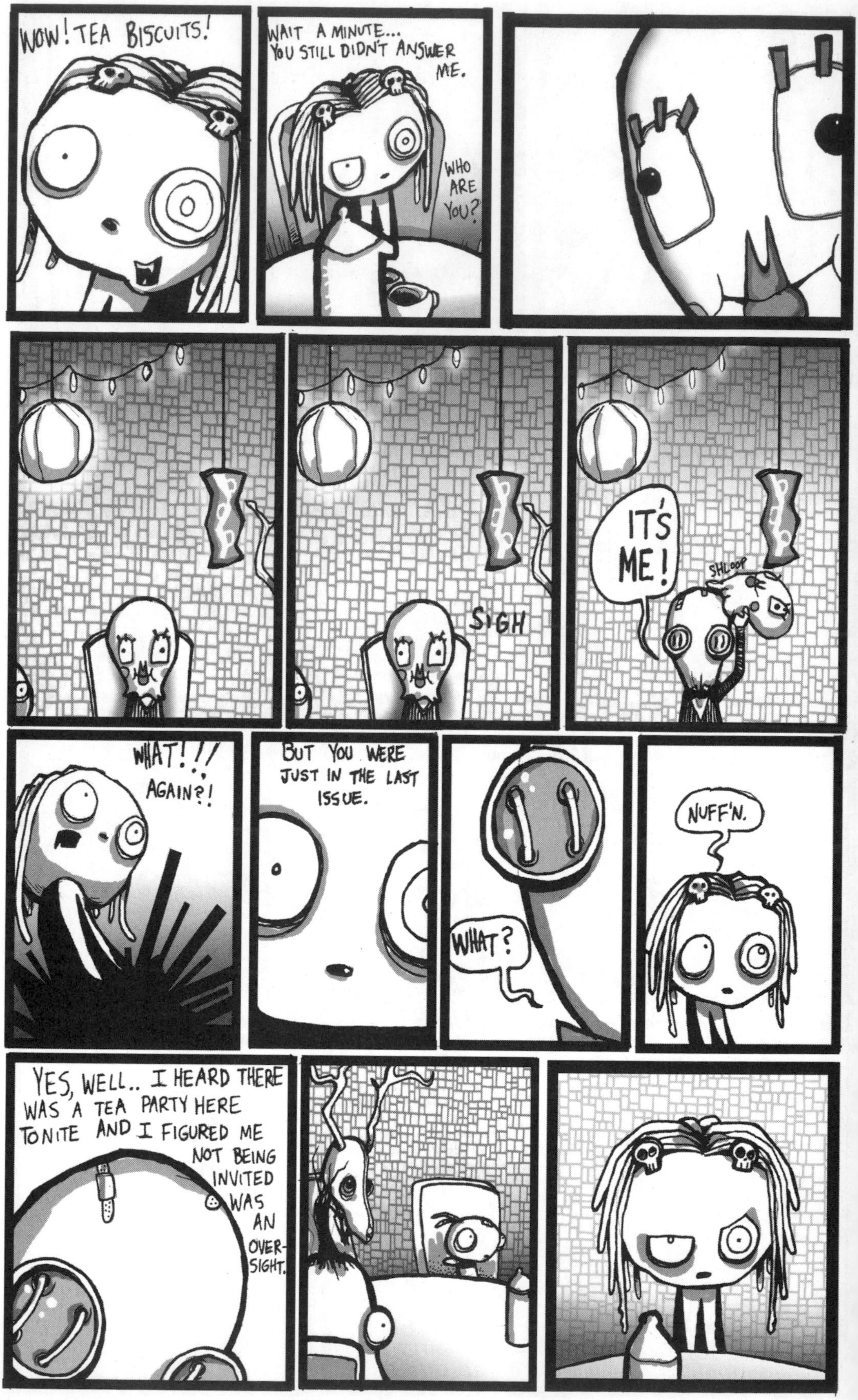
WOW! TEA BISCUITS!
WAIT A MINUTE... YOU STILL DIDN'T ANSWER ME.
WHO ARE YOU?
SIGH
IT'S ME!
SHLOOP
WHAT!!! AGAIN?!
BUT YOU WERE JUST IN THE LAST ISSUE.
WHAT?
NUFF'N.
YES, WELL.. I HEARD THERE WAS A TEA PARTY HERE TONITE AND I FIGURED ME NOT BEING INVITED WAS AN OVERSIGHT.

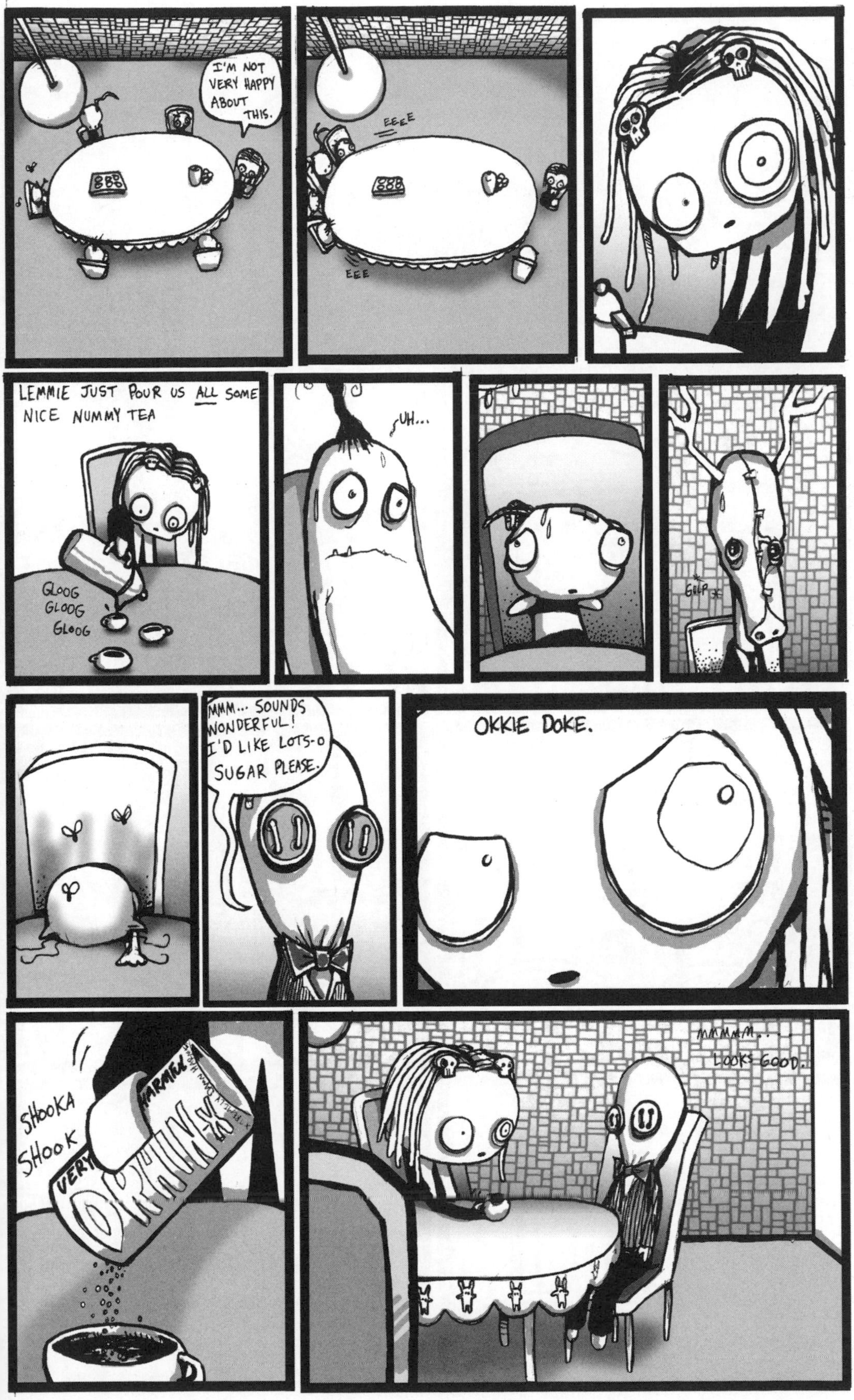
I'M NOT VERY HAPPY ABOUT THIS.
EEEE
EEE
LEMMIE JUST POUR US ALL SOME NICE NUMMY TEA
GLOOG GLOOG GLOOG
UH...
GULP
MMM... SOUNDS WONDERFUL! I'D LIKE LOTS-O SUGAR PLEASE.
OKKIE DOKE.
SHOOKA SHOOK
VERY HARMFUL DRAINX
MMMMM... LOOKS GOOD.

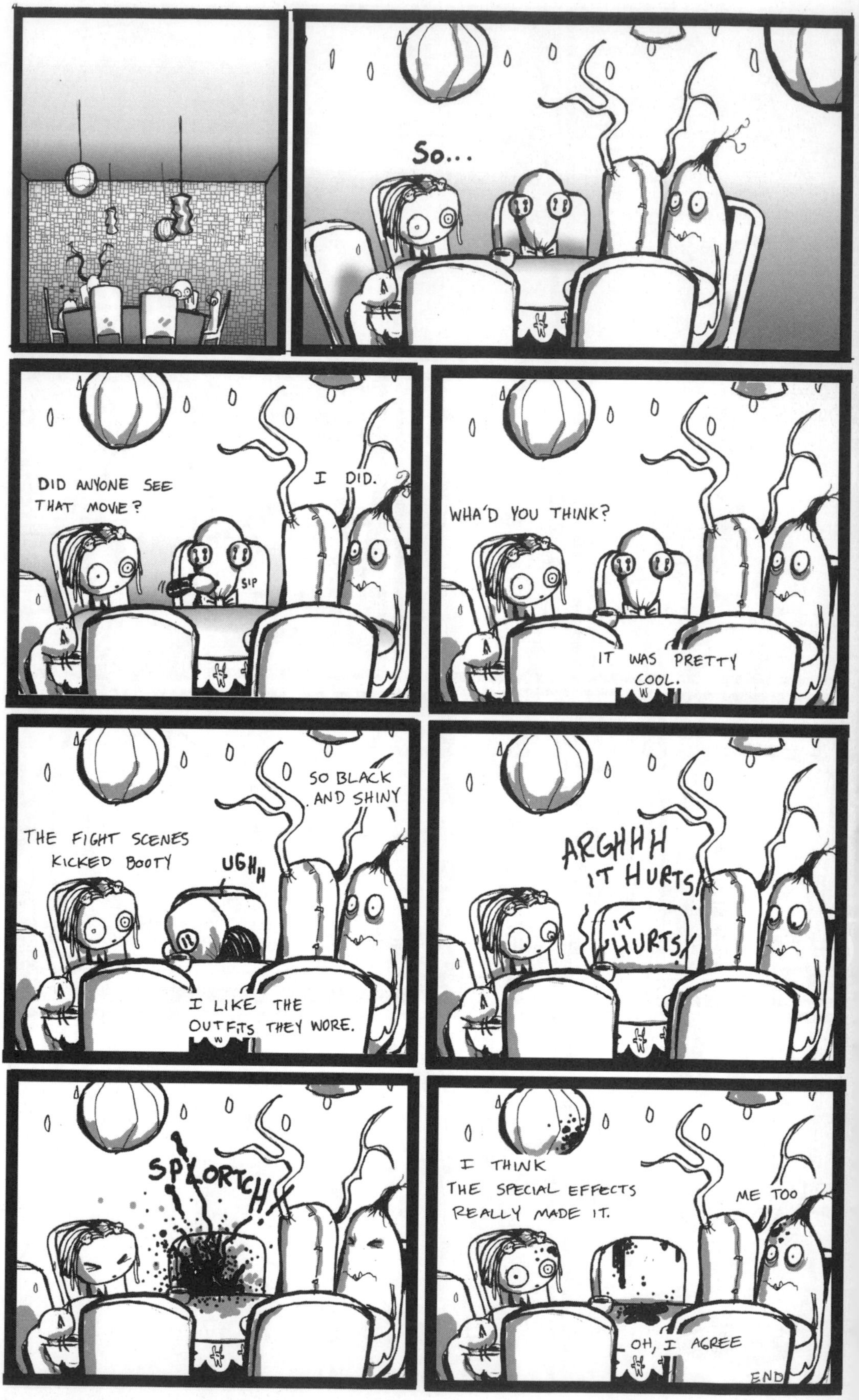
So...
DID ANYONE SEE THAT MOVIE?
I DID.
SIP
WHA'D YOU THINK?
IT WAS PRETTY COOL.
THE FIGHT SCENES KICKED BOOTY
SO BLACK AND SHINY
UGHH
I LIKE THE OUTFITS THEY WORE.
ARGHHH IT HURTS!
IT HURTS!
SPLORTCHH!
I THINK THE SPECIAL EFFECTS REALLY MADE IT.
ME TOO
OH, I AGREE
END

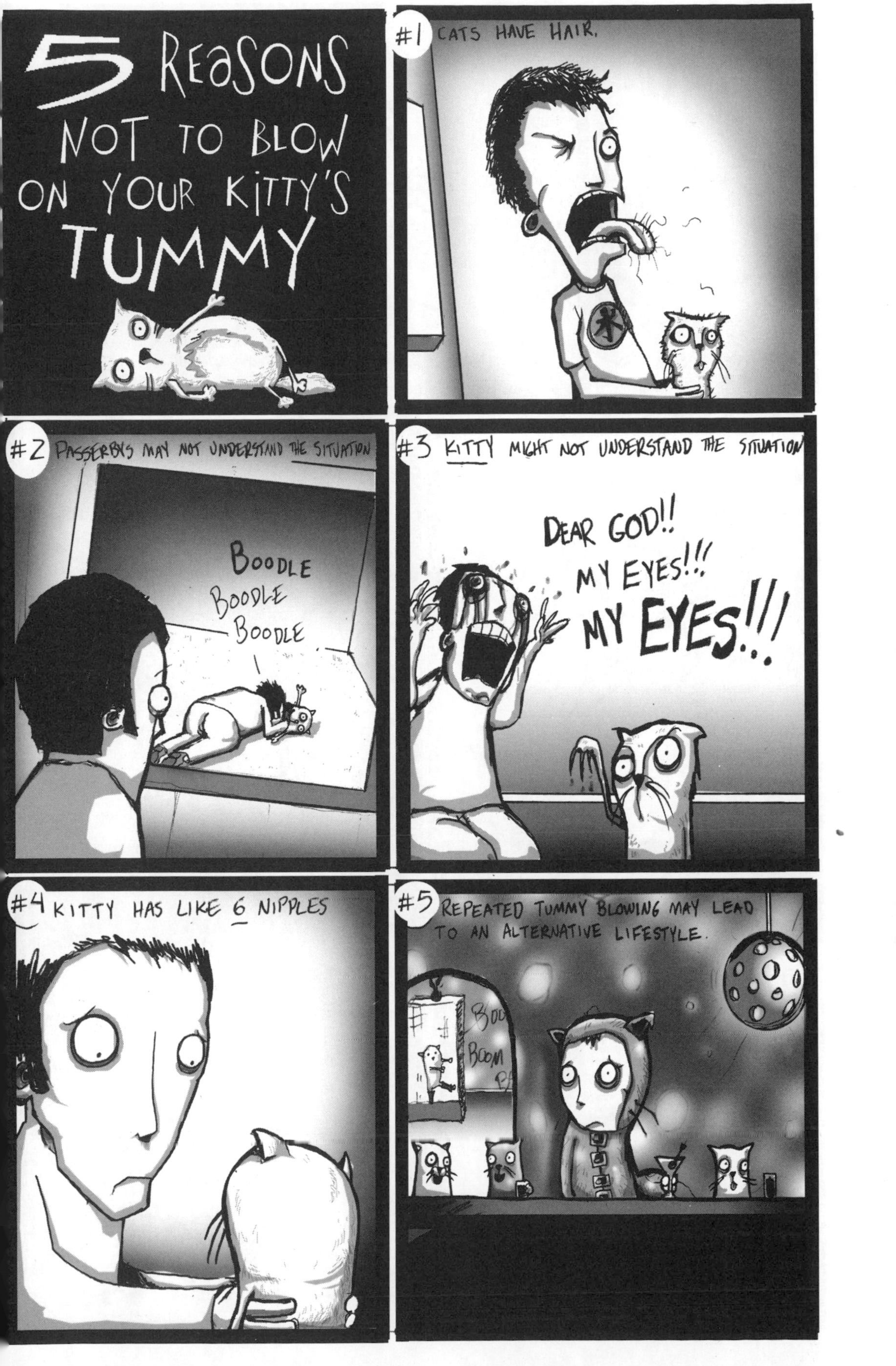
5 REASONS NOT TO BLOW ON YOUR KITTY'S TUMMY
#1 CATS HAVE HAIR.
#2 PASSERBYS MAY NOT UNDERSTAND THE SITUATION
BOODLE
BOODLE
BOODLE
#3 KITTY MIGHT NOT UNDERSTAND THE SITUATION
DEAR GOD!!
MY EYES!!!
MY EYES!!!
#4 KITTY HAS LIKE 6 NIPPLES
#5 REPEATED TUMMY BLOWING MAY LEAD TO AN ALTERNATIVE LIFESTYLE.
BOOM

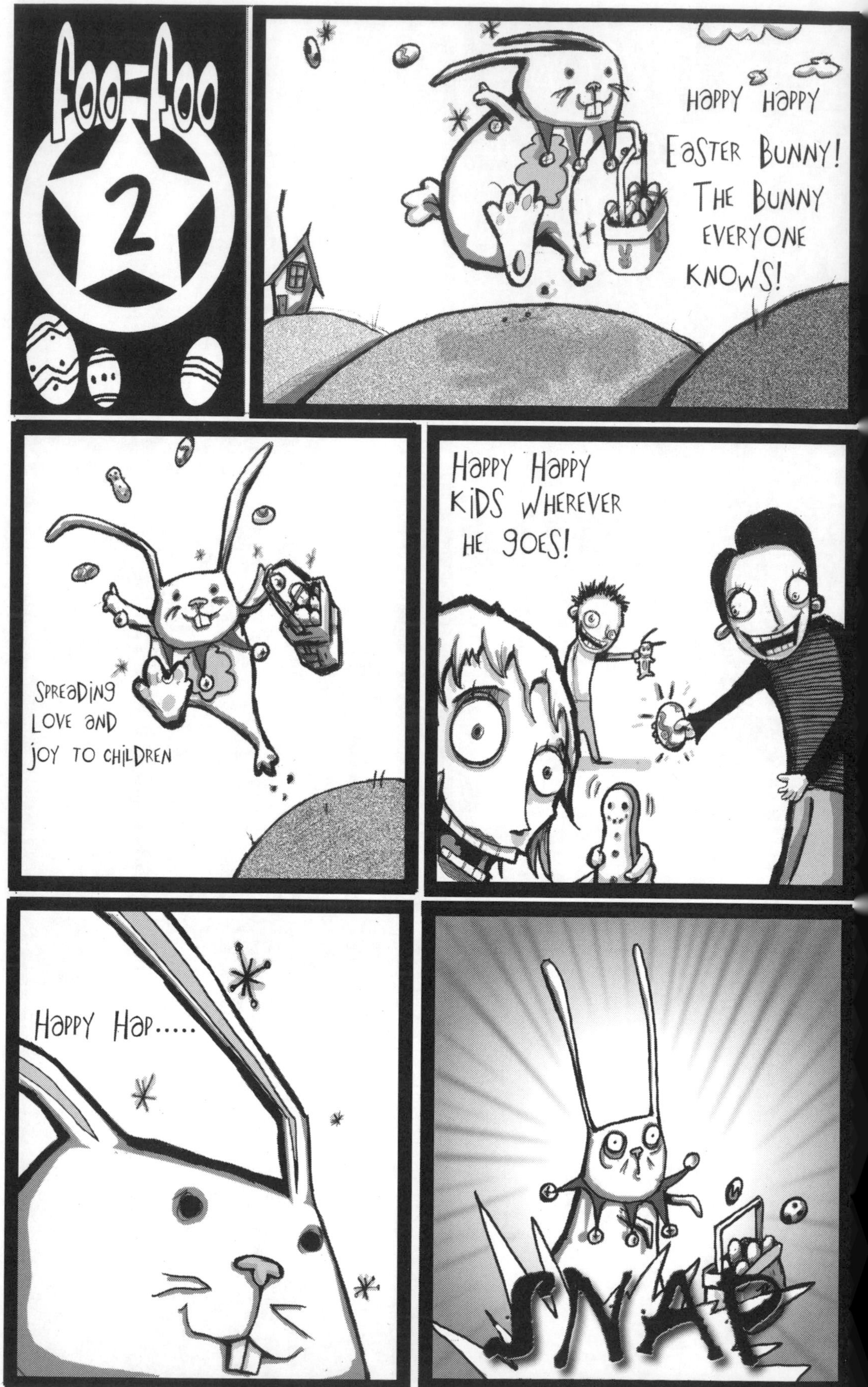
foo-foo
2
HAPPY HAPPY EASTER BUNNY! THE BUNNY EVERYONE KNOWS!
SPREADING LOVE AND JOY TO CHILDREN
HAPPY HAPPY KIDS WHEREVER HE GOES!
HAPPY HAP.....
SNAP

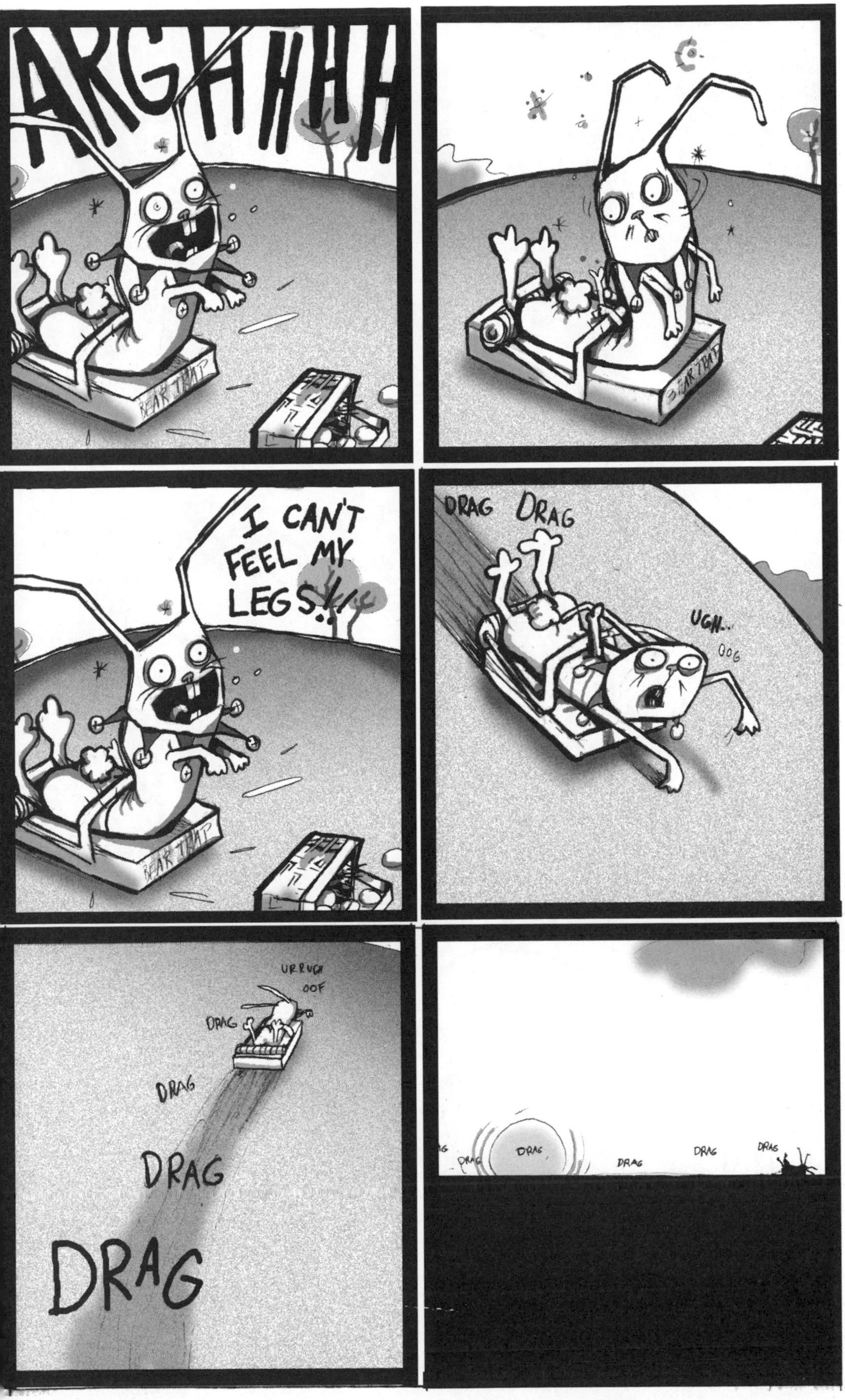
ARGHHHH
BEAR TRAP
BEAR TRAP
I CAN'T FEEL MY LEGS!!!
BEAR TRAP
DRAG DRAG
UGH...
OOG
URRUGH
OOF
DRAG
DRAG
DRAG
DRAG
DRAG
DRAG
DRAG
DRAG
DRAG

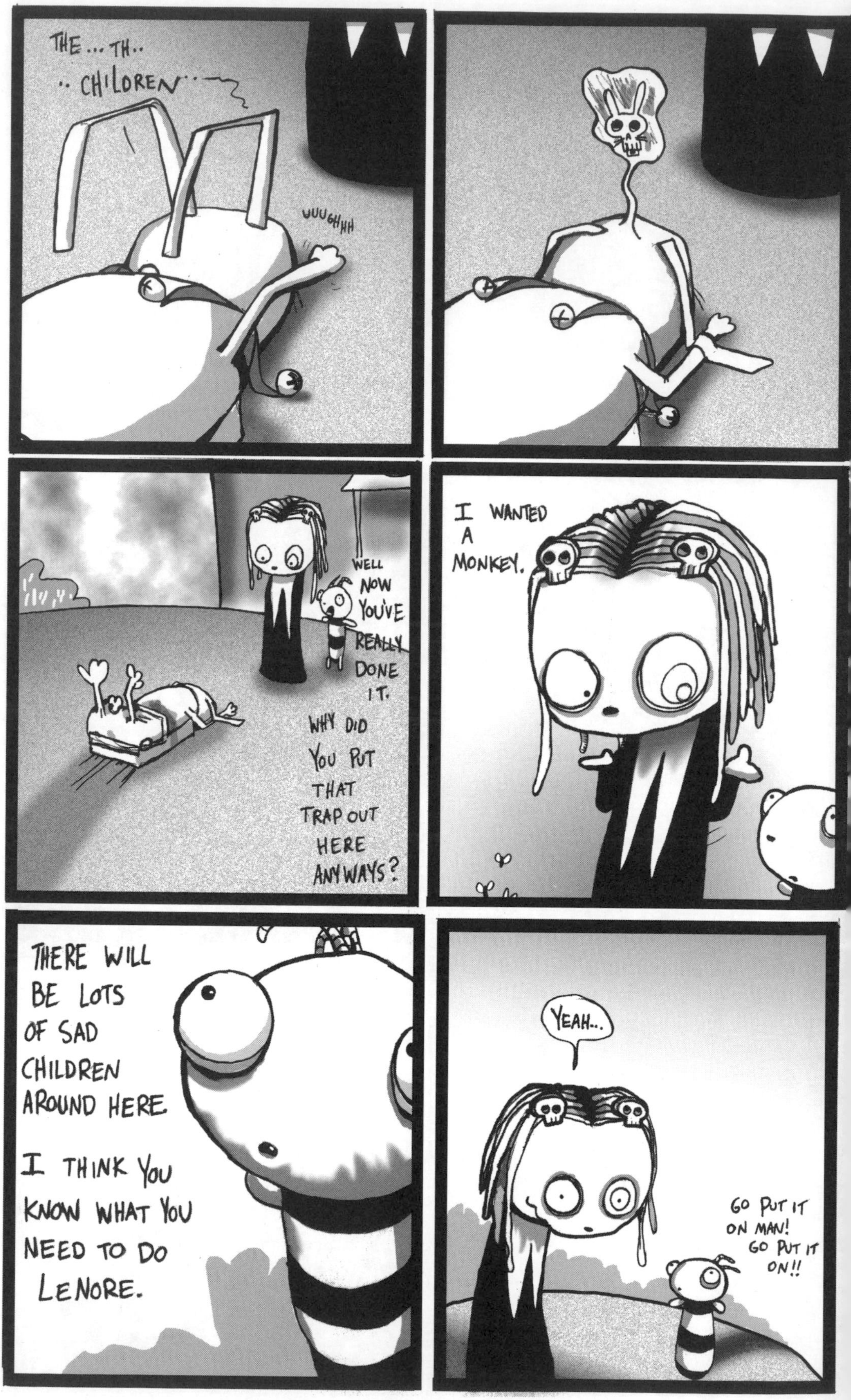
THE... TH..
.. CHILDREN..
UUUGHHH
WELL NOW YOU'VE REALLY DONE IT.
WHY DID YOU PUT THAT TRAP OUT HERE ANYWAYS?
I WANTED A MONKEY.
THERE WILL BE LOTS OF SAD CHILDREN AROUND HERE.
I THINK YOU KNOW WHAT YOU NEED TO DO LENORE.
YEAH...
GO PUT IT ON MAN! GO PUT IT ON!!

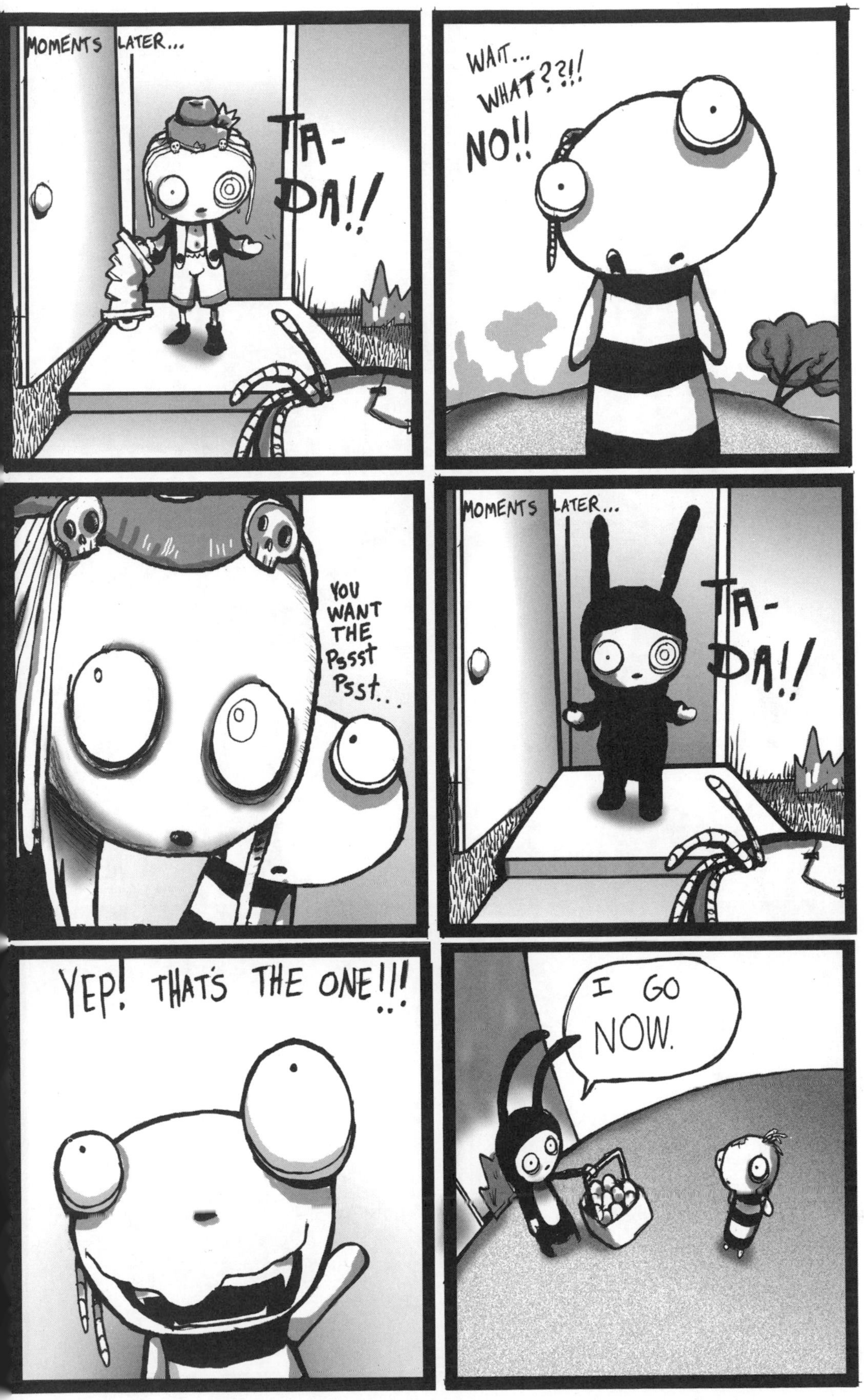
MOMENTS LATER...
TA-DA!!
WAIT...
WHAT??!!
NO!!
YOU WANT THE Pssst Psst...
MOMENTS LATER...
TA-DA!!
YEP! THAT'S THE ONE!!!
I GO NOW.

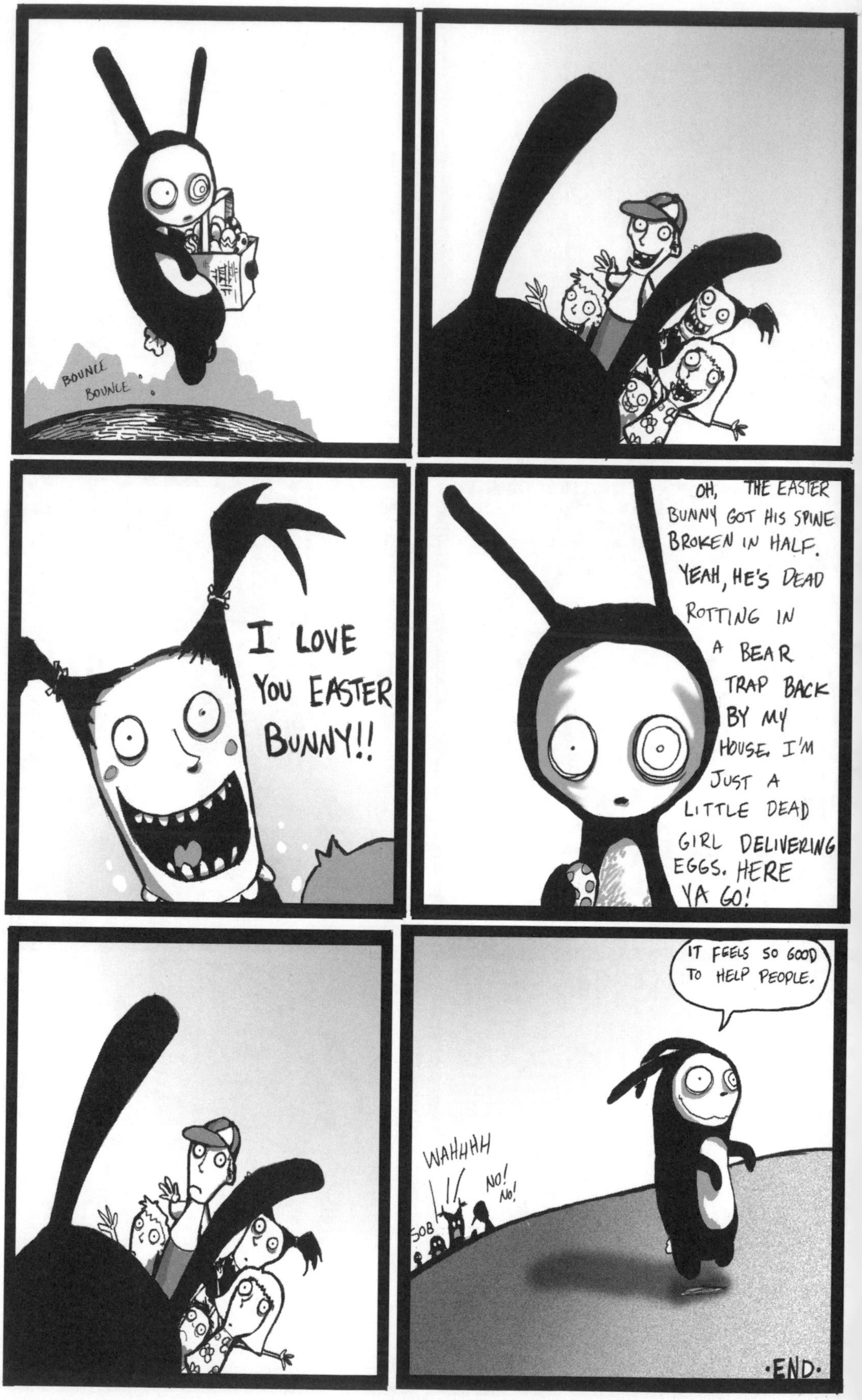
BOUNCE
BOUNCE
I LOVE YOU EASTER BUNNY!!
OH, THE EASTER BUNNY GOT HIS SPINE BROKEN IN HALF. YEAH, HE'S DEAD ROTTING IN A BEAR TRAP BACK BY MY HOUSE. I'M JUST A LITTLE DEAD GIRL DELIVERING EGGS. HERE YA GO!
IT FEELS SO GOOD TO HELP PEOPLE.
WAHHHH
NO!
NO!
SOB
•END•

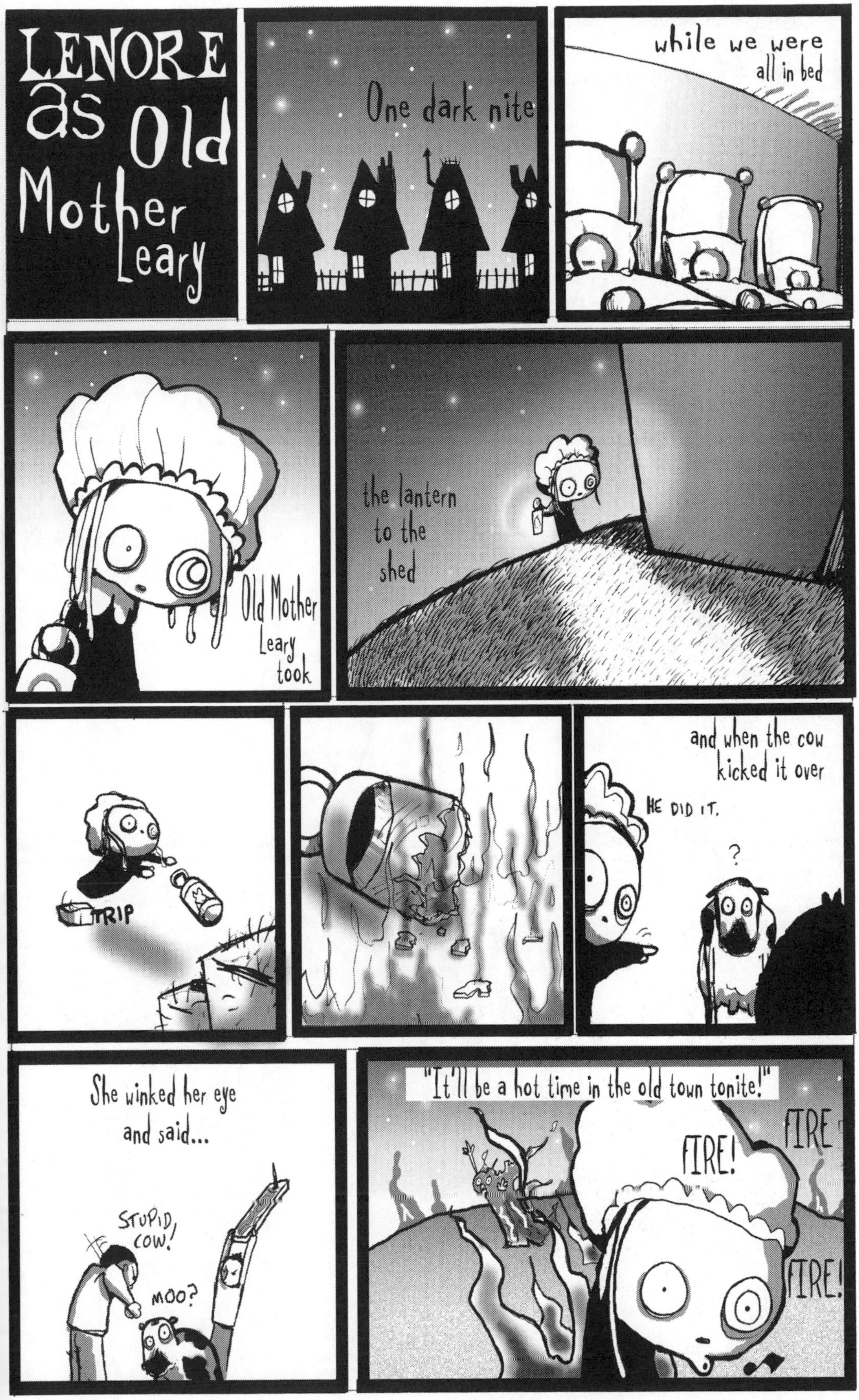
LENORE as Old Mother Leary
One dark nite
while we were all in bed
Old Mother Leary took
the lantern to the shed
TRIP
and when the cow kicked it over
HE DID IT.
?
She winked her eye and said...
STUPID COW!
MOO?
"It'll be a hot time in the old town tonite!"
FIRE!
FIRE
FIRE!

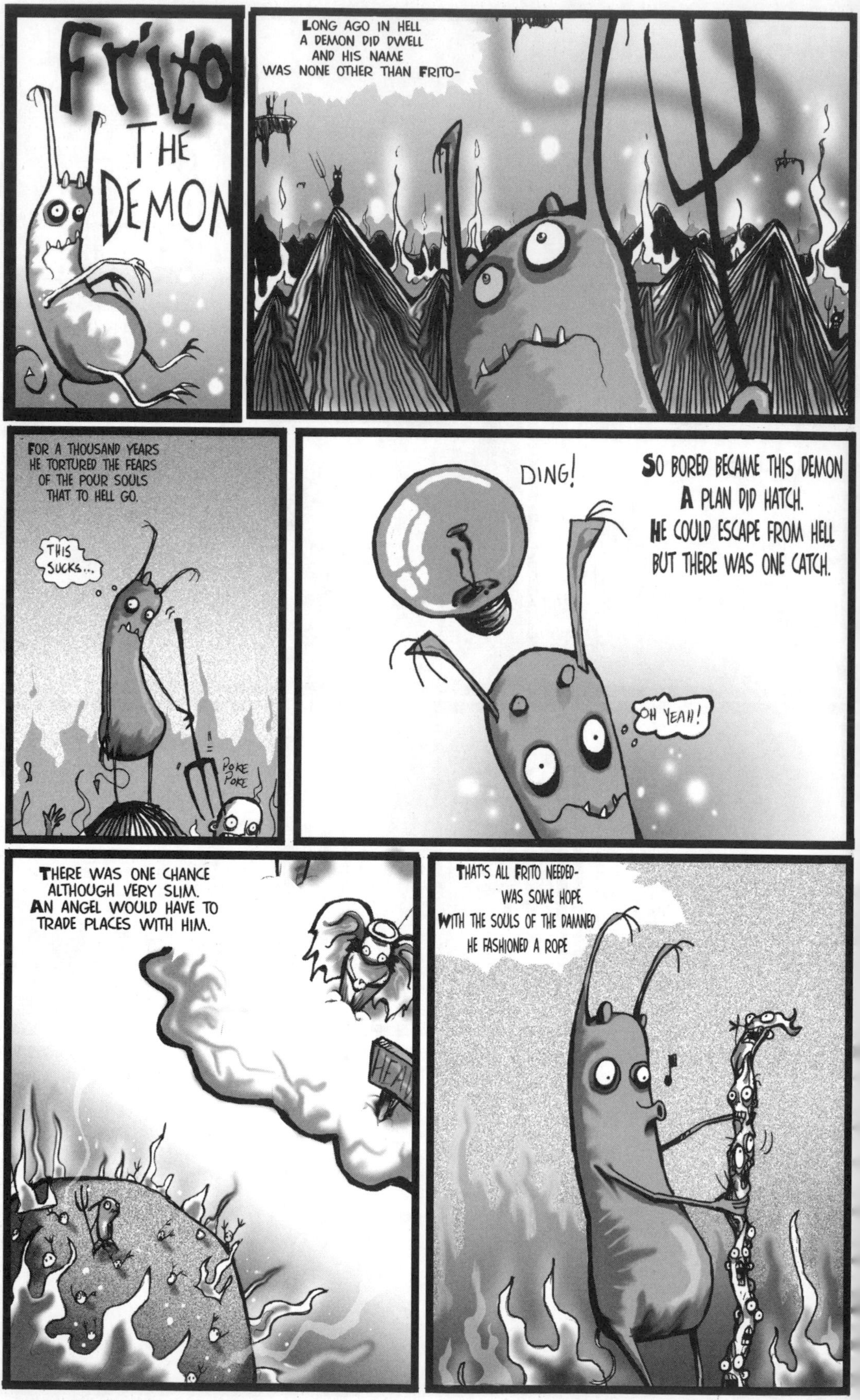
Frito THE DEMON
LONG AGO IN HELL A DEMON DID DWELL AND HIS NAME WAS NONE OTHER THAN FRITO-
FOR A THOUSAND YEARS HE TORTURED THE FEARS OF THE POUR SOULS THAT TO HELL GO.
THIS SUCKS...
POKE POKE
DING!
SO BORED BECAME THIS DEMON A PLAN DID HATCH. HE COULD ESCAPE FROM HELL BUT THERE WAS ONE CATCH.
OH YEAH!
THERE WAS ONE CHANCE ALTHOUGH VERY SLIM. AN ANGEL WOULD HAVE TO TRADE PLACES WITH HIM.
THAT'S ALL FRITO NEEDED- WAS SOME HOPE. WITH THE SOULS OF THE DAMNED HE FASHIONED A ROPE

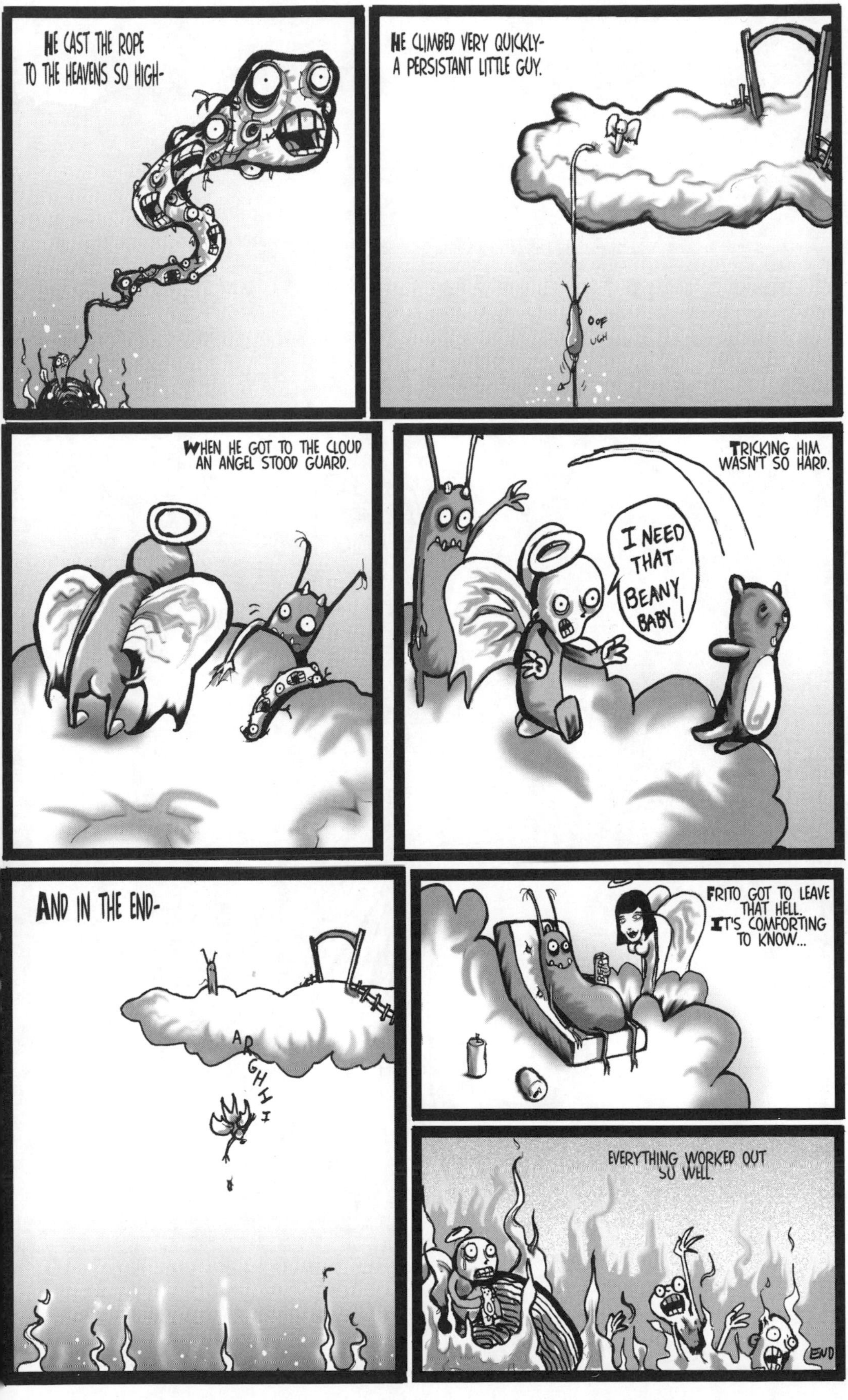
HE CAST THE ROPE
TO THE HEAVENS SO HIGH-
HE CLIMBED VERY QUICKLY-
A PERSISTANT LITTLE GUY.
OOF
UGH
WHEN HE GOT TO THE CLOUD
AN ANGEL STOOD GUARD.
TRICKING HIM
WASN'T SO HARD.
I NEED THAT BEANY BABY!
AND IN THE END-
ARGHHH
FRITO GOT TO LEAVE
THAT HELL.
IT'S COMFORTING
TO KNOW...
BEER
EVERYTHING WORKED OUT
SO WELL.
END

THE THING WHAT CAME FROM THE POOPY CHAIR

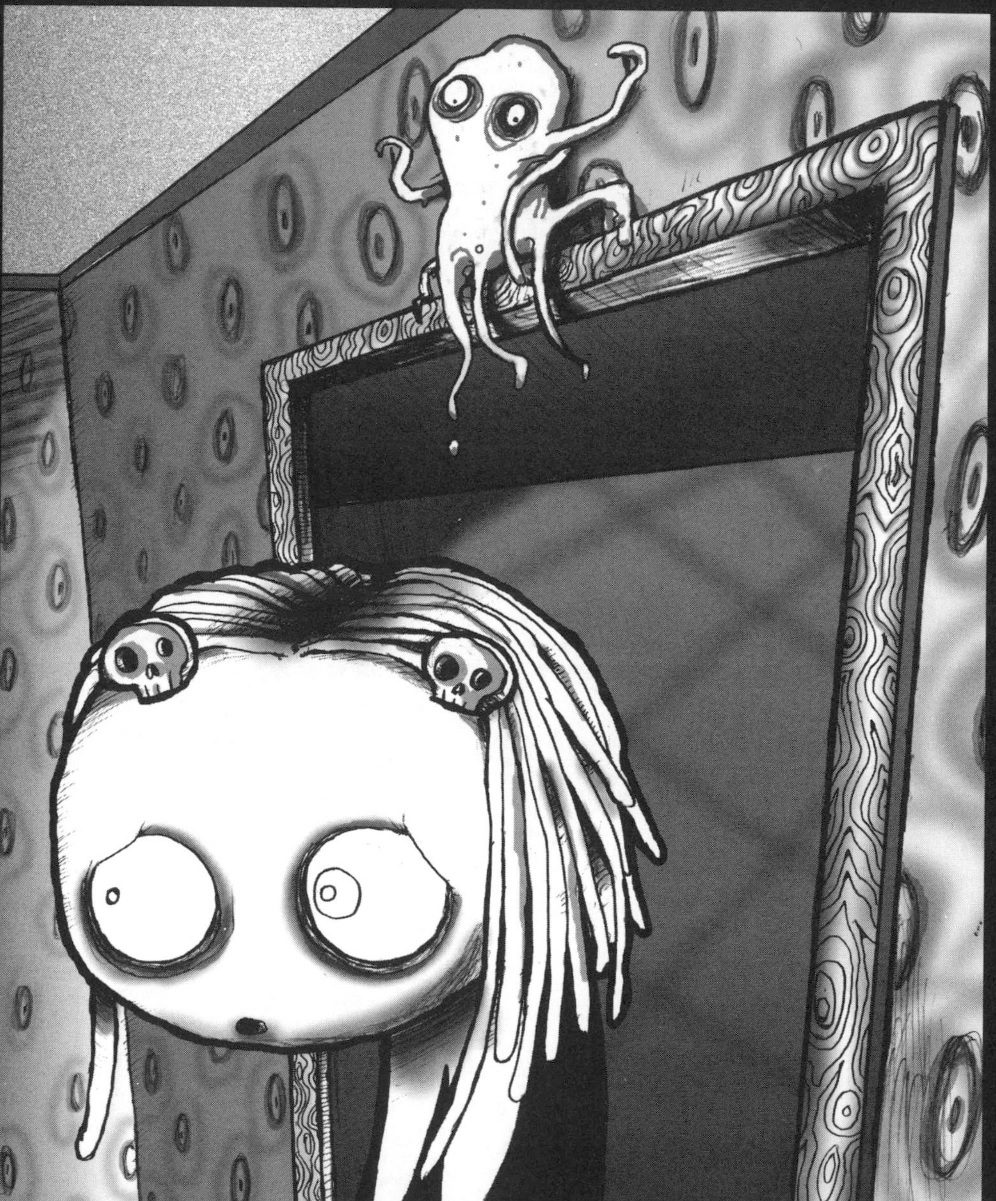

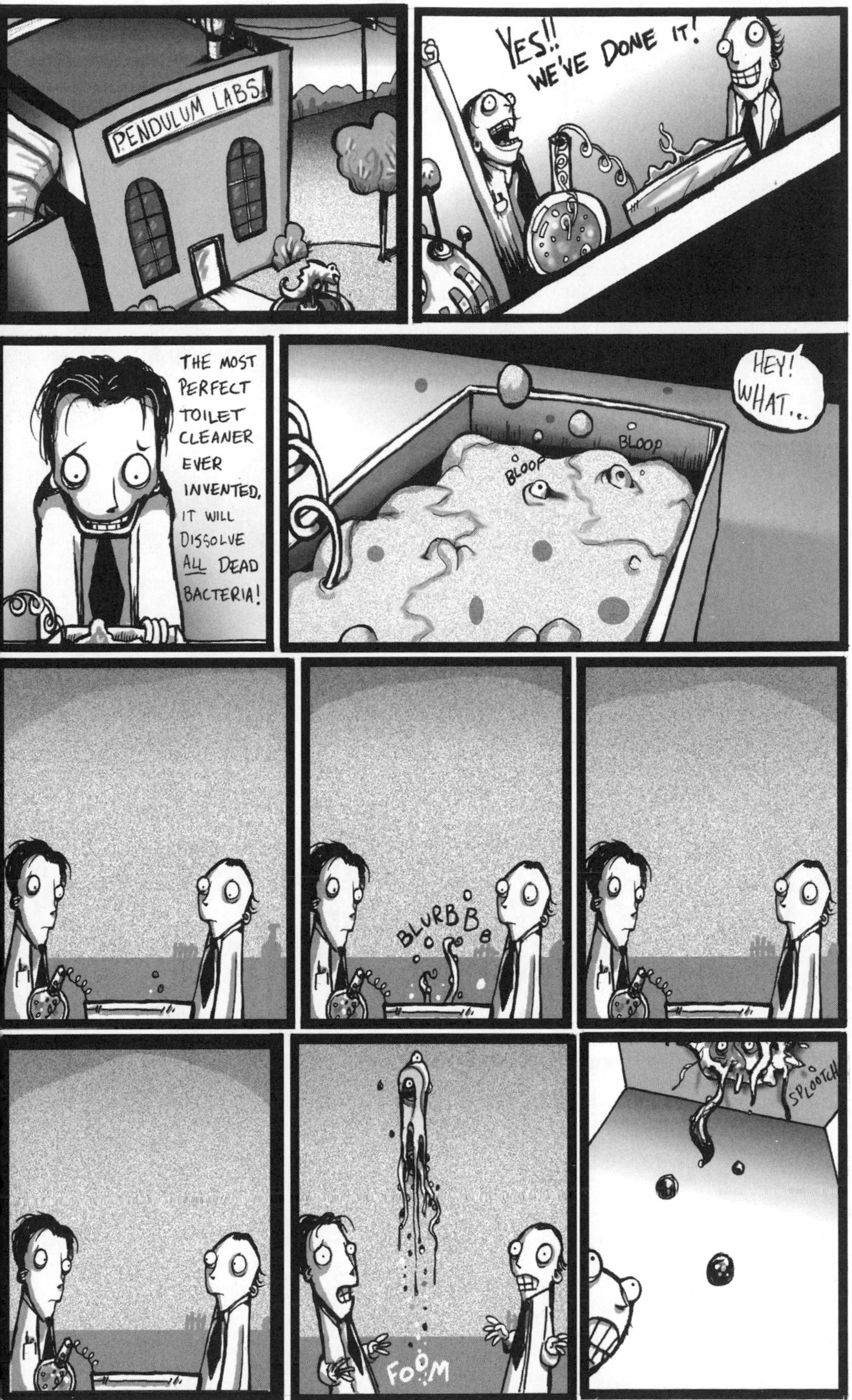
PENDULUM LABS
YES!! WE'VE DONE IT!
THE MOST PERFECT TOILET CLEANER EVER INVENTED. IT WILL DISSOLVE ALL DEAD BACTERIA!
BLOOP
BLOOP
HEY! WHAT...
BLURBBB
FOOM
SPLOOTCH

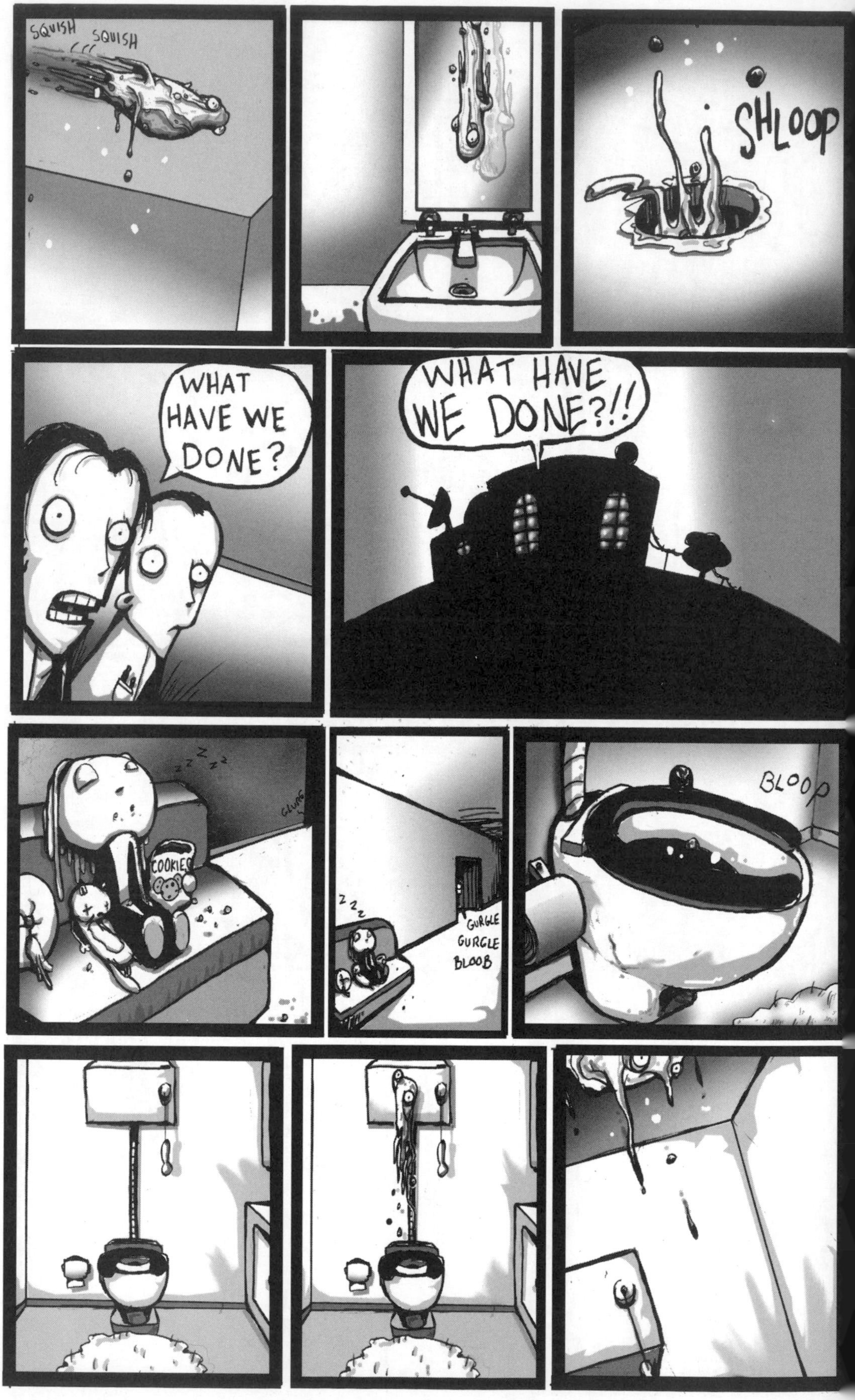
SQUISH SQUISH
SHLOOP
WHAT HAVE WE DONE?
WHAT HAVE WE DONE?!!
COOKIES
GURGLE GURGLE BLOOB
BLOOP

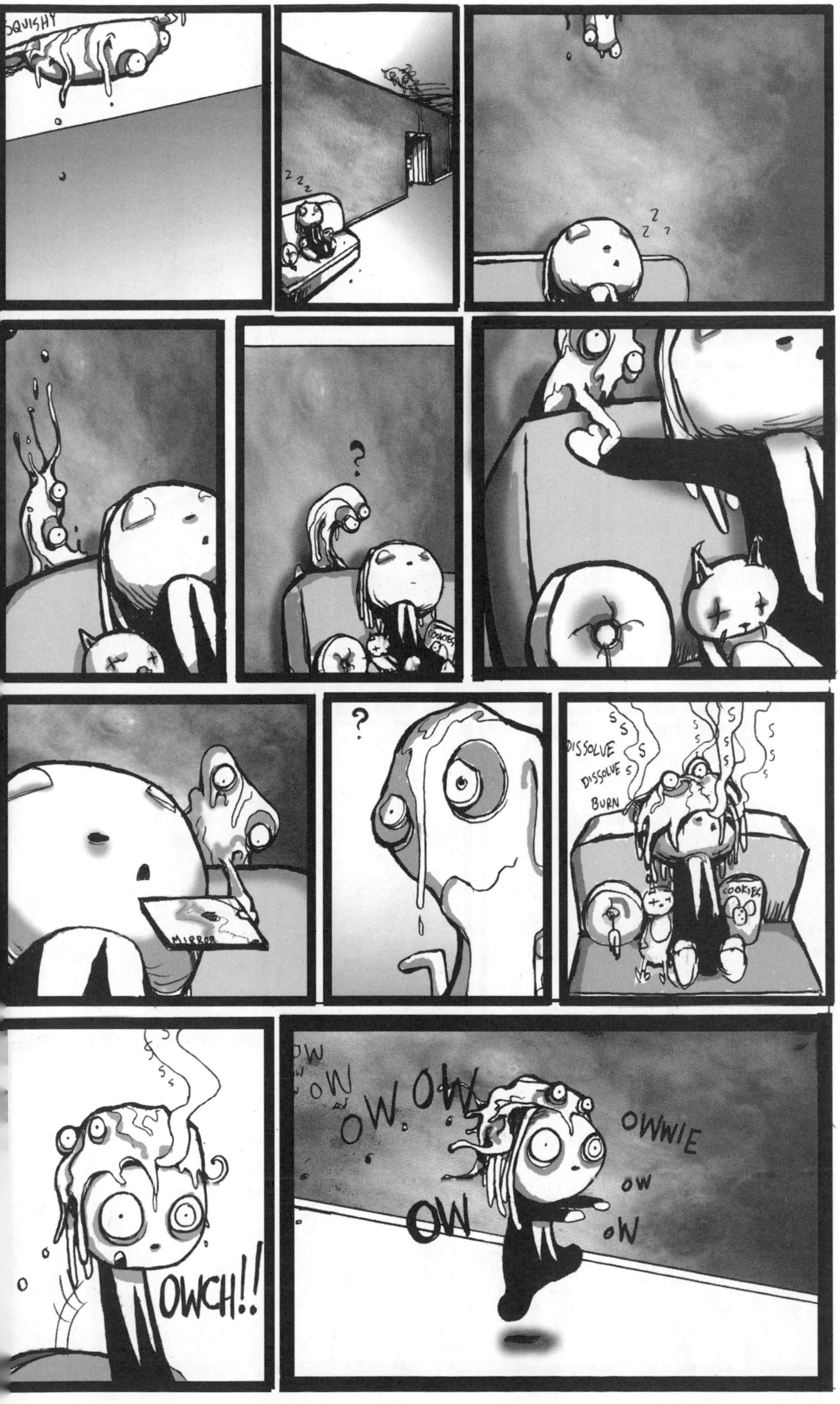
SQUISHY
Z Z Z
Z Z Z
?
COOKIES
MIRROR
?
DISSOLVE
DISSOLVE
BURN
COOKIES
OWCH!!
OW
OW
OW
OW. OW
OWWIE
OW
OW
OW

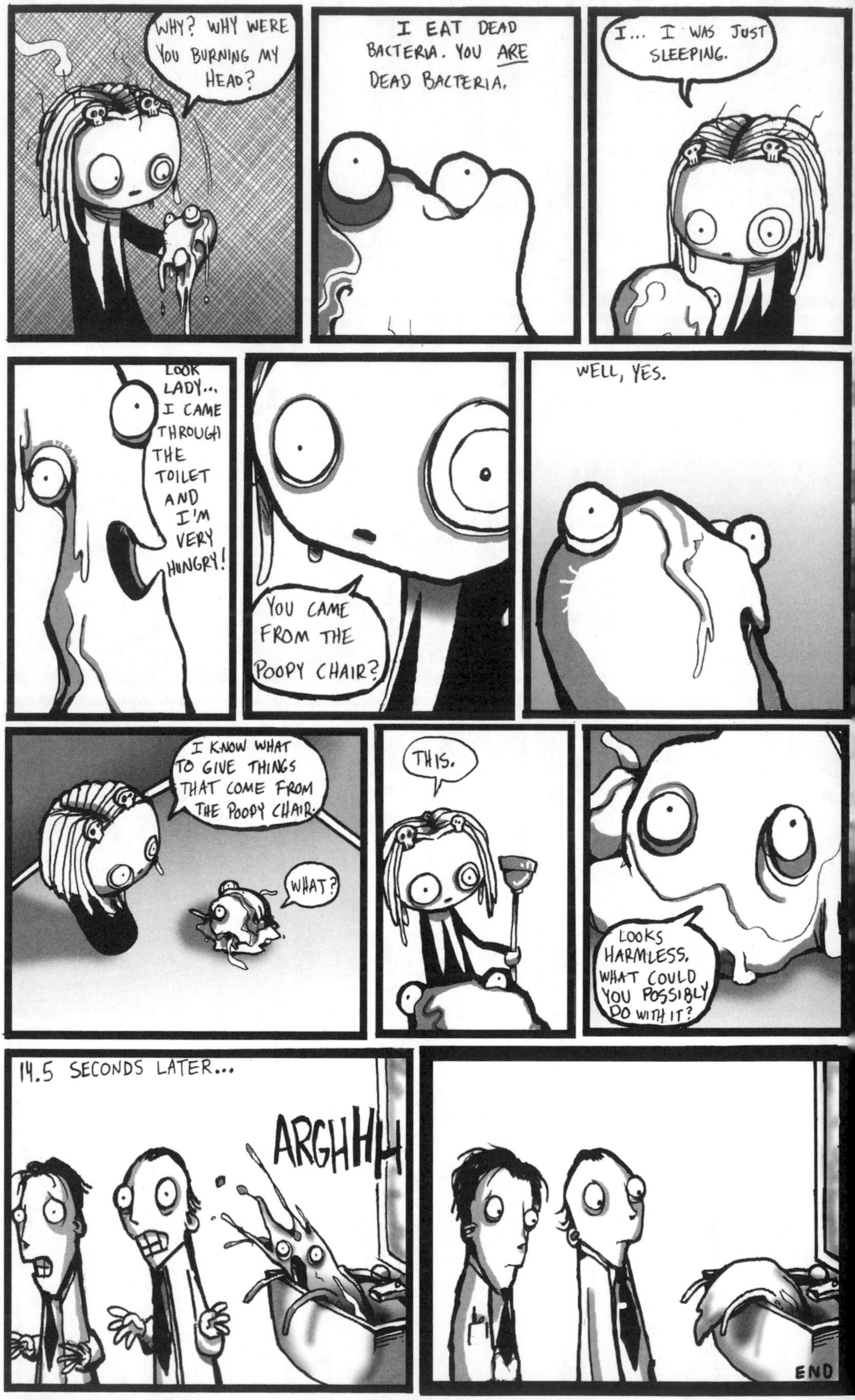
WHY? WHY WERE YOU BURNING MY HEAD?
I EAT DEAD BACTERIA. YOU ARE DEAD BACTERIA.
I... I WAS JUST SLEEPING.
LOOK LADY... I CAME THROUGH THE TOILET AND I'M VERY HUNGRY!
YOU CAME FROM THE POOPY CHAIR?
WELL, YES.
I KNOW WHAT TO GIVE THINGS THAT COME FROM THE POOPY CHAIR.
WHAT?
THIS.
LOOKS HARMLESS. WHAT COULD YOU POSSIBLY DO WITH IT?
14.5 SECONDS LATER...
ARGHHH
END

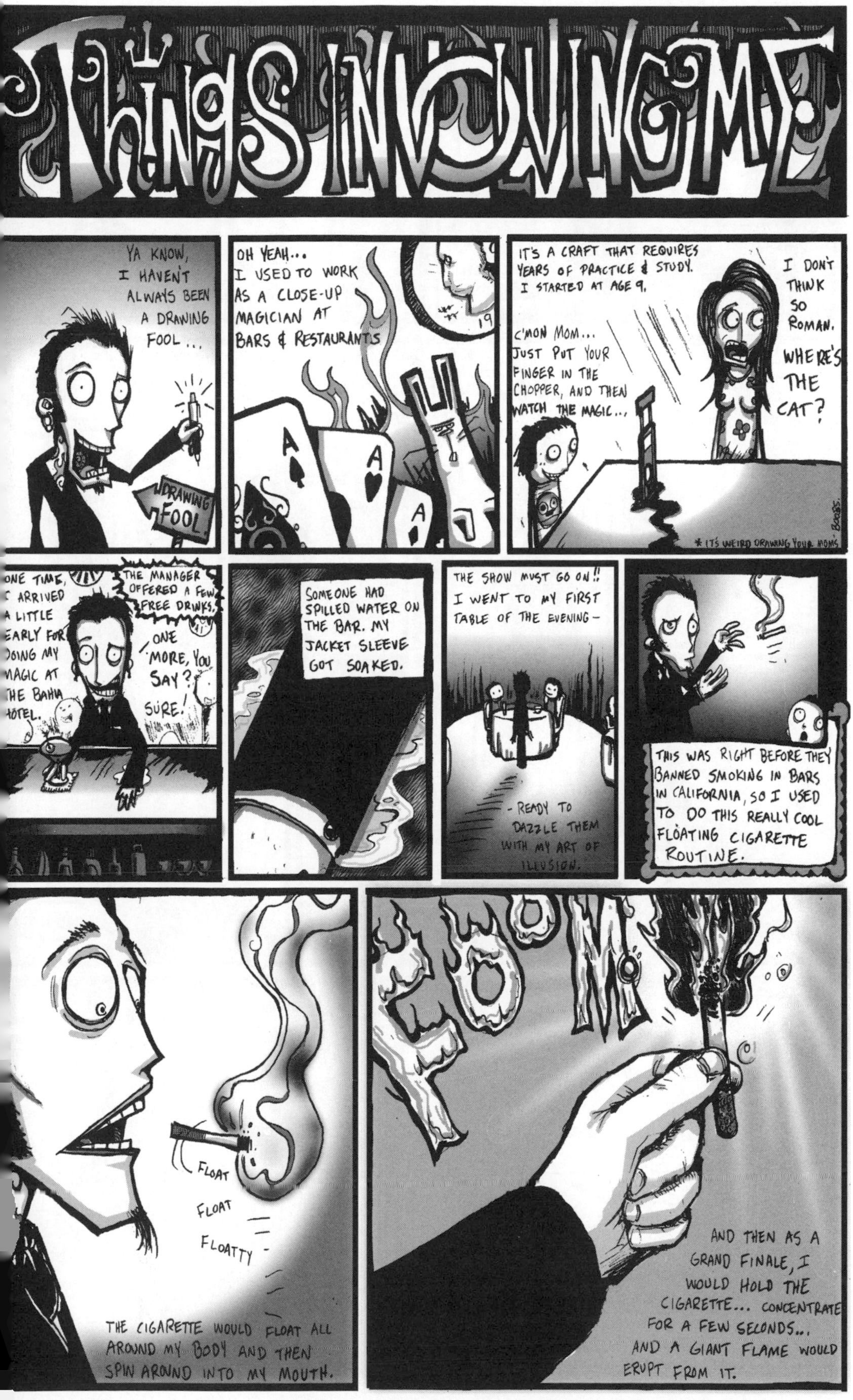
THINGS INVOLVING ME
YA KNOW, I HAVEN'T ALWAYS BEEN A DRAWING FOOL...
DRAWING FOOL
OH YEAH... I USED TO WORK AS A CLOSE-UP MAGICIAN AT BARS & RESTAURANTS
IT'S A CRAFT THAT REQUIRES YEARS OF PRACTICE & STUDY. I STARTED AT AGE 9.
C'MON MOM... JUST PUT YOUR FINGER IN THE CHOPPER, AND THEN WATCH THE MAGIC...
I DON'T THINK SO ROMAN. WHERE'S THE CAT?
* ITS WEIRD DRAWING YOUR MOMS BOOBS.
ONE TIME, I ARRIVED A LITTLE EARLY FOR DOING MY MAGIC AT THE BAHIA HOTEL.
THE MANAGER OFFERED A FEW FREE DRINKS.
ONE MORE, YOU SAY? SURE!
SOMEONE HAD SPILLED WATER ON THE BAR. MY JACKET SLEEVE GOT SOAKED.
THE SHOW MUST GO ON!! I WENT TO MY FIRST TABLE OF THE EVENING -
- READY TO DAZZLE THEM WITH MY ART OF ILLUSION.
THIS WAS RIGHT BEFORE THEY BANNED SMOKING IN BARS IN CALIFORNIA, SO I USED TO DO THIS REALLY COOL FLOATING CIGARETTE ROUTINE.
FLOAT
FLOAT
FLOATTY
THE CIGARETTE WOULD FLOAT ALL AROUND MY BODY AND THEN SPIN AROUND INTO MY MOUTH.
FOOM!
AND THEN AS A GRAND FINALE, I WOULD HOLD THE CIGARETTE... CONCENTRATE FOR A FEW SECONDS... AND A GIANT FLAME WOULD ERUPT FROM IT.

AND I MEAN A **FLAME**!

WOOSH!

THIS WHOLE ACT WAS VERY SPOOKY AND VERY MAGICAL....

WHEW THANK YOU!

THIS NITE HOWEVER, WAS TO BECOME A LITTLE MORE "MAGICAL."

EXCUSE ME, YOUR ARM IS ON FIRE.

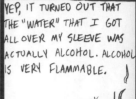

YEP, IT TURNED OUT THAT THE "WATER" THAT I GOT ALL OVER MY SLEEVE WAS ACTUALLY ALCOHOL. ALCOHOL IS VERY FLAMMABLE.

CRACK SIZZLE

IN THE TWO YEARS THAT I HAD BEEN DOING MAGIC PROFESSIONALLY, I HAD NEVER MESSED UP A TRICK BEFORE. I WAS DETERMINED TO SOMEHOW PLAY THIS SITUATION OFF....

OH, NO... I'M NOT REALLY ON FIRE.

POP SCORR!

IT'S JUST AN ILLUSION!

WHAT?!! DEAR GOD MAN!! YOU'RE GOING UP IN FLAMES!!

NOPE. IT'S MAGIC!

PLEASE GET HELP!!!!

PLEASE?

SEEMS ALMOST REAL... DOESN'T IT?

SIZZLE SIZZLE

BUT.... I CAN SMELL YOUR FLESH...

O.K. WELL LOOKS LIKE MY JOB IS DONE. YOU'VE BEEN A WONDERFUL AUDIENCE.

I'LL BE HERE ALL WEEK. GOOD NITE!

PLOD PLOD PLOD...

WHAT HAPPENED TO YOU?!!

MAGIC...

DOCTOR BOB

更

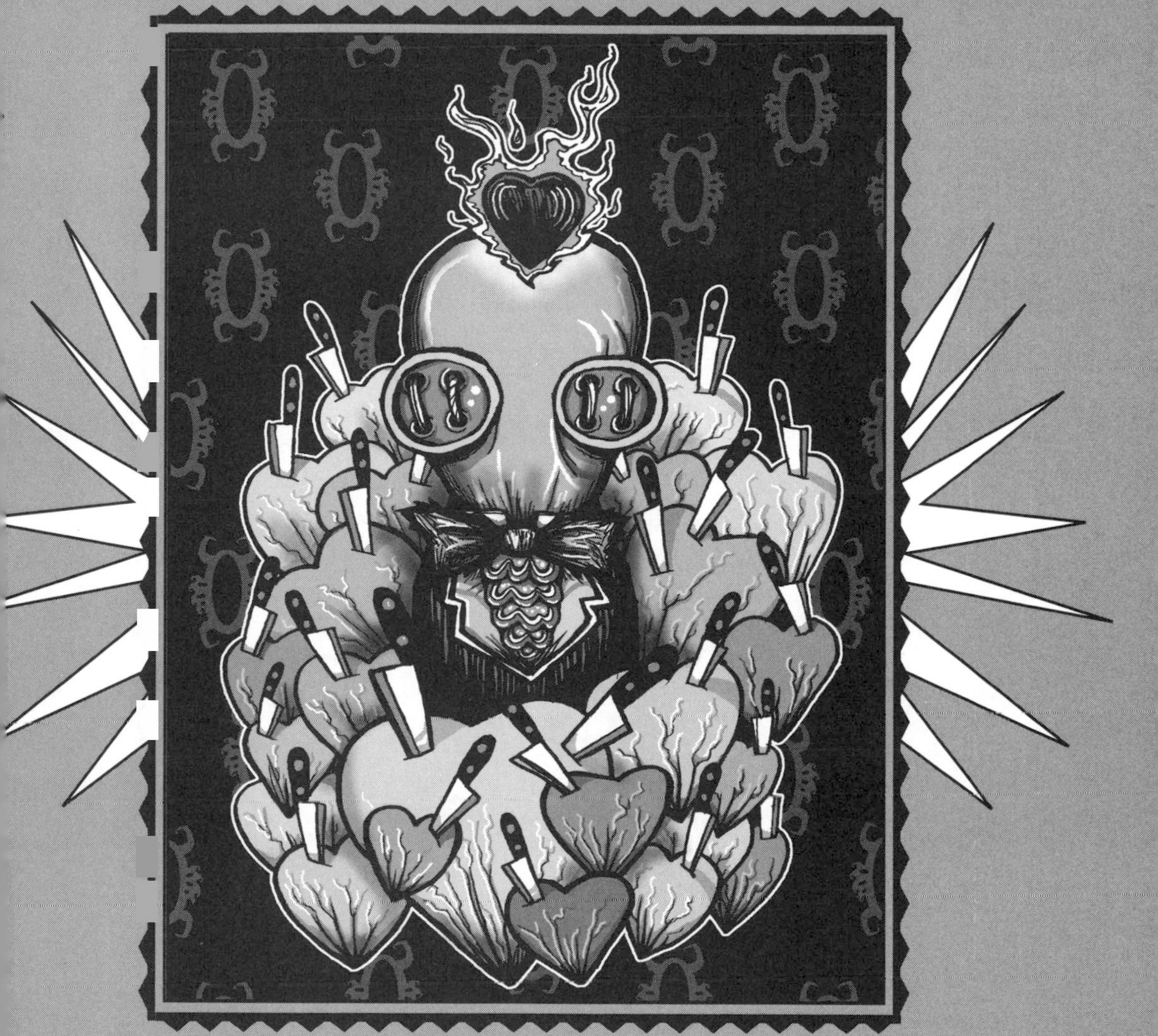

issue six

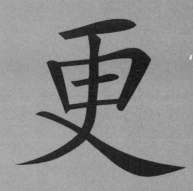

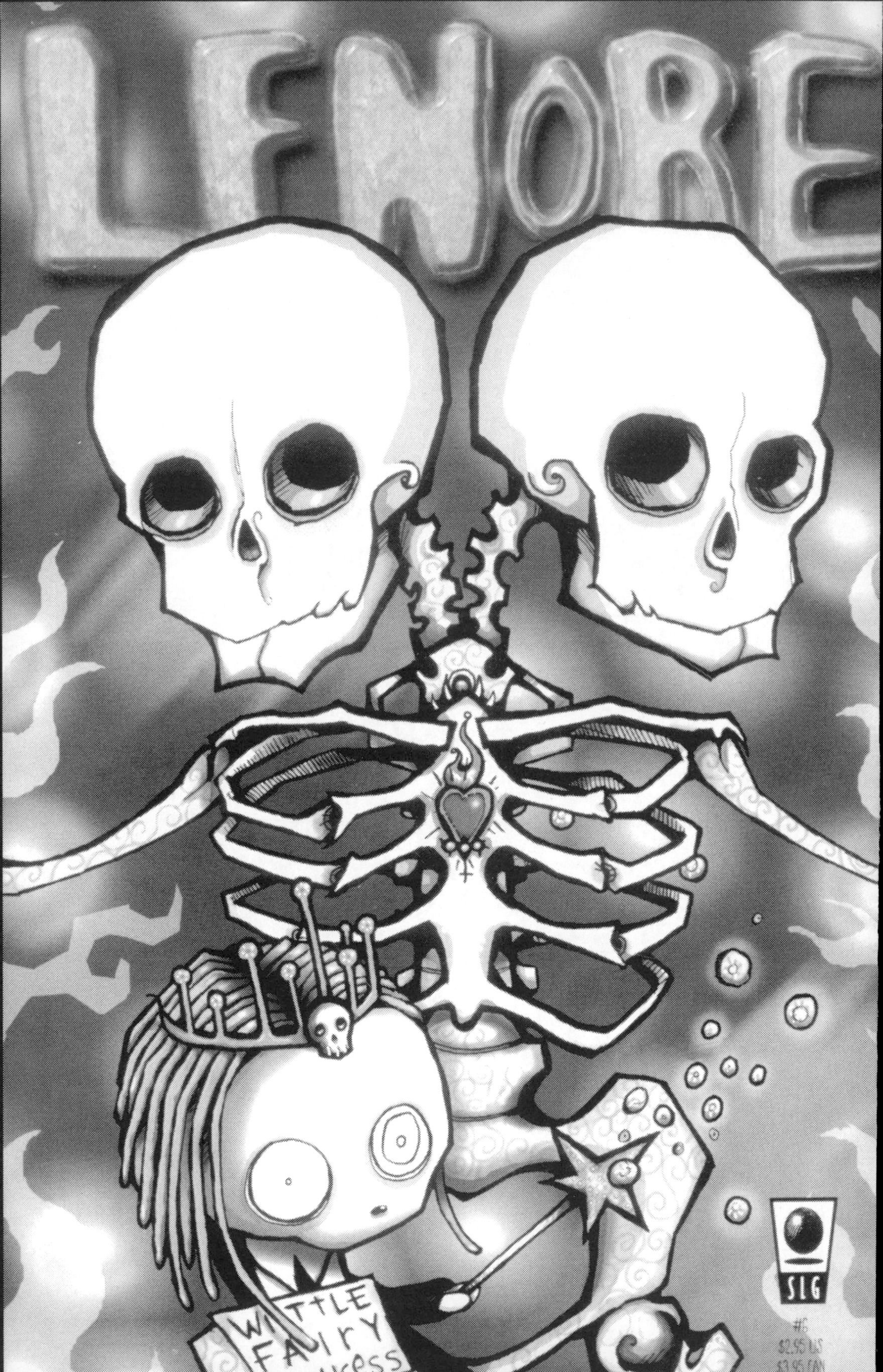
LENORE
Wittle
Fairy
Princess
SLG
#6
$2.95 US
$3.95 CAN

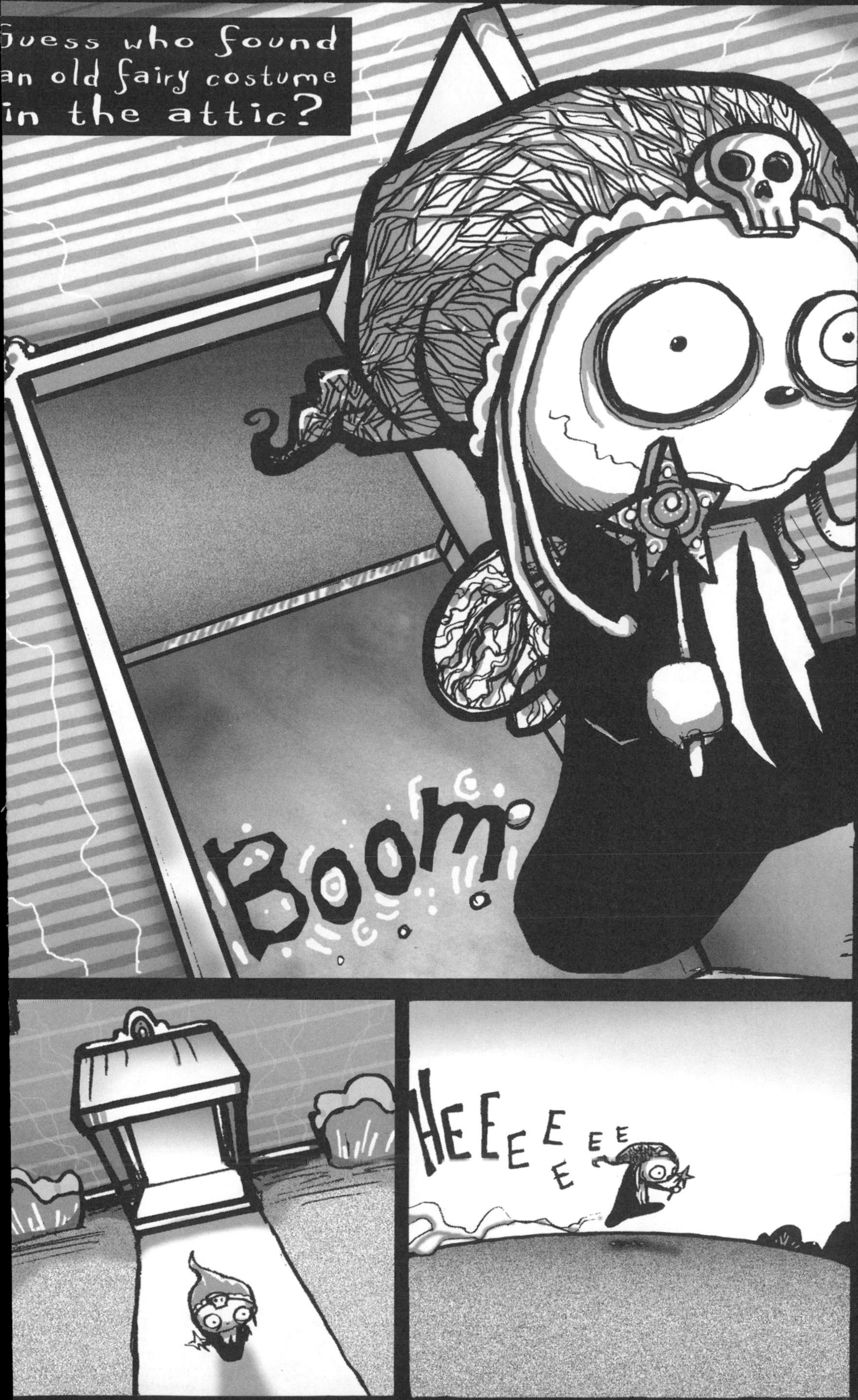
Guess who found an old fairy costume in the attic?
Boom
HEEEEEEEE

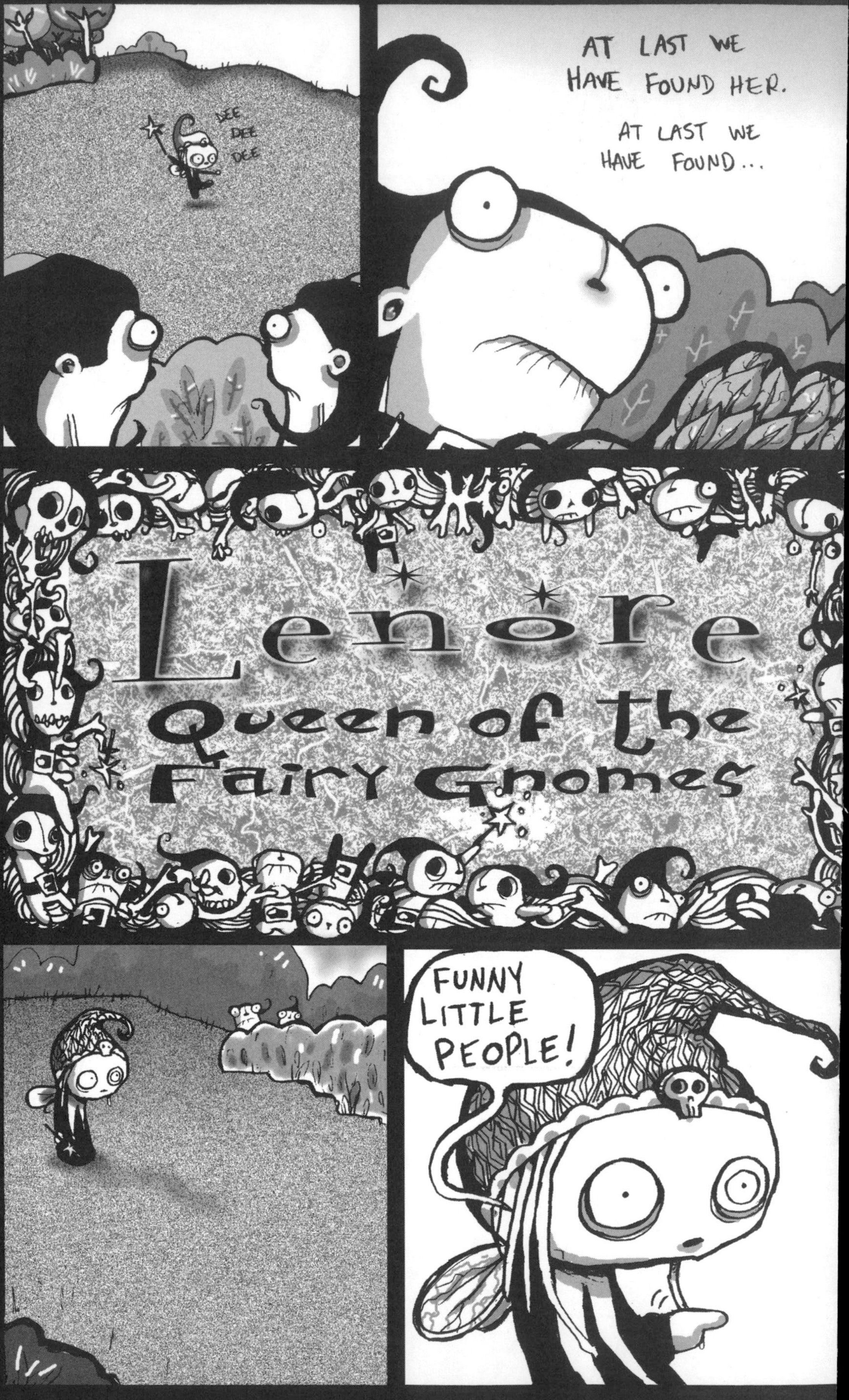
DEE DEE DEE
AT LAST WE HAVE FOUND HER.
AT LAST WE HAVE FOUND...
Lenore
Queen of the Fairy Gnomes
FUNNY LITTLE PEOPLE!

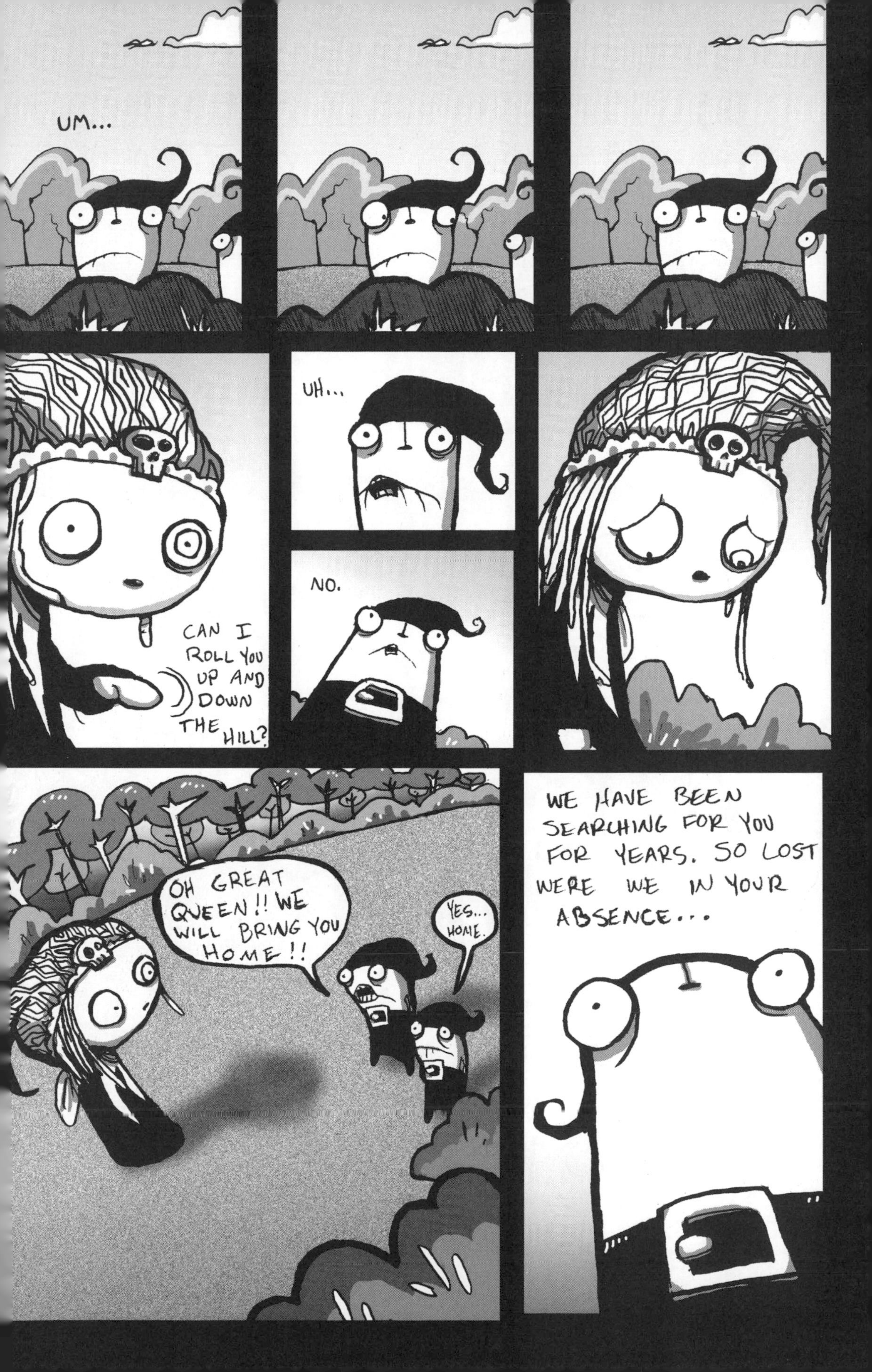
UM...
UH...
CAN I ROLL YOU UP AND DOWN THE HILL?
NO.
OH GREAT QUEEN!! WE WILL BRING YOU HOME!!
YES... HOME.
WE HAVE BEEN SEARCHING FOR YOU FOR YEARS. SO LOST WERE WE IN YOUR ABSENCE...

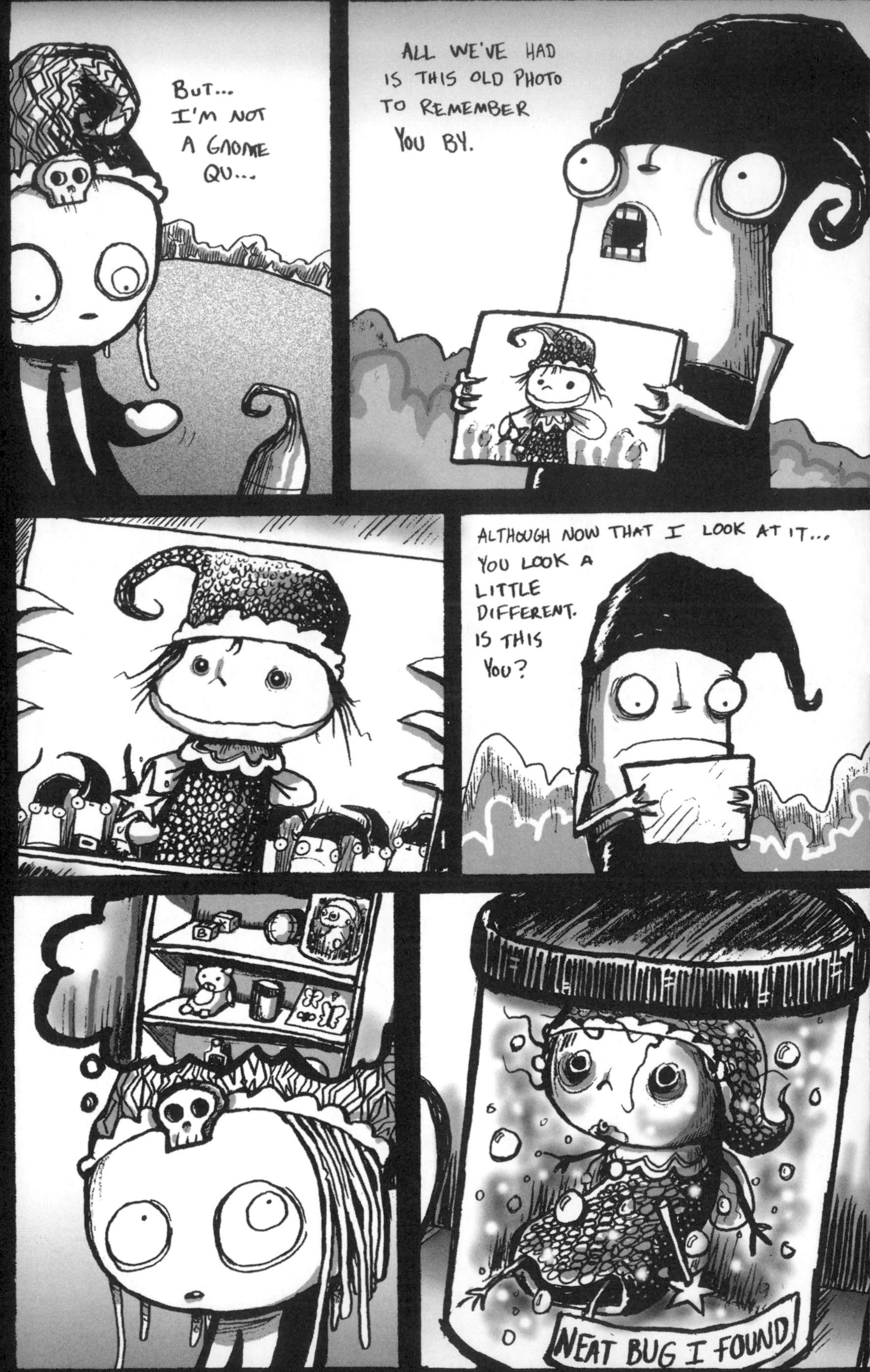
BUT...
I'M NOT
A GNOME
QU...
ALL WE'VE HAD
IS THIS OLD PHOTO
TO REMEMBER
YOU BY.
ALTHOUGH NOW THAT I LOOK AT IT...
YOU LOOK A
LITTLE
DIFFERENT.
IS THIS
YOU?
NEAT BUG I FOUND

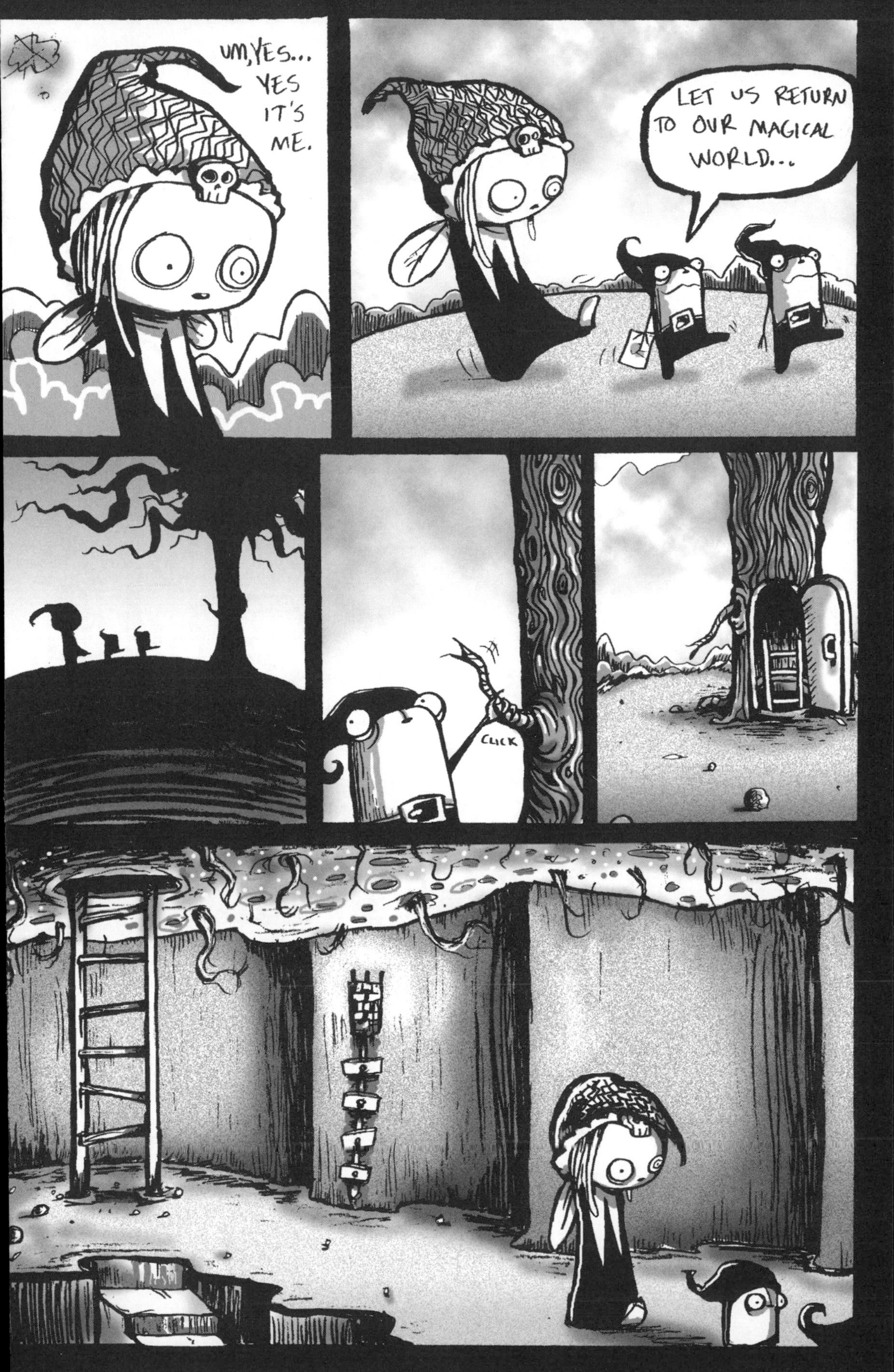
UM, YES... YES IT'S ME.
LET US RETURN TO OUR MAGICAL WORLD...
CLICK

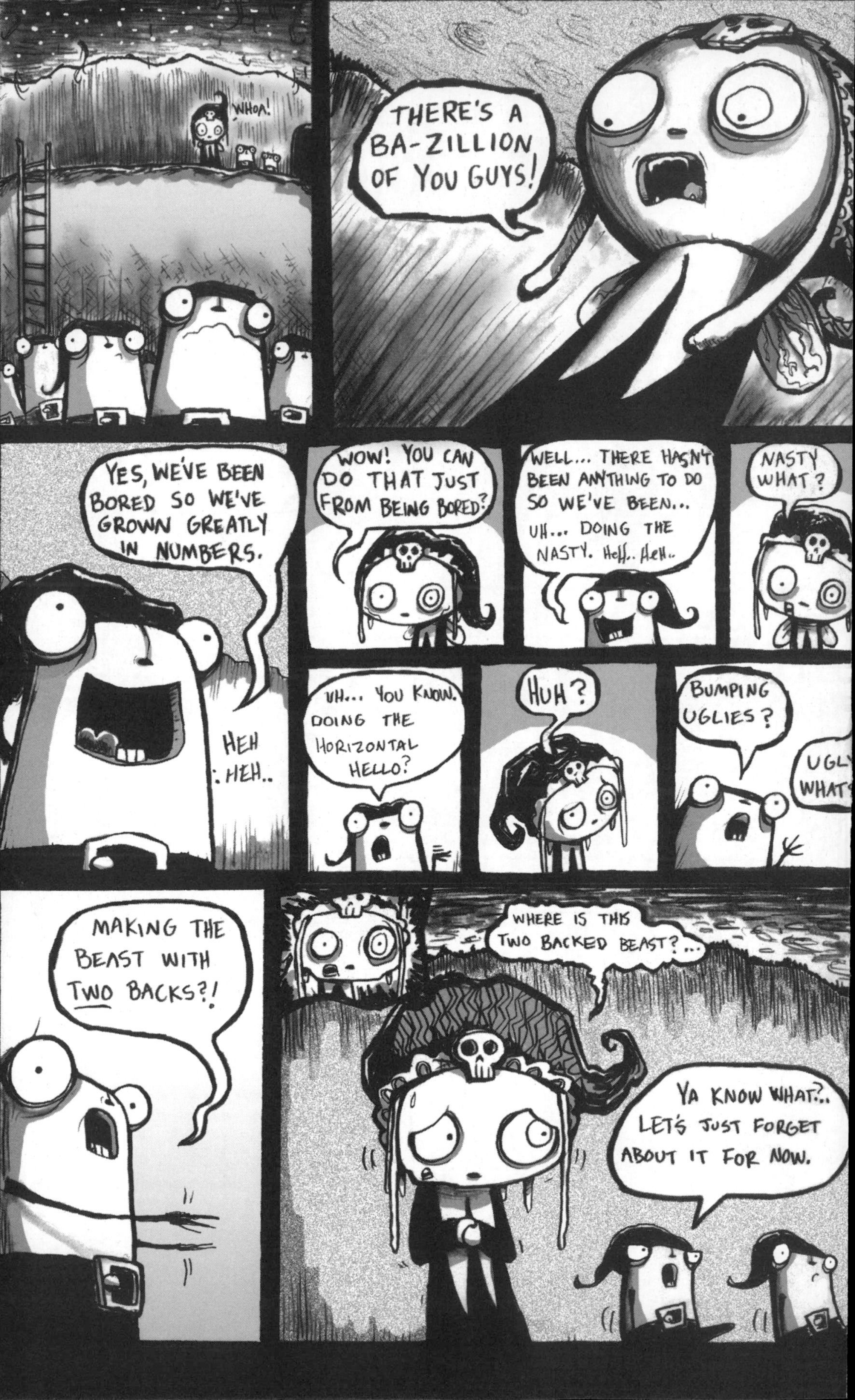
WHOA!
THERE'S A BA-ZILLION OF YOU GUYS!
YES, WE'VE BEEN BORED SO WE'VE GROWN GREATLY IN NUMBERS.
HEH HEH..
WOW! YOU CAN DO THAT JUST FROM BEING BORED?
WELL... THERE HASN'T BEEN ANYTHING TO DO SO WE'VE BEEN.. UH... DOING THE NASTY. HEH.. HEH..
NASTY WHAT?
UH... YOU KNOW. DOING THE HORIZONTAL HELLO?
HUH?
BUMPING UGLIES?
MAKING THE BEAST WITH TWO BACKS?!
WHERE IS THIS TWO BACKED BEAST?...
YA KNOW WHAT?.. LET'S JUST FORGET ABOUT IT FOR NOW.

OH MY GOD!!! LOOK! IT'S THE GREAT QUEEN!! ARE YOU LOOKING? HUH?

RUMBLE RUMBLE RUMBLE RUMBLE RUMB

WOOWIE!

JOY! HAPPY DAY!

AND NOW... MYSTERIOUS NARRATOR OUT OF NOWHERE...

AND TO THIS DAY, NO ONE IS SURE WHAT LED UP TO CAUSE THE SERIES OF EVENTS THAT FOLLOWED NEXT.

SOME SAY THAT IT WAS HER DIET EARLIER THAT DAY...

GURGLE

SUGAR CRAPPIES

SODA BUZZ

POP ROCK

CHOCOLATE COVERED ESPRESSO BEANS

OTHERS SAY THAT IT WAS BECAUSE OF THAT TIME SHE GOT "BEANED" BY A LAWNGNOME FROM LITTLE BILLY NIPKISS

STILL, EVEN OTHERS THINK IT RELATES TO BILLY NIPKISS' MYSTERIOUS SOCK PUPPET ACCIDENT IMMEDIATELY AFTER..

WHAT?

BILLY NIPKISS R.I.P LITTLE FELLA

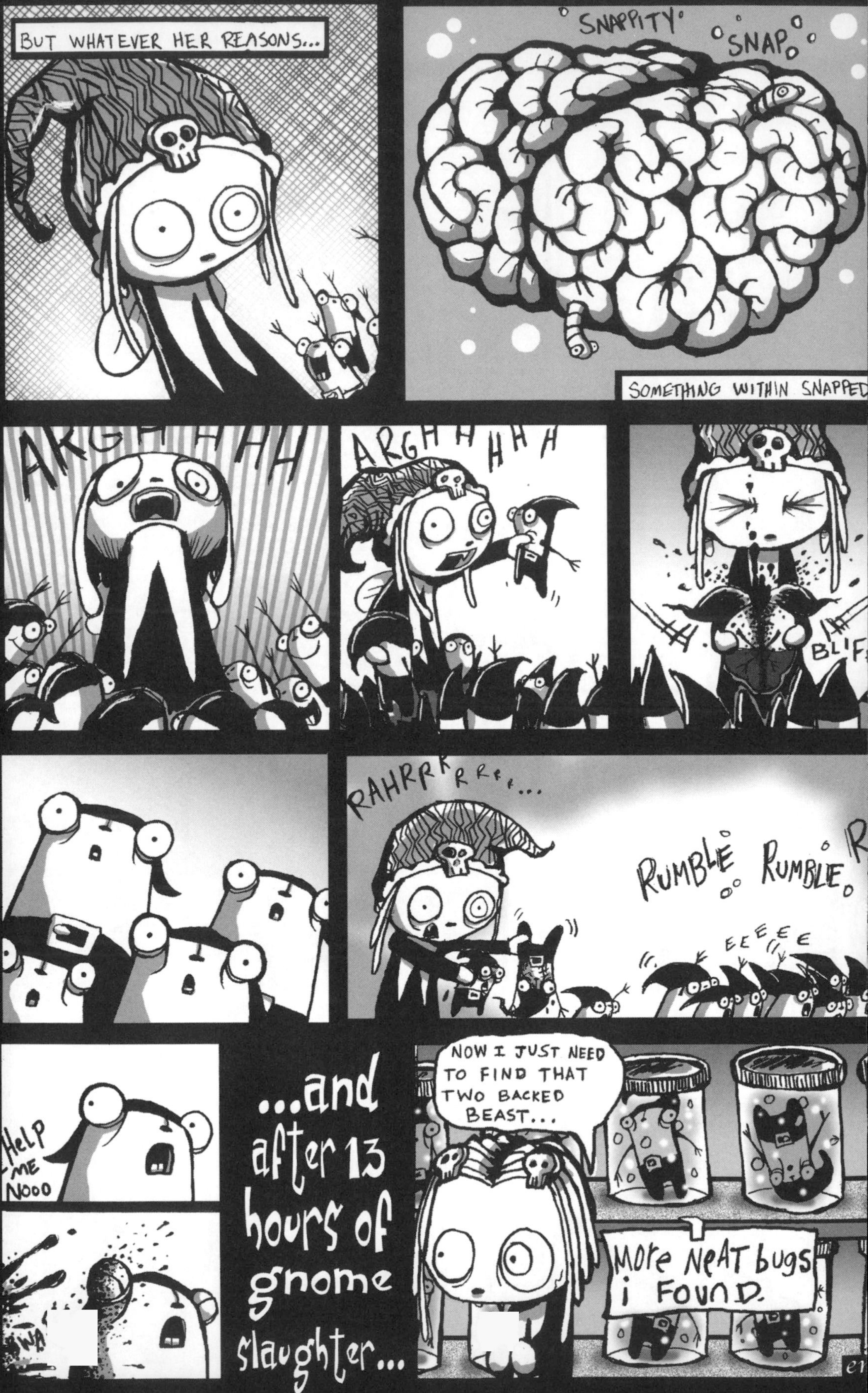
BUT WHATEVER HER REASONS...
SNAPPITY SNAP
SOMETHING WITHIN SNAPPED
ARGHHHHH
ARGHHHHH
BLIF
RAHRRRRRR...
RUMBLE RUMBLE
EEEEEE
HELP ME NOOO
WA
...and after 13 hours of gnome slaughter...
NOW I JUST NEED TO FIND THAT TWO BACKED BEAST...
MORE NEAT BUGS i FOUND.

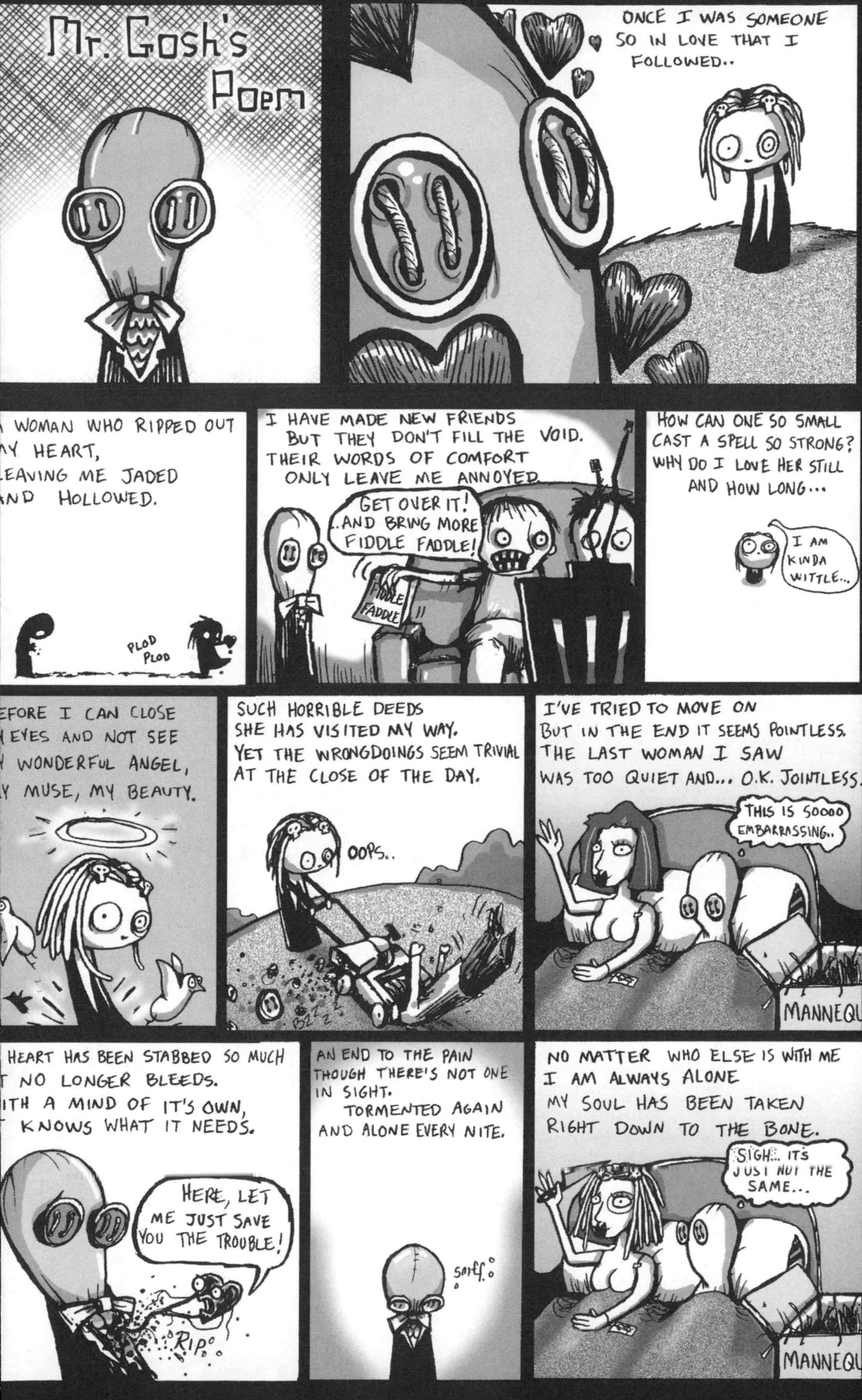
Mr. Gosh's Poem
ONCE I WAS SOMEONE SO IN LOVE THAT I FOLLOWED..
WOMAN WHO RIPPED OUT
Y HEART,
EAVING ME JADED
ND HOLLOWED.
PLOD PLOD
I HAVE MADE NEW FRIENDS BUT THEY DON'T FILL THE VOID. THEIR WORDS OF COMFORT ONLY LEAVE ME ANNOYED.
GET OVER IT! ..AND BRING MORE FIDDLE FADDLE!
FIDDLE FADDLE
HOW CAN ONE SO SMALL CAST A SPELL SO STRONG? WHY DO I LOVE HER STILL AND HOW LONG...
I AM KINDA WITTLE...
EFORE I CAN CLOSE
EYES AND NOT SEE
WONDERFUL ANGEL,
MUSE, MY BEAUTY.
SUCH HORRIBLE DEEDS SHE HAS VISITED MY WAY. YET THE WRONGDOINGS SEEM TRIVIAL AT THE CLOSE OF THE DAY.
OOPS..
BZZZZ
I'VE TRIED TO MOVE ON BUT IN THE END IT SEEMS POINTLESS. THE LAST WOMAN I SAW WAS TOO QUIET AND... O.K. JOINTLESS.
THIS IS SOOOO EMBARRASSING..
MANNEQU
HEART HAS BEEN STABBED SO MUCH
T NO LONGER BLEEDS.
ITH A MIND OF IT'S OWN,
KNOWS WHAT IT NEEDS.
HERE, LET ME JUST SAVE YOU THE TROUBLE!
RIP
AN END TO THE PAIN THOUGH THERE'S NOT ONE IN SIGHT. TORMENTED AGAIN AND ALONE EVERY NITE.
sniff.
NO MATTER WHO ELSE IS WITH ME I AM ALWAYS ALONE MY SOUL HAS BEEN TAKEN RIGHT DOWN TO THE BONE.
SIGH.. IT'S JUST NOT THE SAME...
MANNEQU

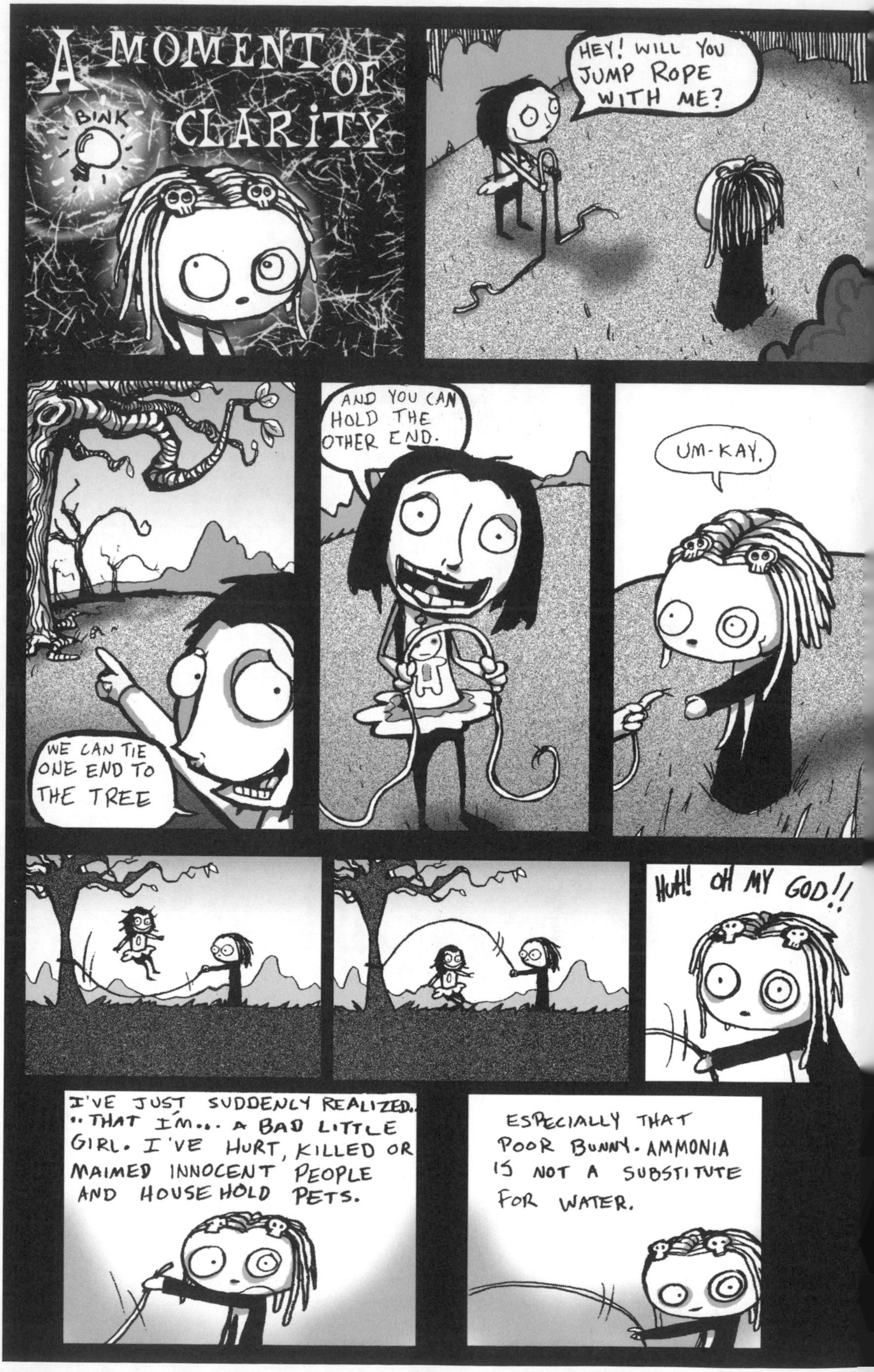
A MOMENT OF CLARITY
BINK
HEY! WILL YOU JUMP ROPE WITH ME?
WE CAN TIE ONE END TO THE TREE
AND YOU CAN HOLD THE OTHER END.
UM-KAY.
HUH! OH MY GOD!!
I'VE JUST SUDDENLY REALIZED.. ..THAT I'M... A BAD LITTLE GIRL. I'VE HURT, KILLED OR MAIMED INNOCENT PEOPLE AND HOUSEHOLD PETS.
ESPECIALLY THAT POOR BUNNY. AMMONIA IS NOT A SUBSTITUTE FOR WATER.

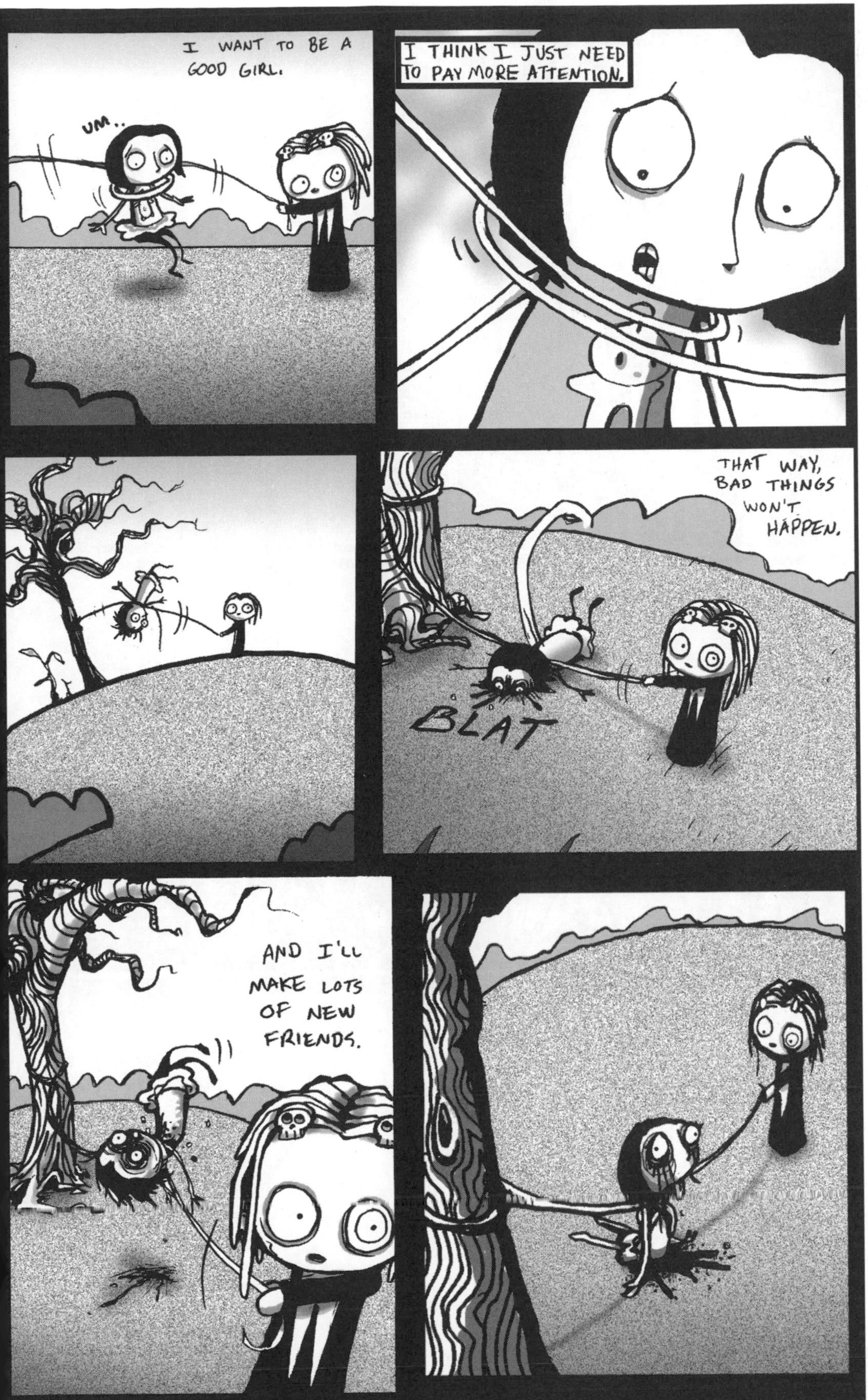
I WANT TO BE A GOOD GIRL.
UM..
I THINK I JUST NEED TO PAY MORE ATTENTION.
THAT WAY, BAD THINGS WON'T HAPPEN.
BLAT
AND I'LL MAKE LOTS OF NEW FRIENDS.

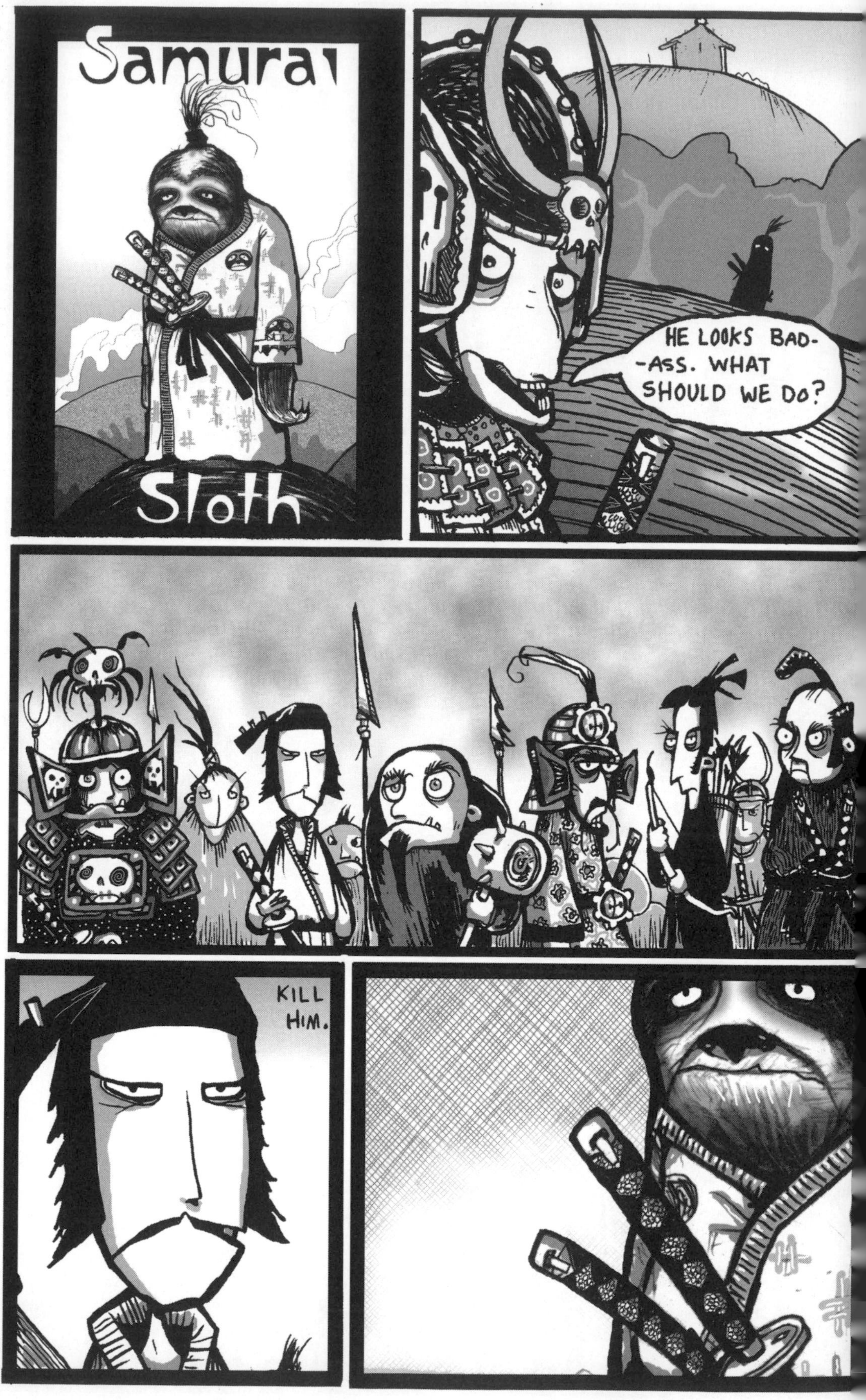
Samurai
Sloth
HE LOOKS BAD-
-ASS. WHAT
SHOULD WE DO?
KILL
HIM.

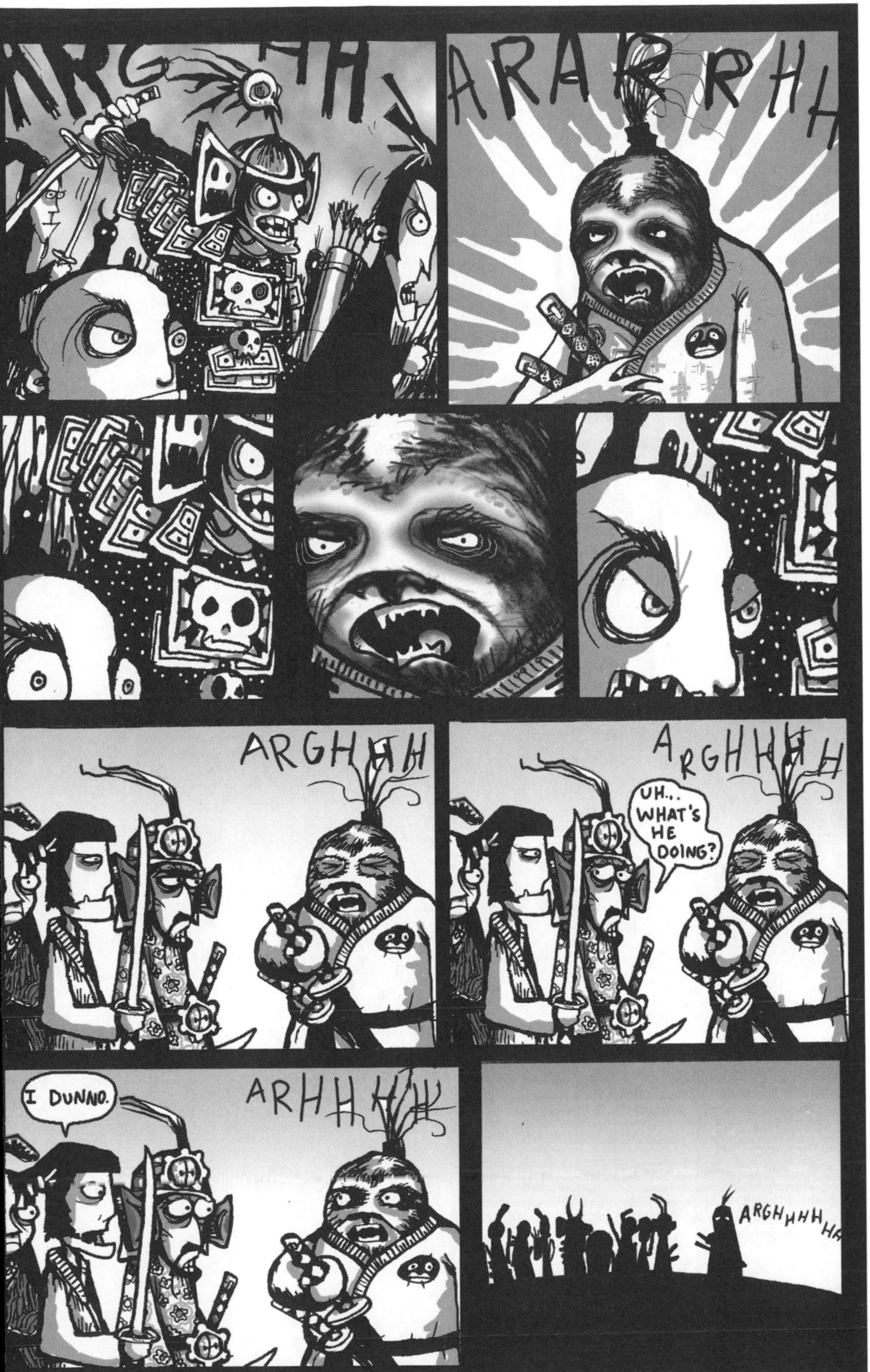
ARGHH
ARARRHH
ARGHHH
ARGHHHH
UH... WHAT'S HE DOING?
I DUNNO.
ARHHHH
ARGHHHHHA

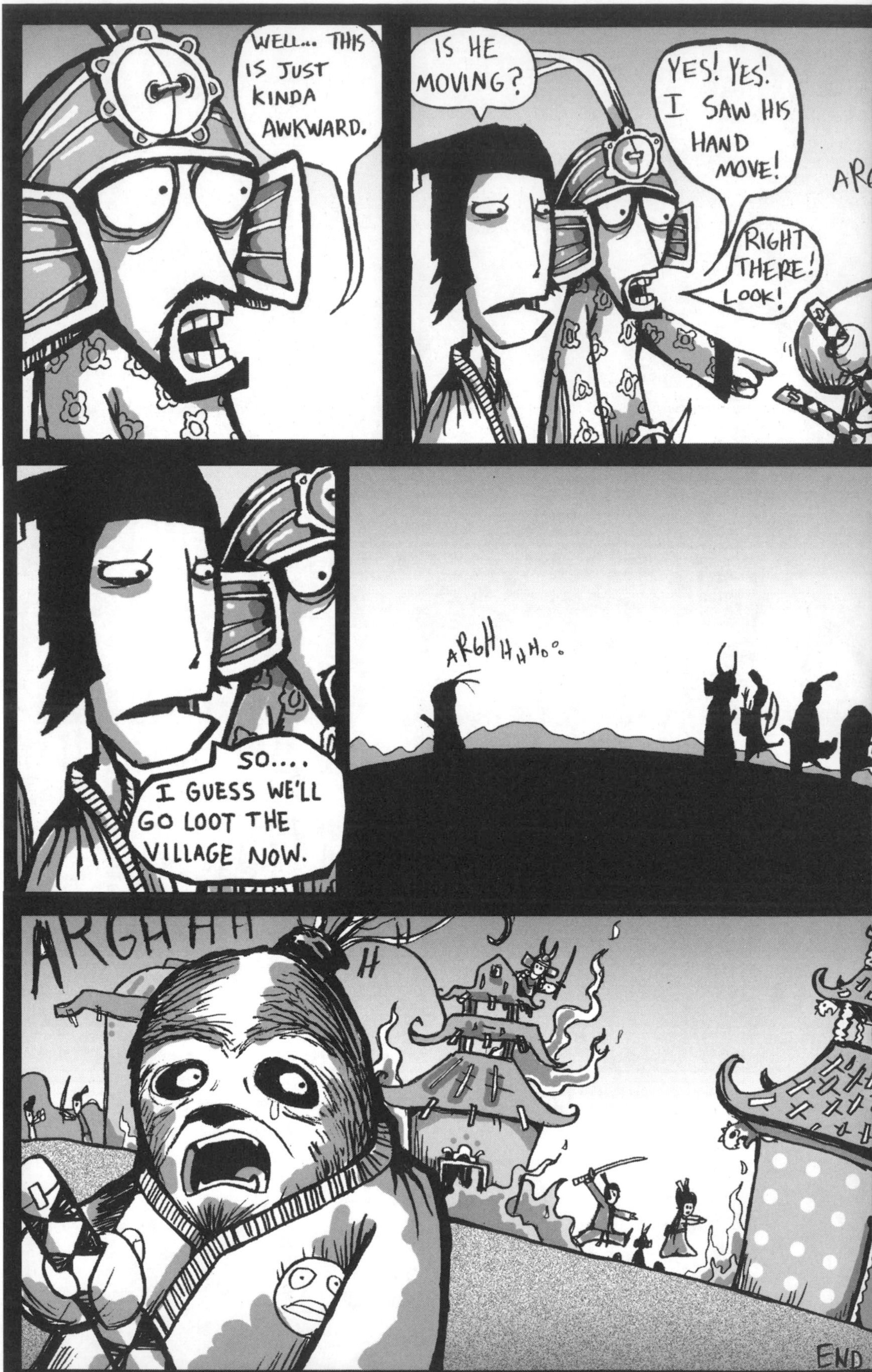
WELL... THIS IS JUST KINDA AWKWARD.
IS HE MOVING?
YES! YES! I SAW HIS HAND MOVE!
RIGHT THERE! LOOK!
SO.... I GUESS WE'LL GO LOOT THE VILLAGE NOW.
ARGHHHHHoo
ARGHHH
H
END

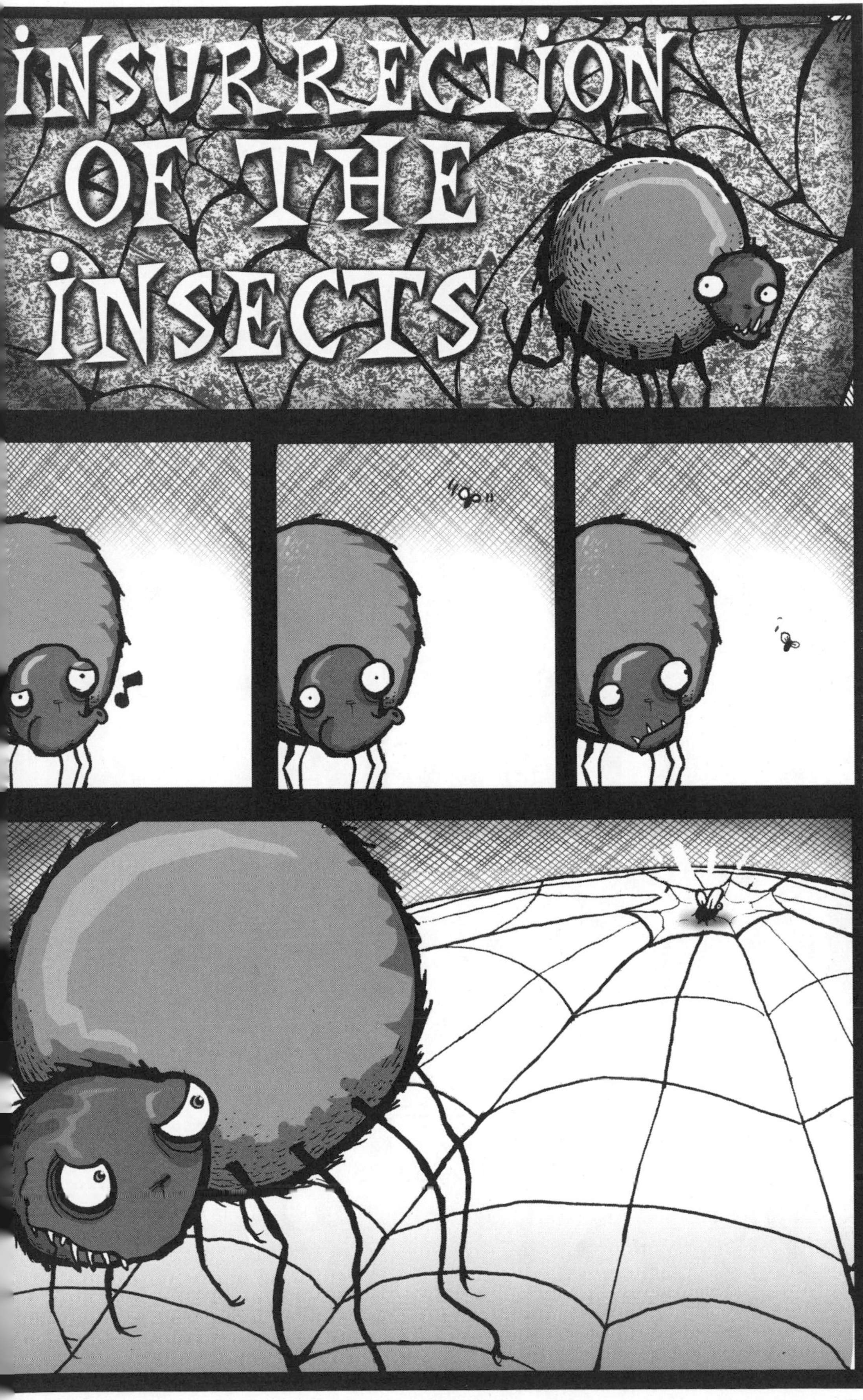
INSURRECTION OF THE INSECTS

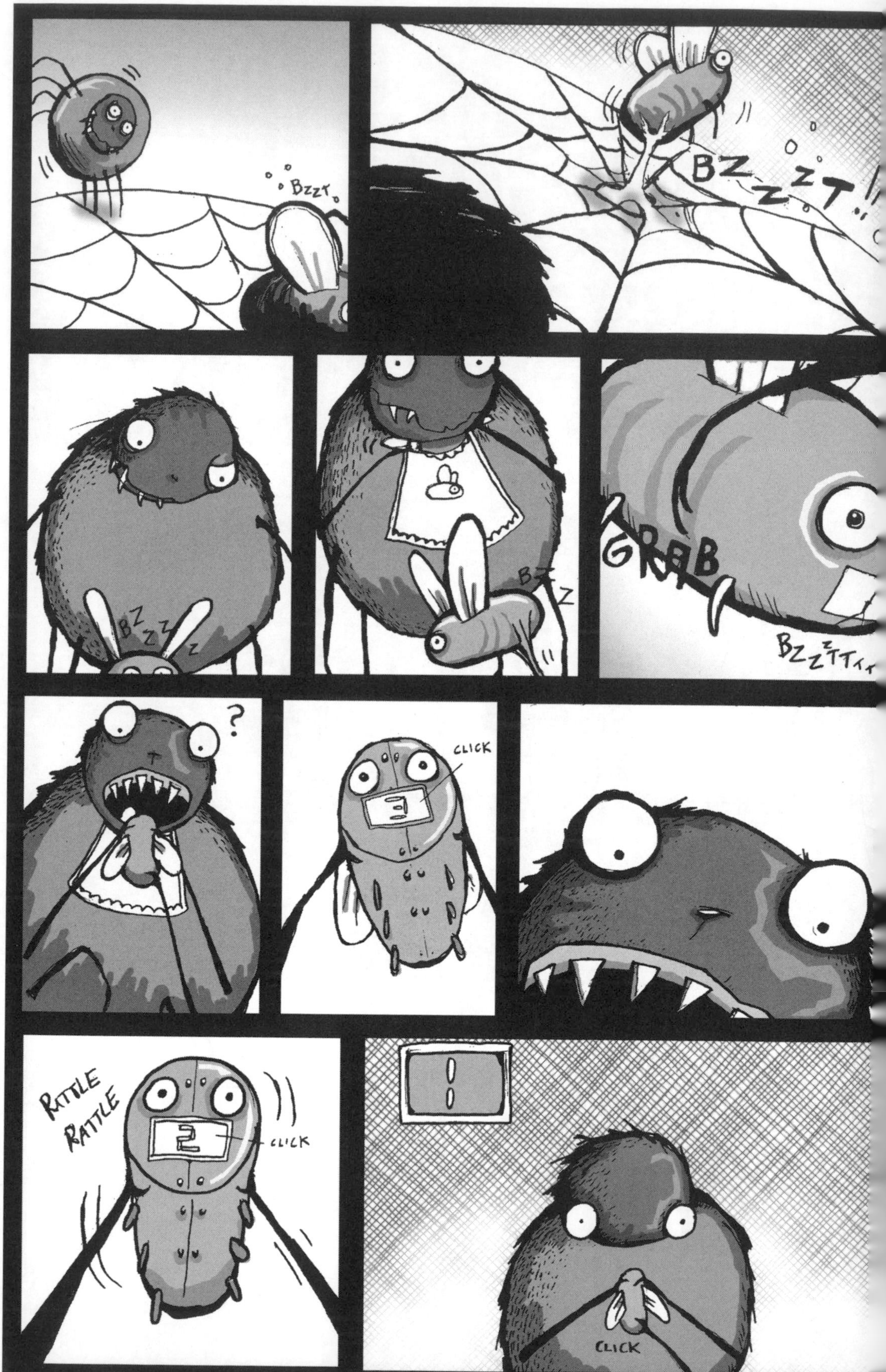
Bzzt
BZZZT!!
BZZZ
BZZ
GRAB
BZZTTT
?
CLICK
RATTLE RATTLE
CLICK
CLICK

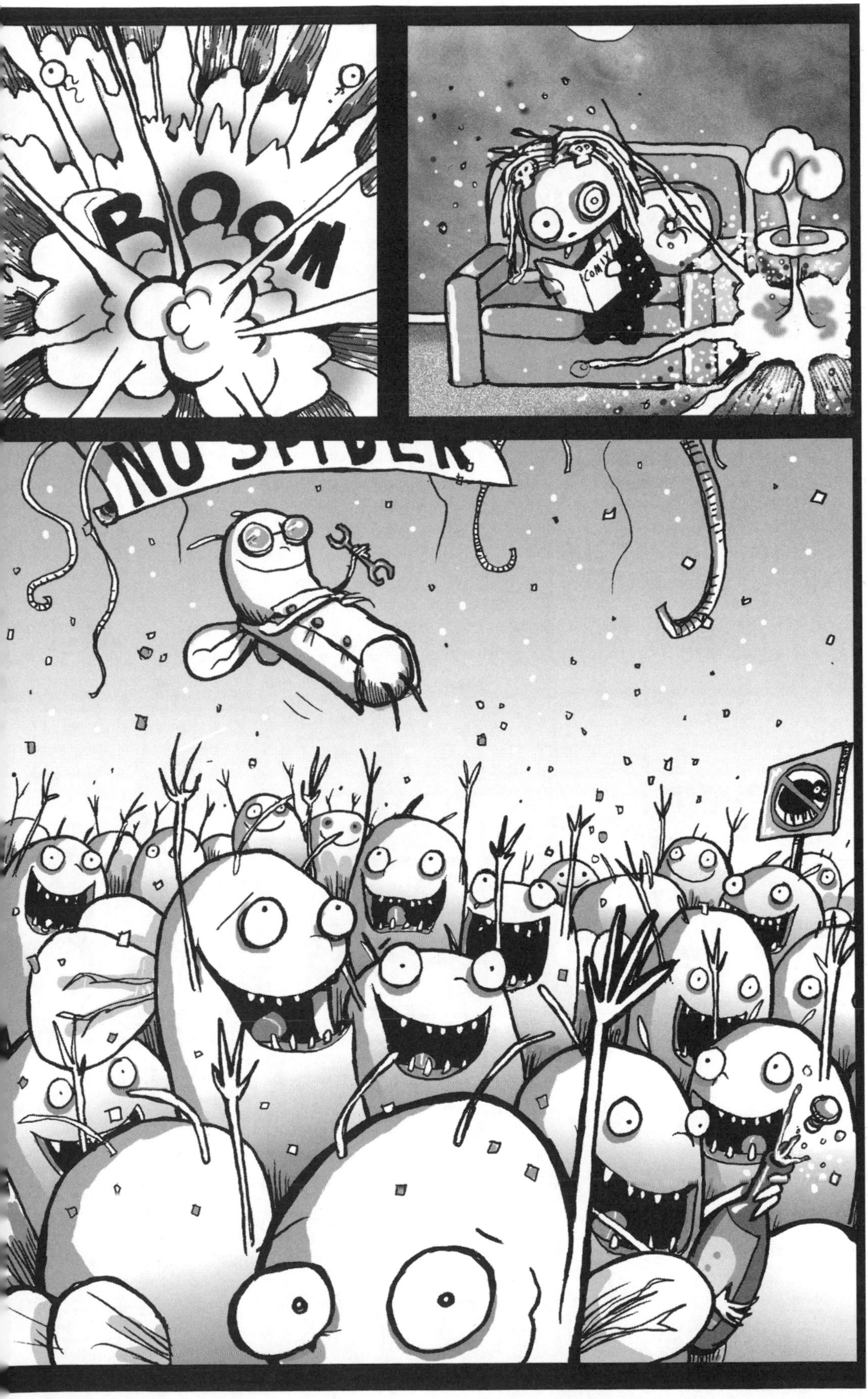
BOOM
COMIX

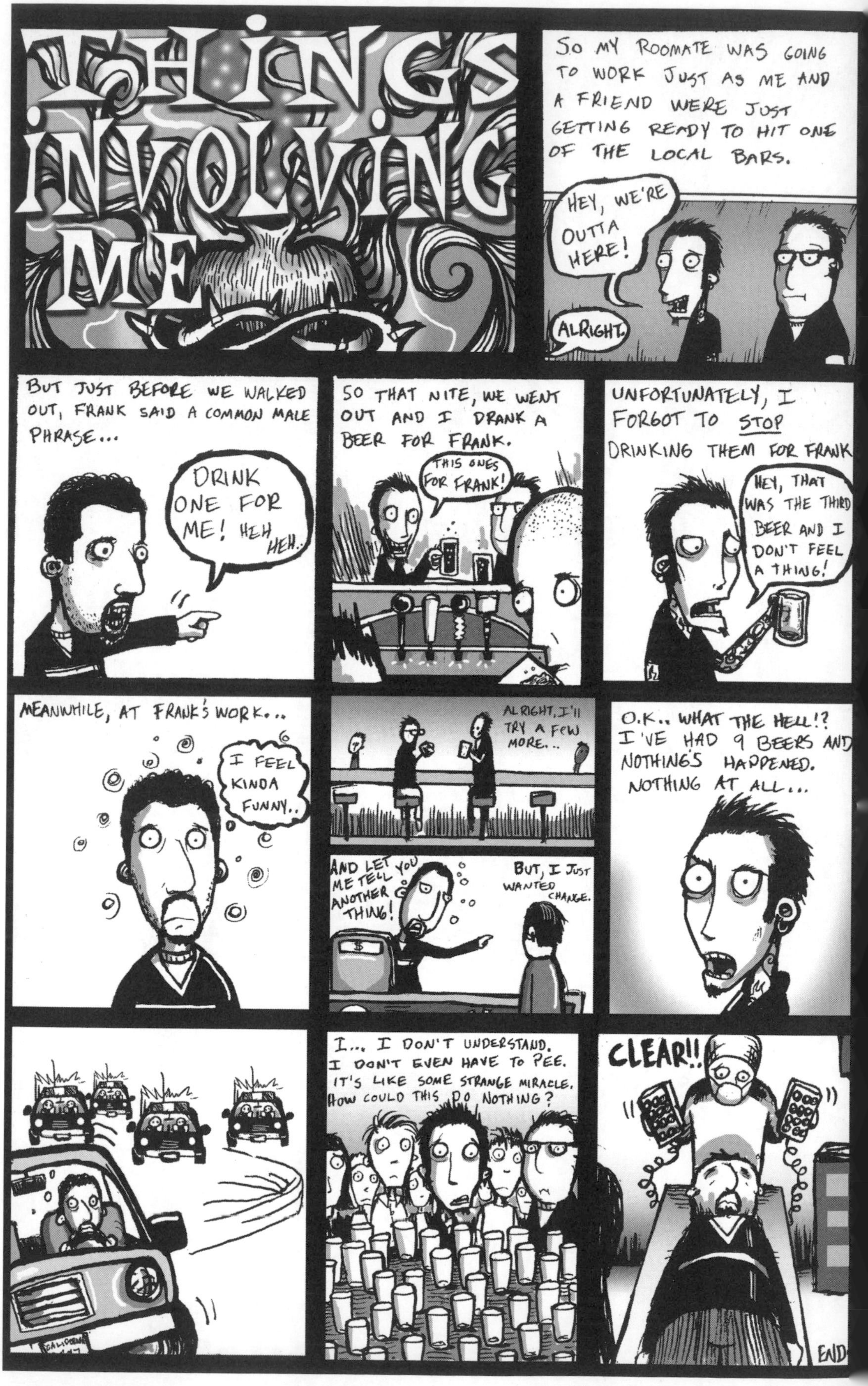
THINGS INVOLVING ME
SO MY ROOMATE WAS GOING TO WORK JUST AS ME AND A FRIEND WERE JUST GETTING READY TO HIT ONE OF THE LOCAL BARS.
HEY, WE'RE OUTTA HERE!
ALRIGHT.
BUT JUST BEFORE WE WALKED OUT, FRANK SAID A COMMON MALE PHRASE...
DRINK ONE FOR ME! HEH HEH..
SO THAT NITE, WE WENT OUT AND I DRANK A BEER FOR FRANK.
THIS ONES FOR FRANK!
UNFORTUNATELY, I FORGOT TO STOP DRINKING THEM FOR FRANK
HEY, THAT WAS THE THIRD BEER AND I DON'T FEEL A THING!
MEANWHILE, AT FRANK'S WORK...
I FEEL KINDA FUNNY..
ALRIGHT, I'LL TRY A FEW MORE...
AND LET ME TELL YOU ANOTHER THING!
BUT, I JUST WANTED CHANGE.
O.K.. WHAT THE HELL!? I'VE HAD 9 BEERS AND NOTHING'S HAPPENED. NOTHING AT ALL...
I... I DON'T UNDERSTAND. I DON'T EVEN HAVE TO PEE. IT'S LIKE SOME STRANGE MIRACLE. HOW COULD THIS DO NOTHING?
CLEAR!!
END

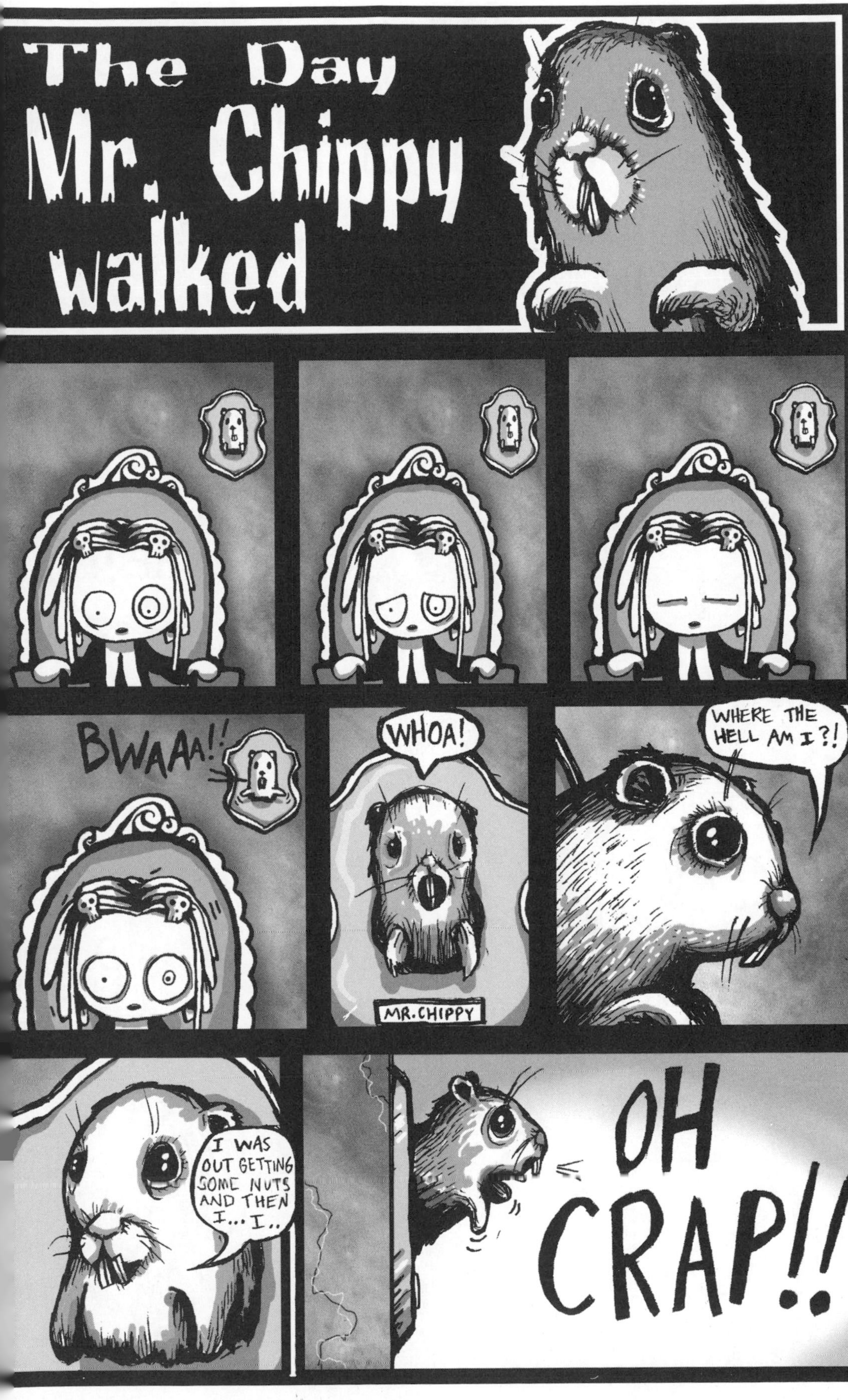
The Day
Mr. Chippy
walked
BWAAA!!
WHOA!
MR. CHIPPY
WHERE THE HELL AM I ?!
I WAS OUT GETTING SOME NUTS AND THEN I... I..
OH CRAP!!

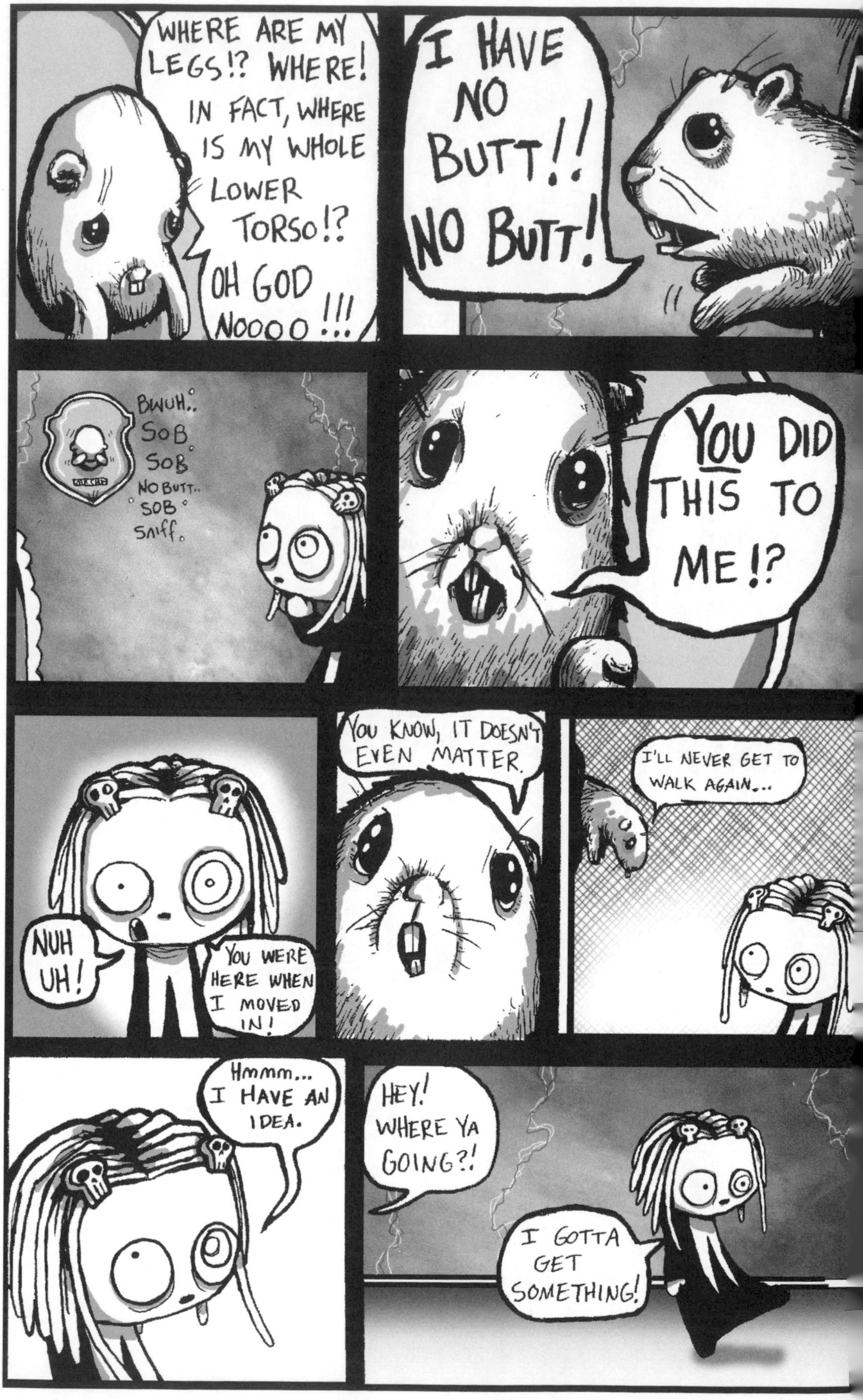
WHERE ARE MY LEGS!? WHERE! IN FACT, WHERE IS MY WHOLE LOWER TORSO!? OH GOD NOOOO!!!
I HAVE NO BUTT!! NO BUTT!
BWUH.. SOB SOB NO BUTT.. SOB SNIFF.
YOU DID THIS TO ME!?
NUH UH!
YOU WERE HERE WHEN I MOVED IN!
YOU KNOW, IT DOESN'T EVEN MATTER.
I'LL NEVER GET TO WALK AGAIN...
Hmmm... I HAVE AN IDEA.
HEY! WHERE YA GOING?!
I GOTTA GET SOMETHING!

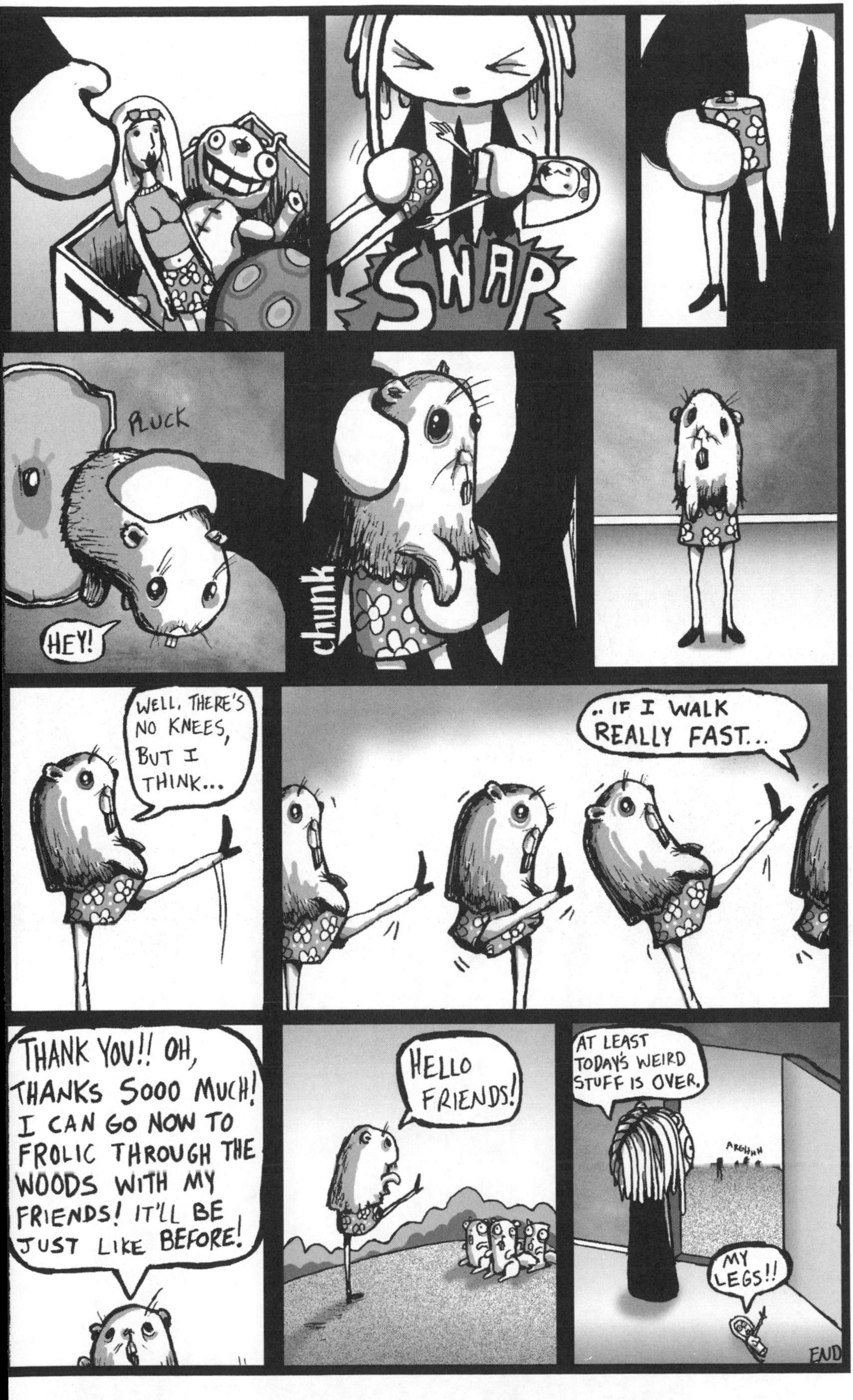
SNAP
PLUCK
HEY!
chunk
WELL, THERE'S NO KNEES, BUT I THINK...
.. IF I WALK REALLY FAST...
THANK YOU!! OH, THANKS SOOO MUCH! I CAN GO NOW TO FROLIC THROUGH THE WOODS WITH MY FRIENDS! IT'LL BE JUST LIKE BEFORE!
HELLO FRIENDS!
AT LEAST TODAY'S WEIRD STUFF IS OVER.
MY LEGS!!
END

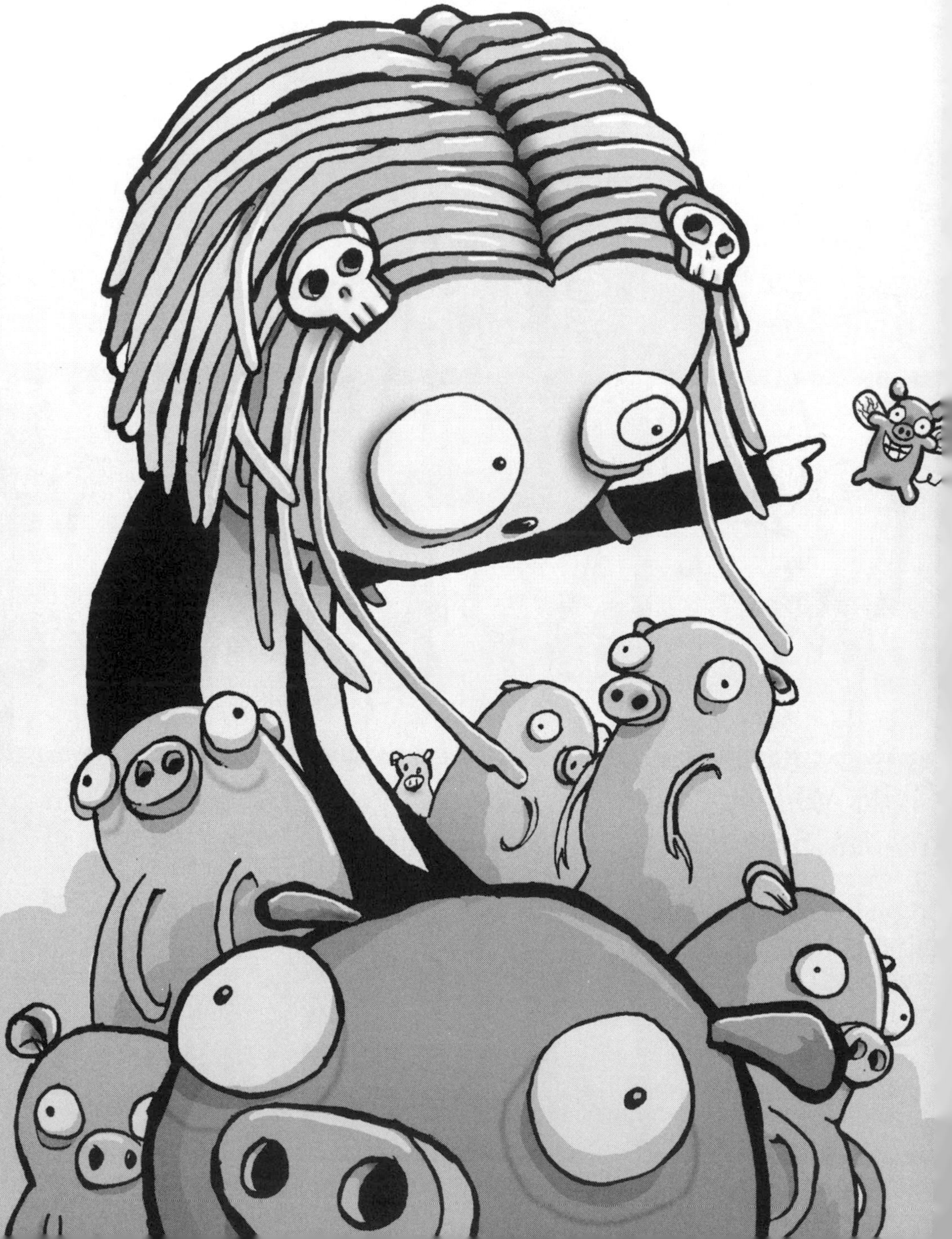

光

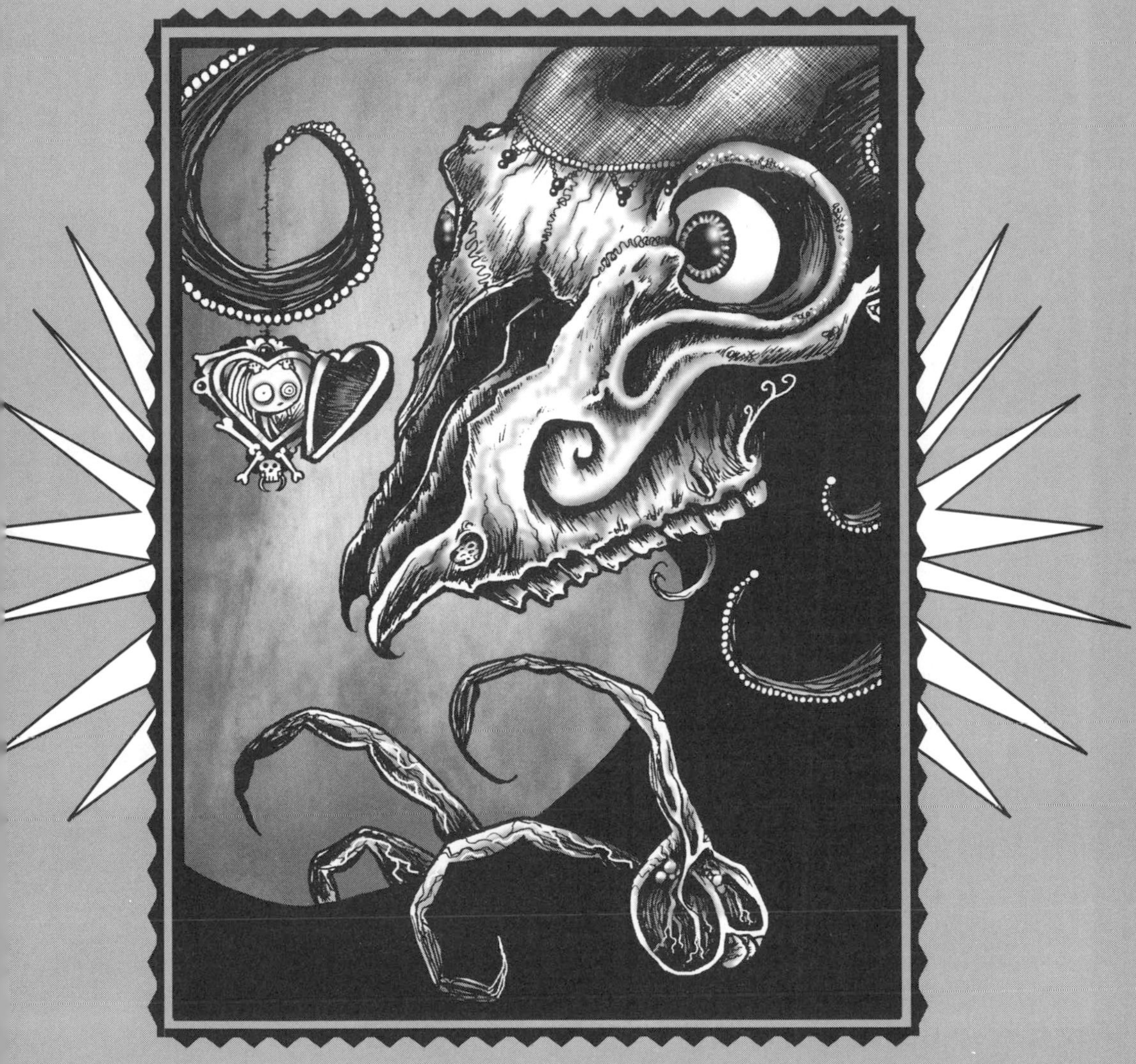

issue seven

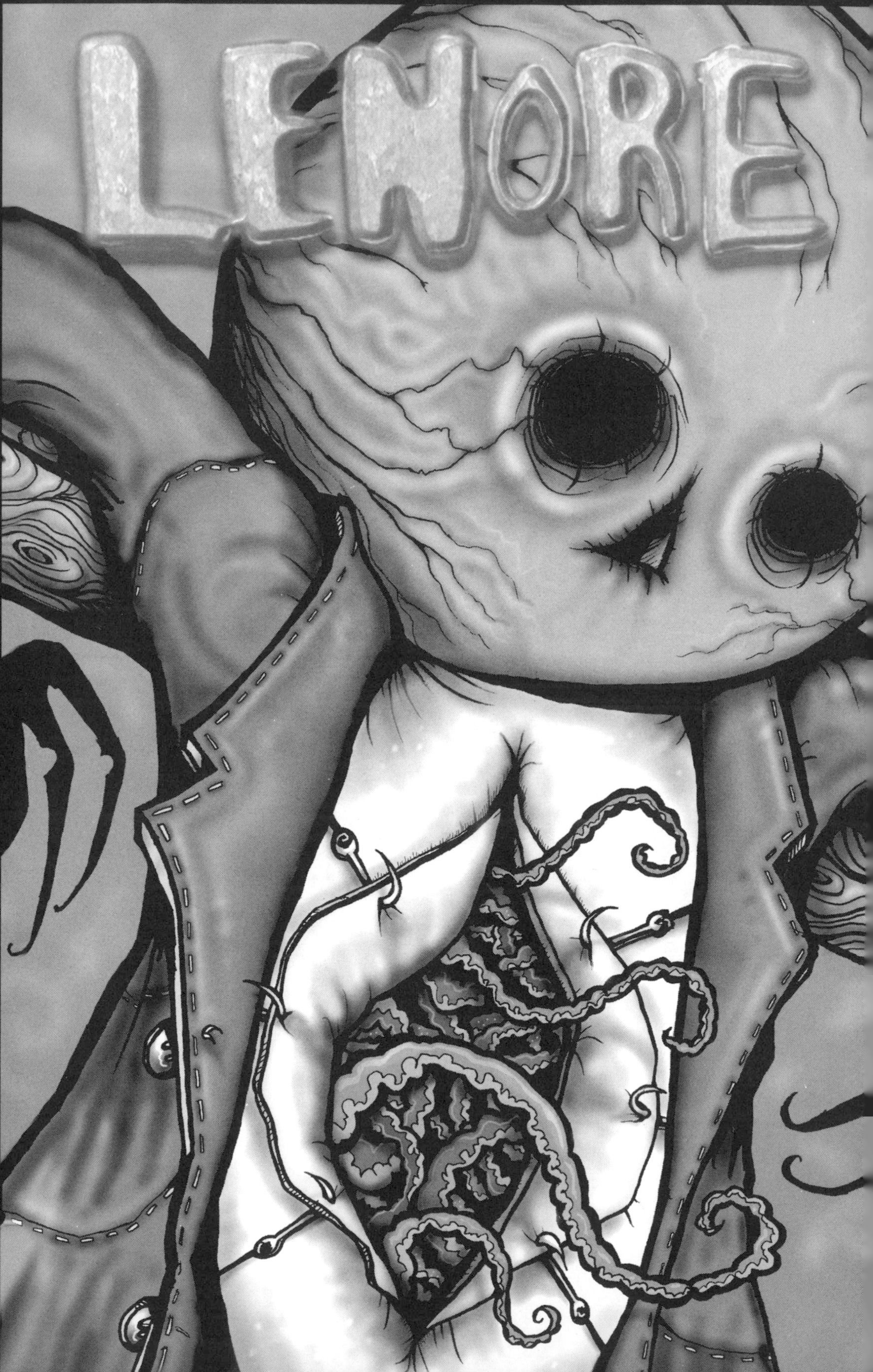
LENORE

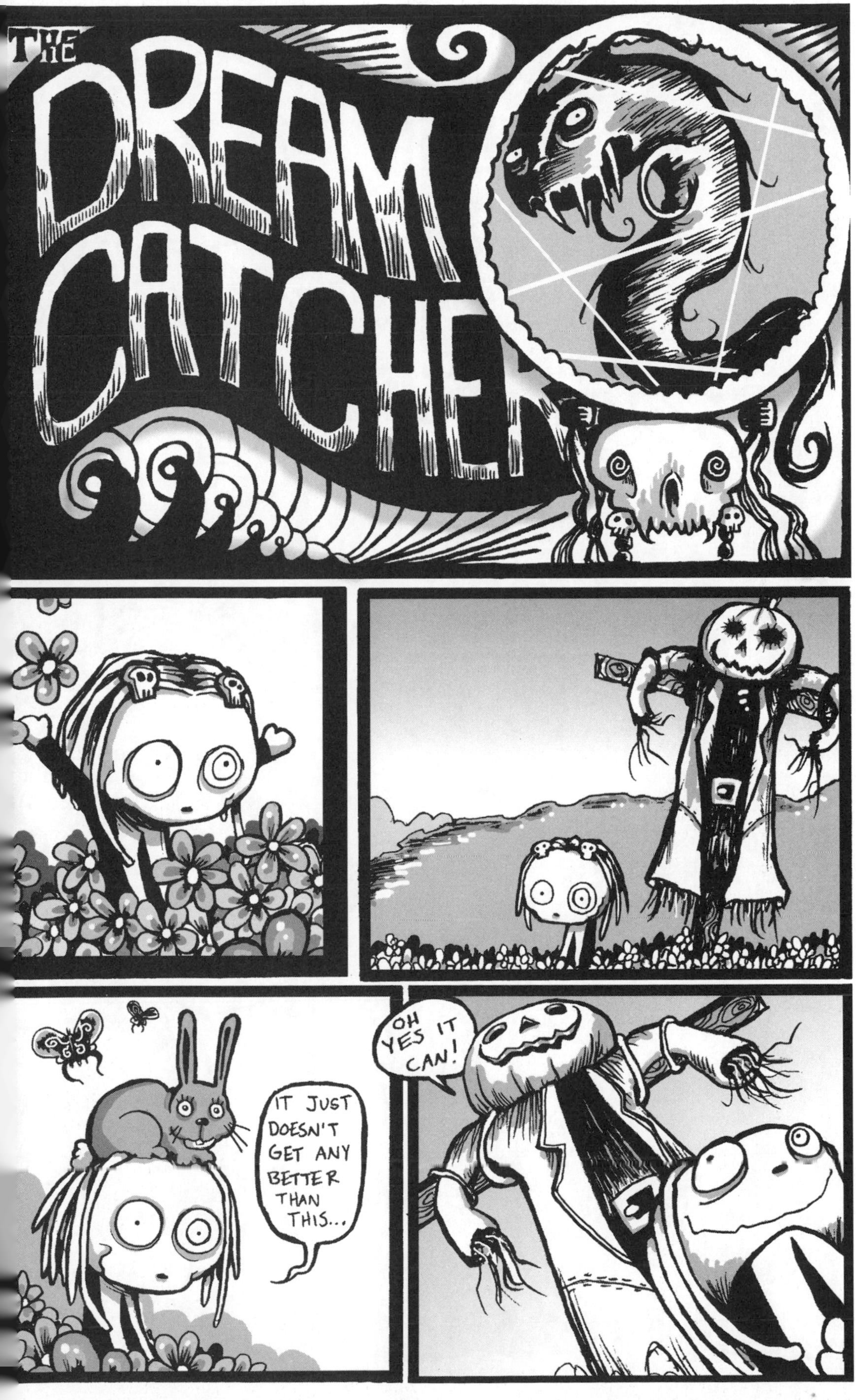
THE DREAM CATCHER
IT JUST DOESN'T GET ANY BETTER THAN THIS...
OH YES IT CAN!

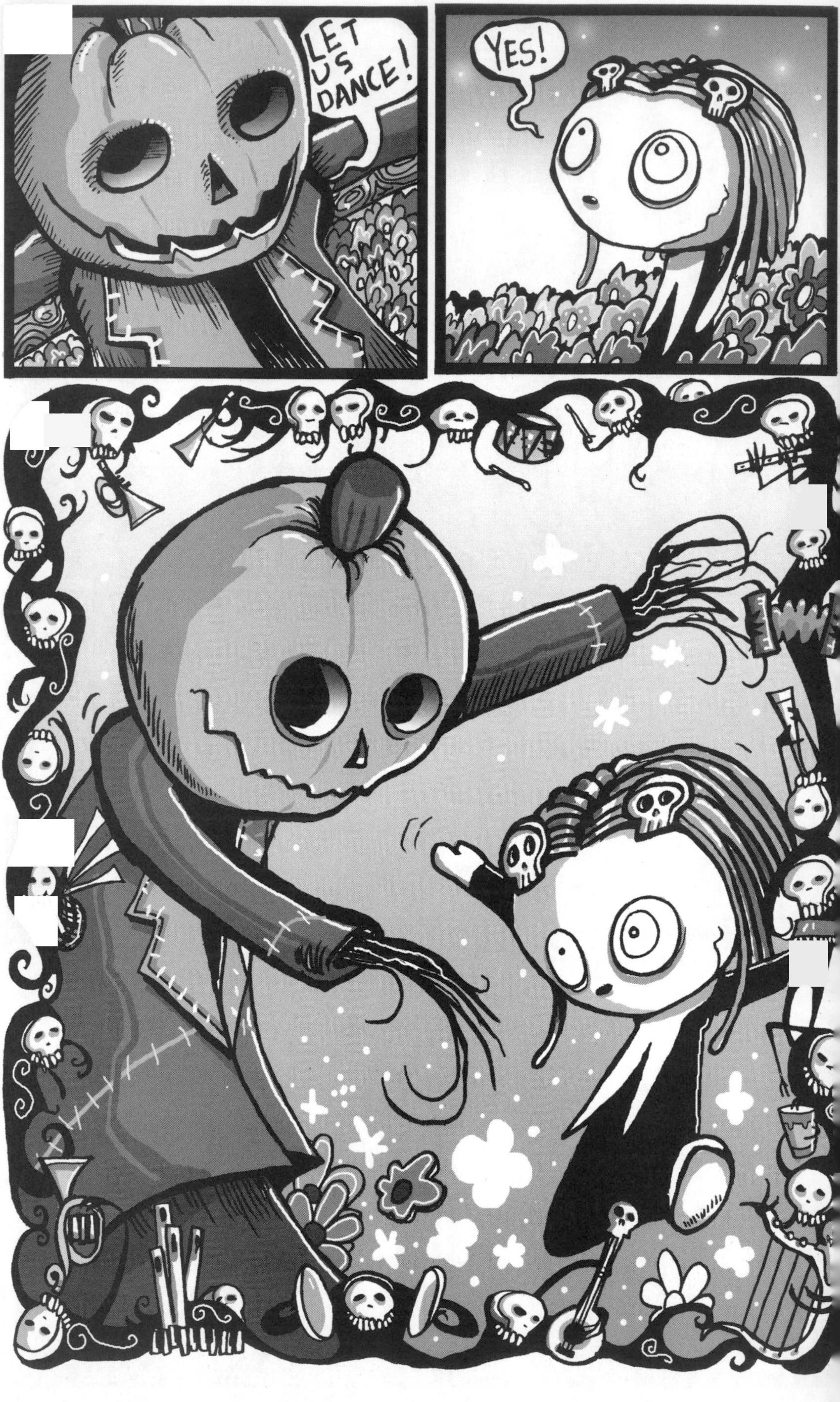
LET US DANCE!
YES!

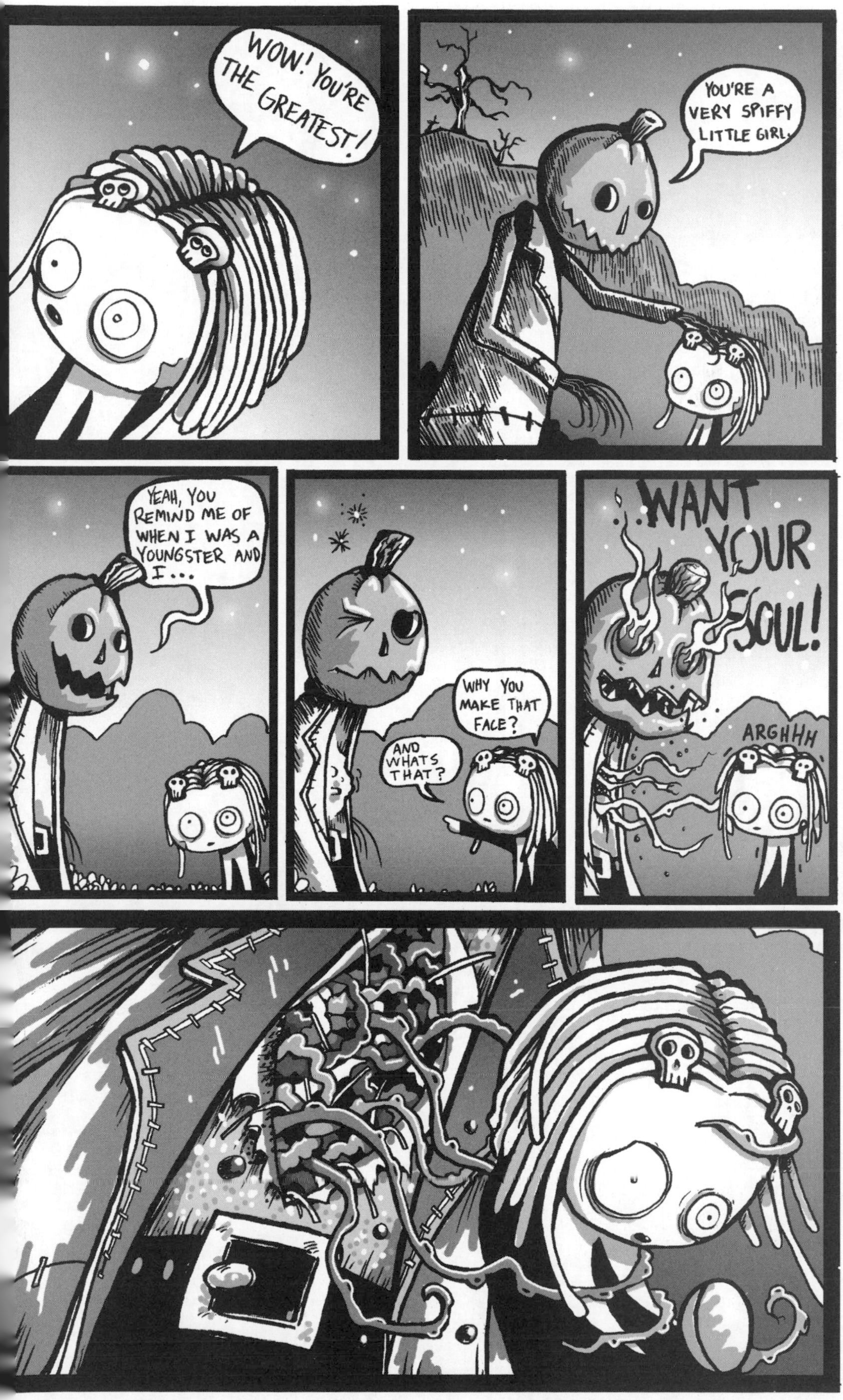
WOW! YOU'RE THE GREATEST!
YOU'RE A VERY SPIFFY LITTLE GIRL.
YEAH, YOU REMIND ME OF WHEN I WAS A YOUNGSTER AND I...
WHY YOU MAKE THAT FACE?
AND WHATS THAT?
WANT YOUR SOUL!
ARGHHH

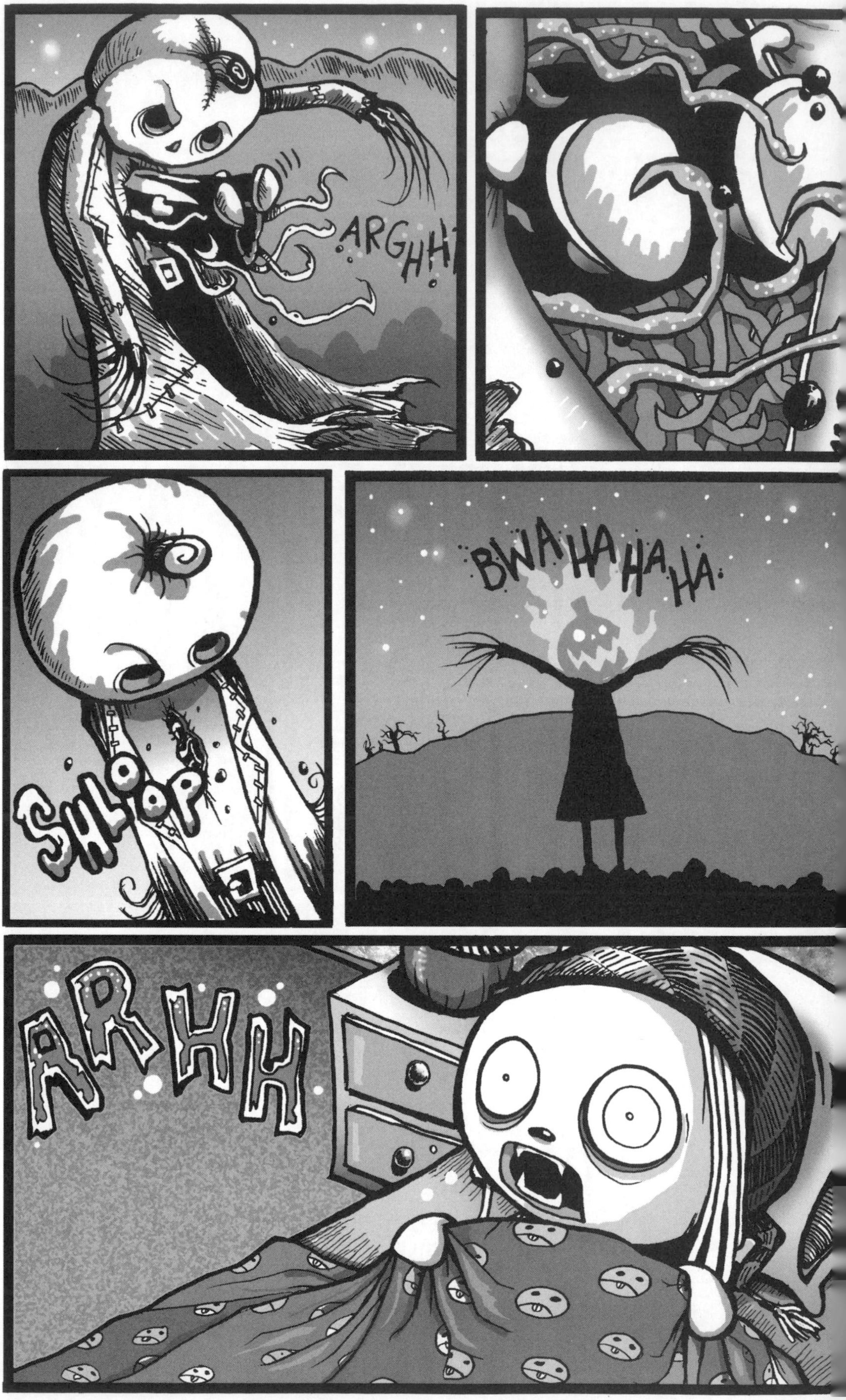
ARGH
SHLOOP
BWAHAHAHAHA
ARHH

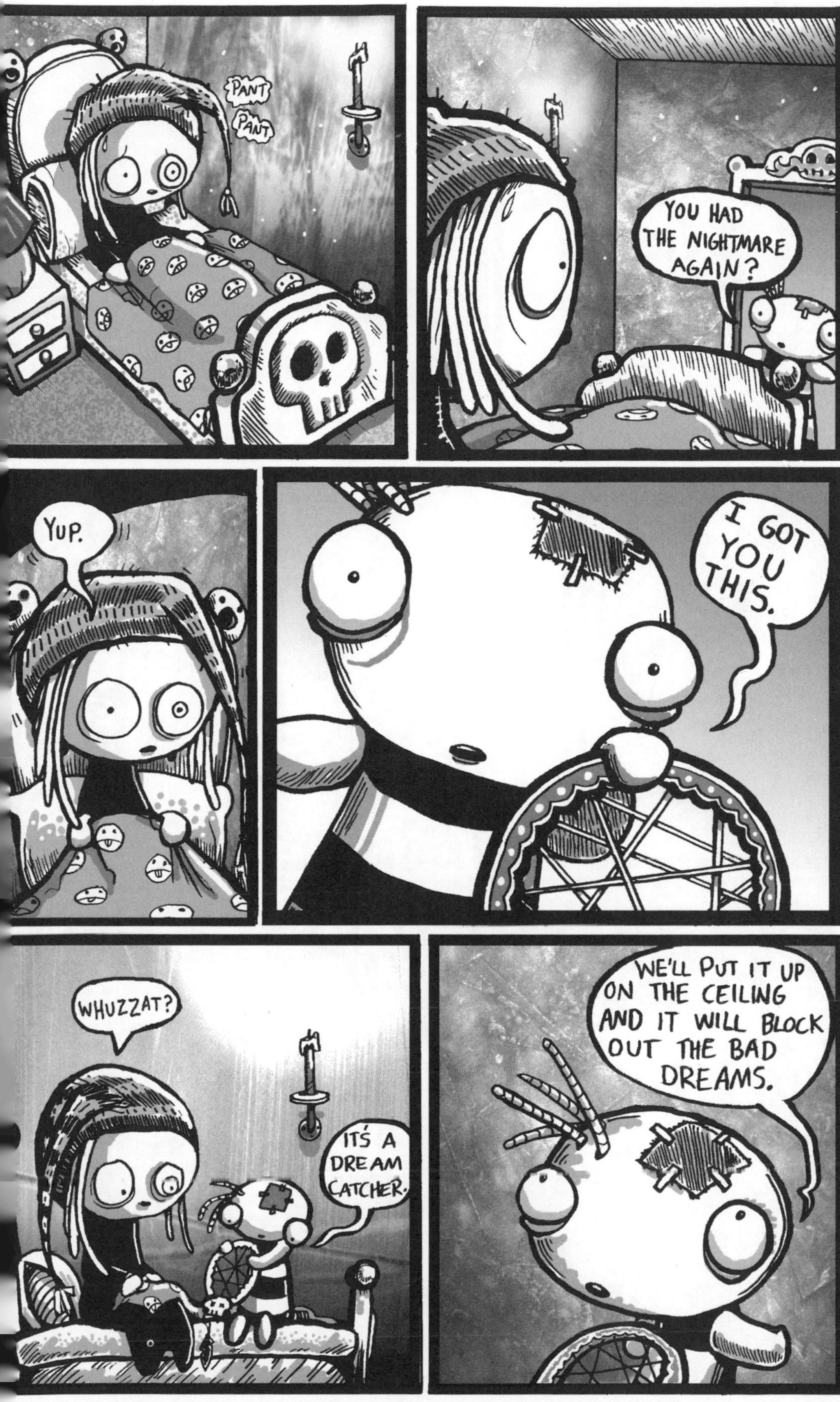
PANT
PANT
YOU HAD THE NIGHTMARE AGAIN?
YUP.
I GOT YOU THIS.
WHUZZAT?
IT'S A DREAM CATCHER.
WE'LL PUT IT UP ON THE CEILING AND IT WILL BLOCK OUT THE BAD DREAMS.

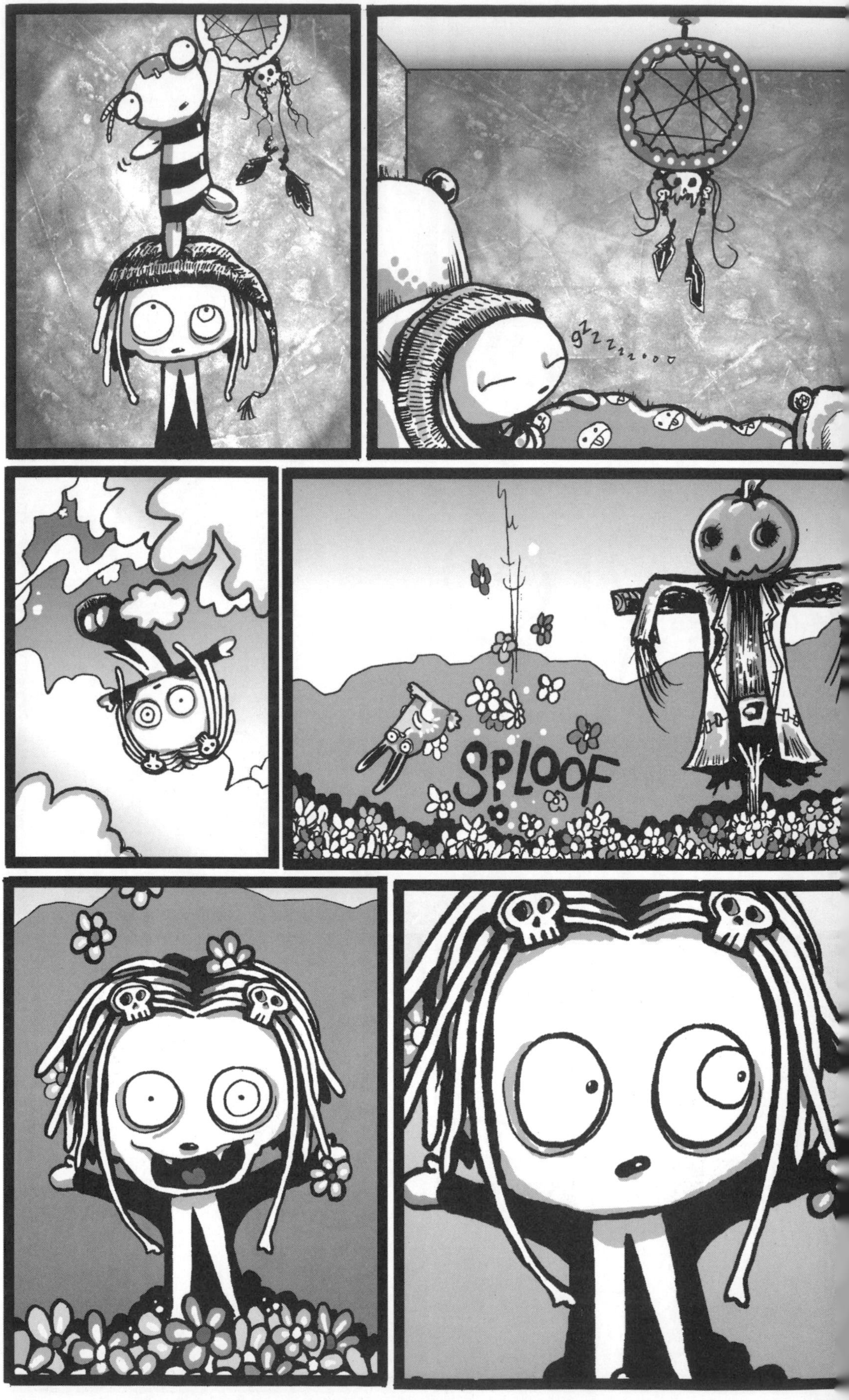
SPLOOF

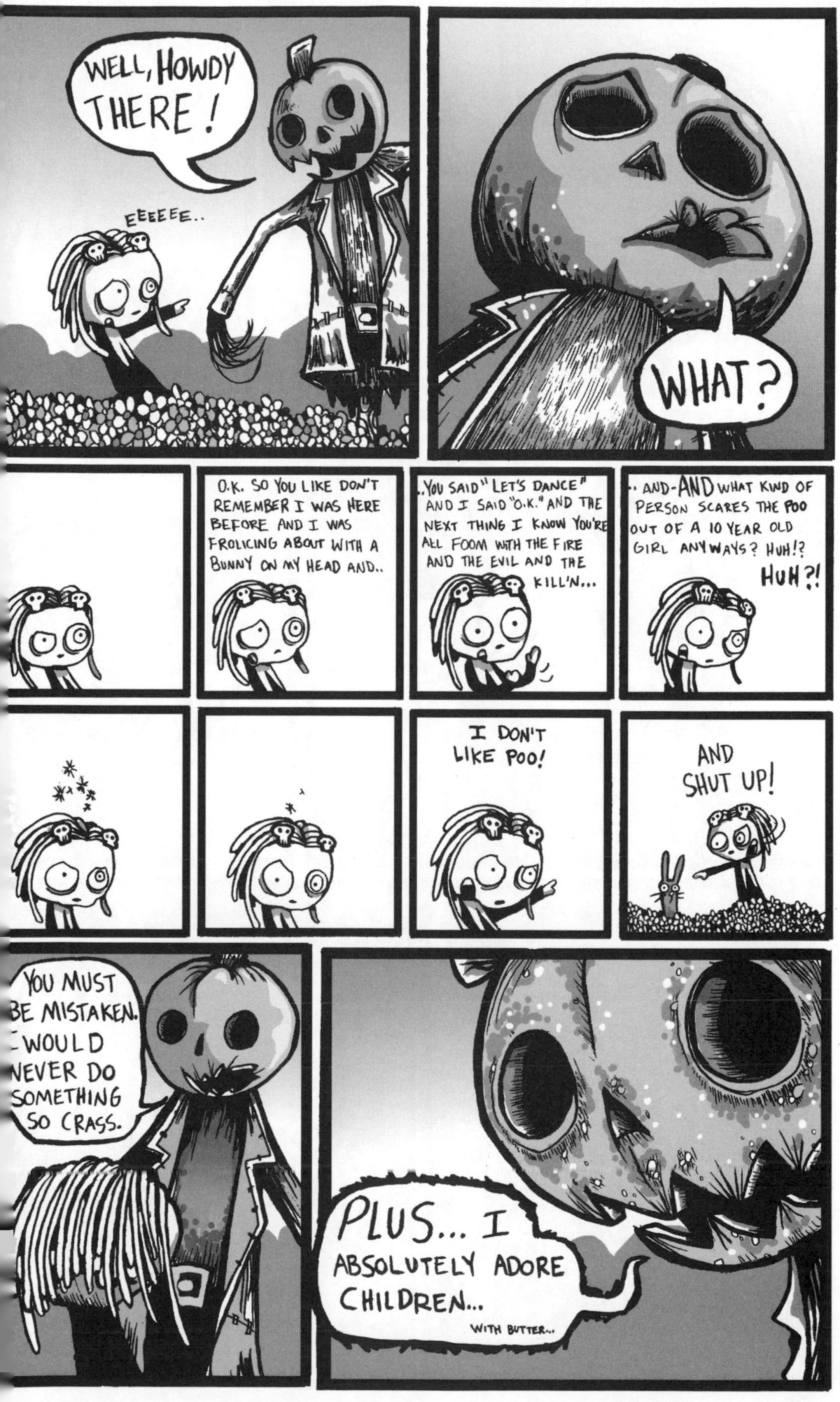
WELL, HOWDY THERE!
EEEEEE..
WHAT?
O.K. SO YOU LIKE DON'T REMEMBER I WAS HERE BEFORE AND I WAS FROLICING ABOUT WITH A BUNNY ON MY HEAD AND..
..YOU SAID "LET'S DANCE" AND I SAID "O.K." AND THE NEXT THING I KNOW YOU'RE ALL FOOM WITH THE FIRE AND THE EVIL AND THE KILL'N...
..AND-AND WHAT KIND OF PERSON SCARES THE POO OUT OF A 10 YEAR OLD GIRL ANYWAYS? HUH!?
HUH?!
I DON'T LIKE POO!
AND SHUT UP!
YOU MUST BE MISTAKEN. I WOULD NEVER DO SOMETHING SO CRASS.
PLUS... I ABSOLUTELY ADORE CHILDREN...
WITH BUTTER...

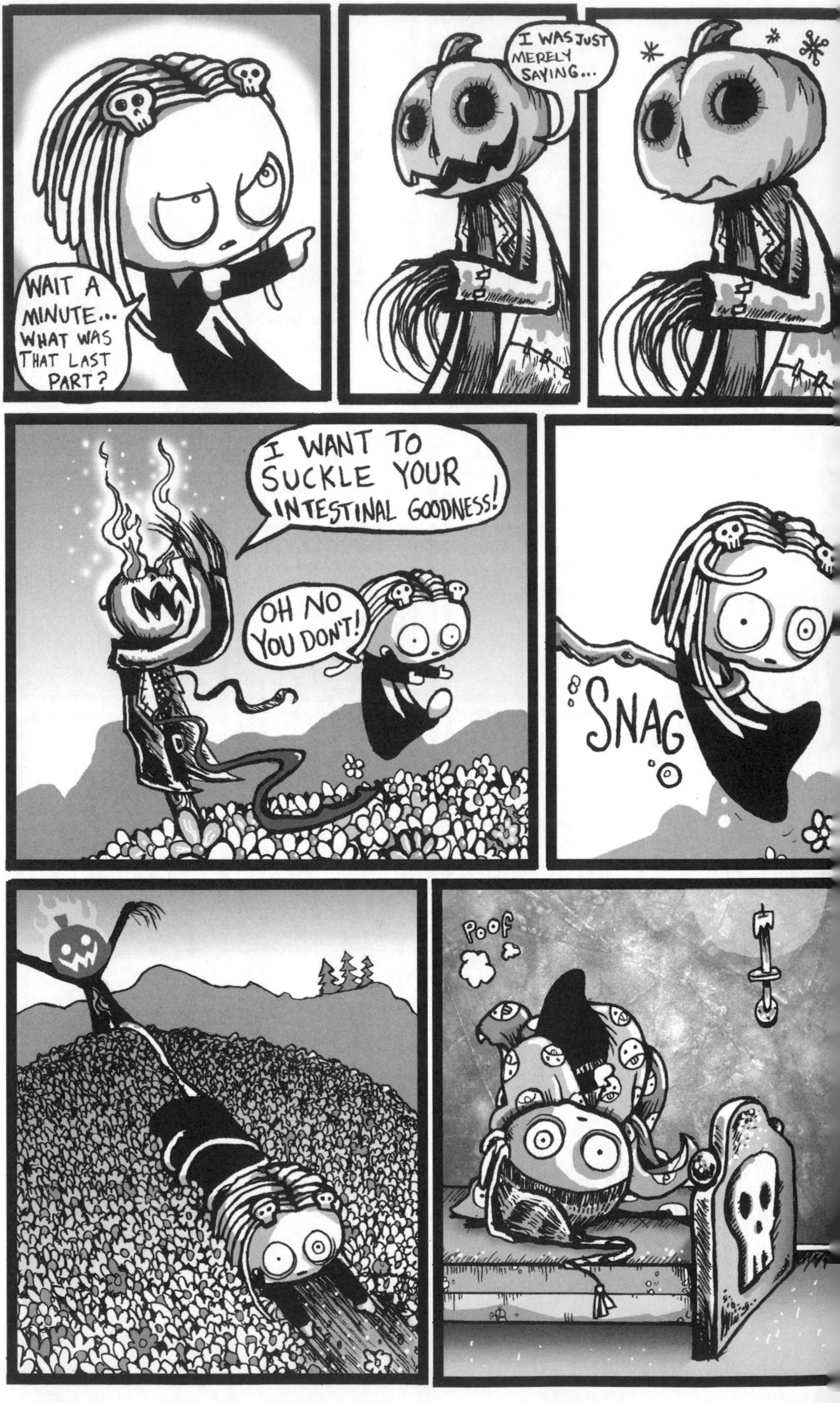
WAIT A MINUTE... WHAT WAS THAT LAST PART?
I WAS JUST MERELY SAYING...
I WANT TO SUCKLE YOUR INTESTINAL GOODNESS!
OH NO YOU DON'T!
SNAG
POOF

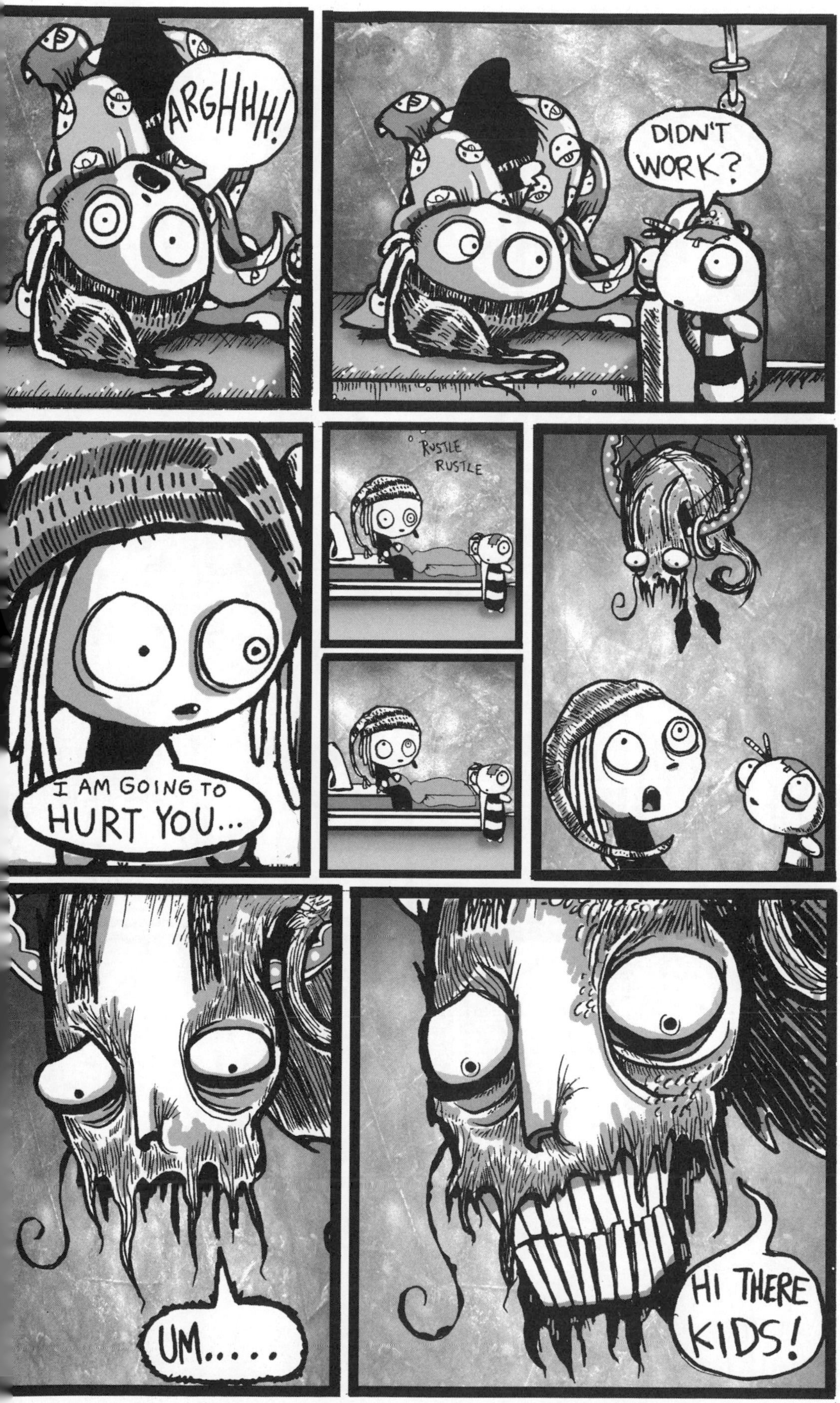
ARGHHH!
DIDN'T WORK?
I AM GOING TO HURT YOU...
RUSTLE RUSTLE
UM.....
HI THERE KIDS!

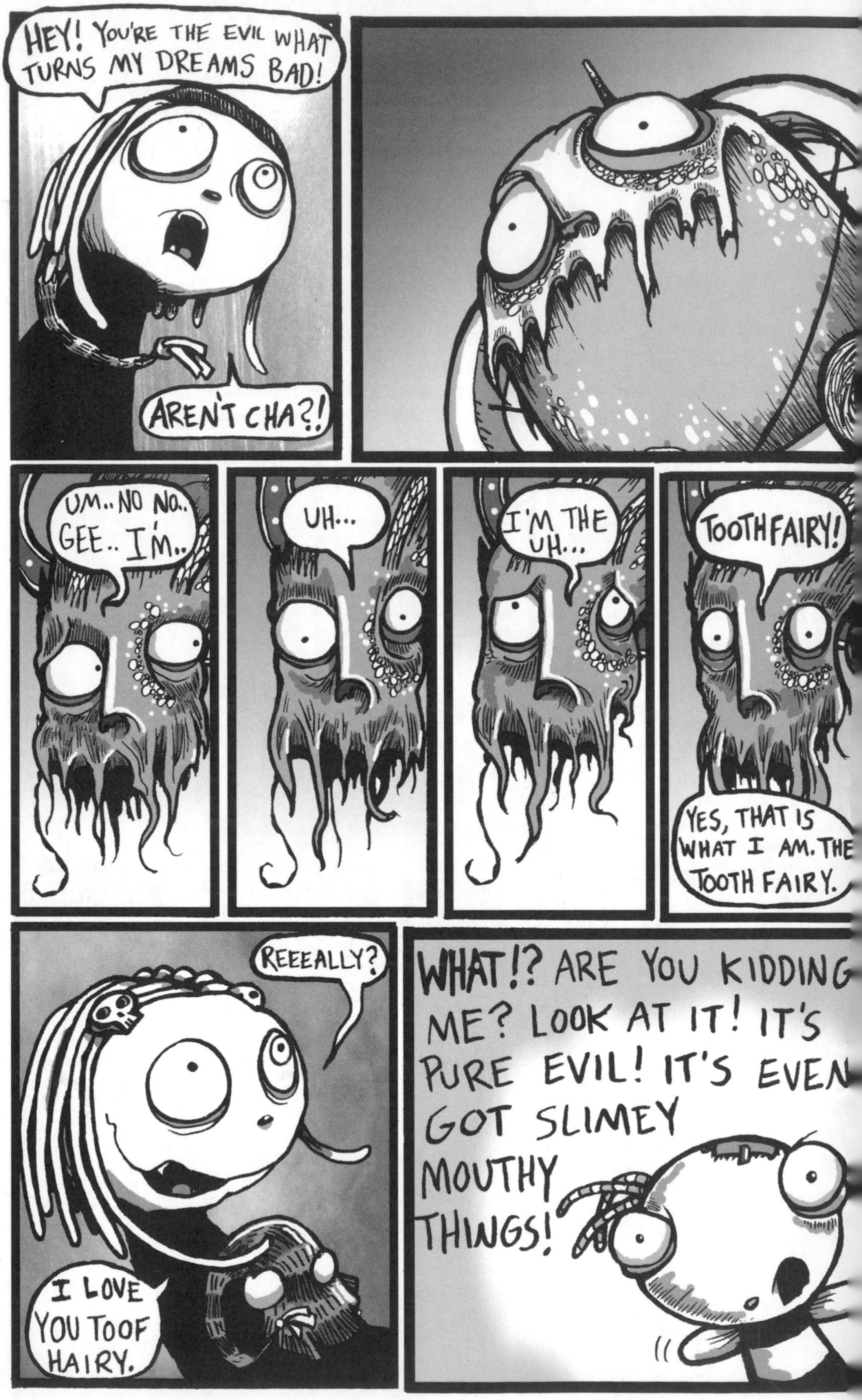
HEY! YOU'RE THE EVIL WHAT TURNS MY DREAMS BAD!
AREN'T CHA?!
UM.. NO NO.. GEE.. I'M..
UH...
I'M THE UH...
TOOTHFAIRY!
YES, THAT IS WHAT I AM. THE TOOTH FAIRY.
REEEALLY?
I LOVE YOU TOOF HAIRY.
WHAT!? ARE YOU KIDDING ME? LOOK AT IT! IT'S PURE EVIL! IT'S EVEN GOT SLIMEY MOUTHY THINGS!

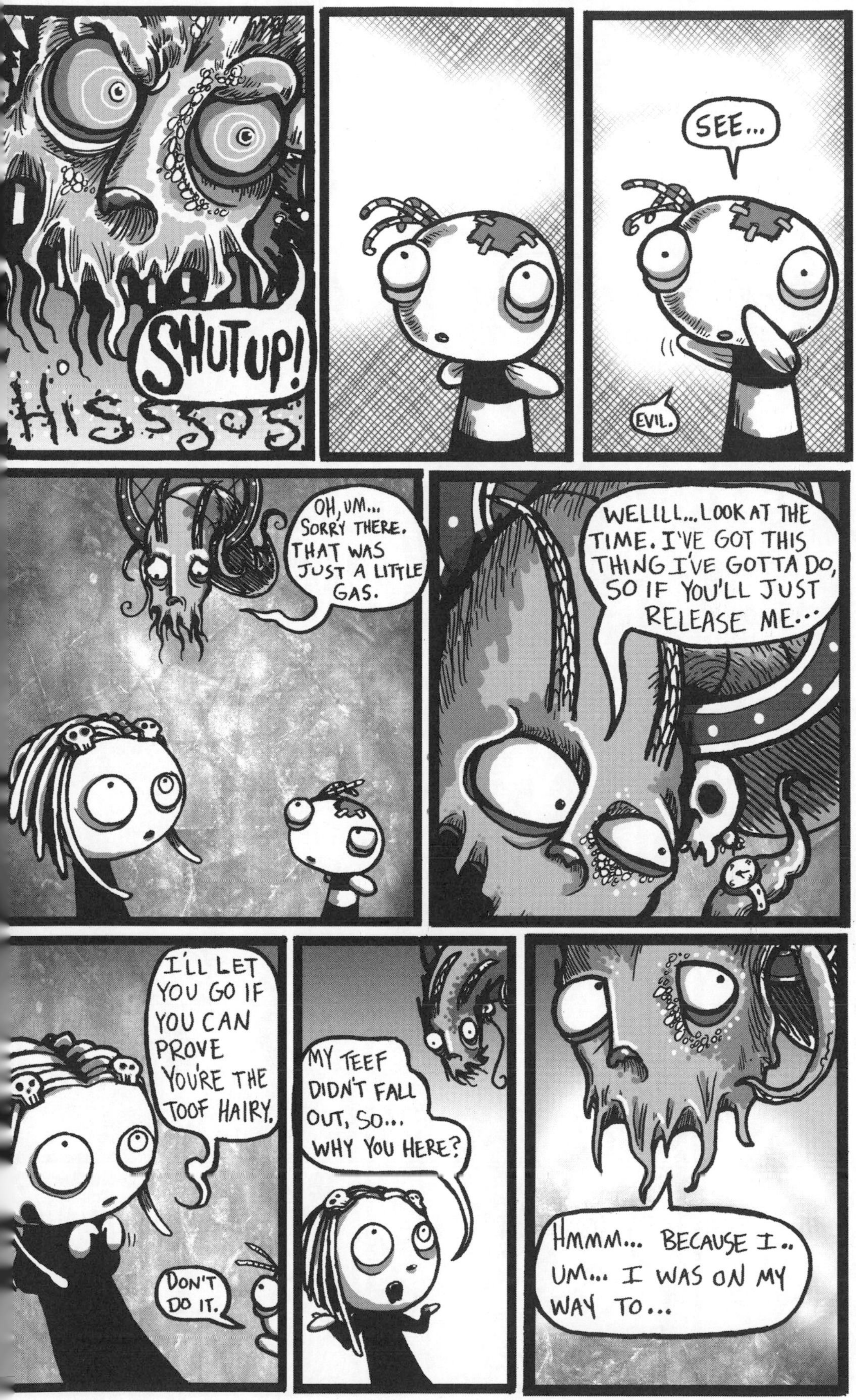
SHUTUP!
HISSSSS
SEE...
EVIL.
OH, UM... SORRY THERE. THAT WAS JUST A LITTLE GAS.
WELLLL... LOOK AT THE TIME. I'VE GOT THIS THING I'VE GOTTA DO, SO IF YOU'LL JUST RELEASE ME...
I'LL LET YOU GO IF YOU CAN PROVE YOU'RE THE TOOF HAIRY.
DON'T DO IT.
MY TEEF DIDN'T FALL OUT, SO... WHY YOU HERE?
HMMM... BECAUSE I.. UM... I WAS ON MY WAY TO...

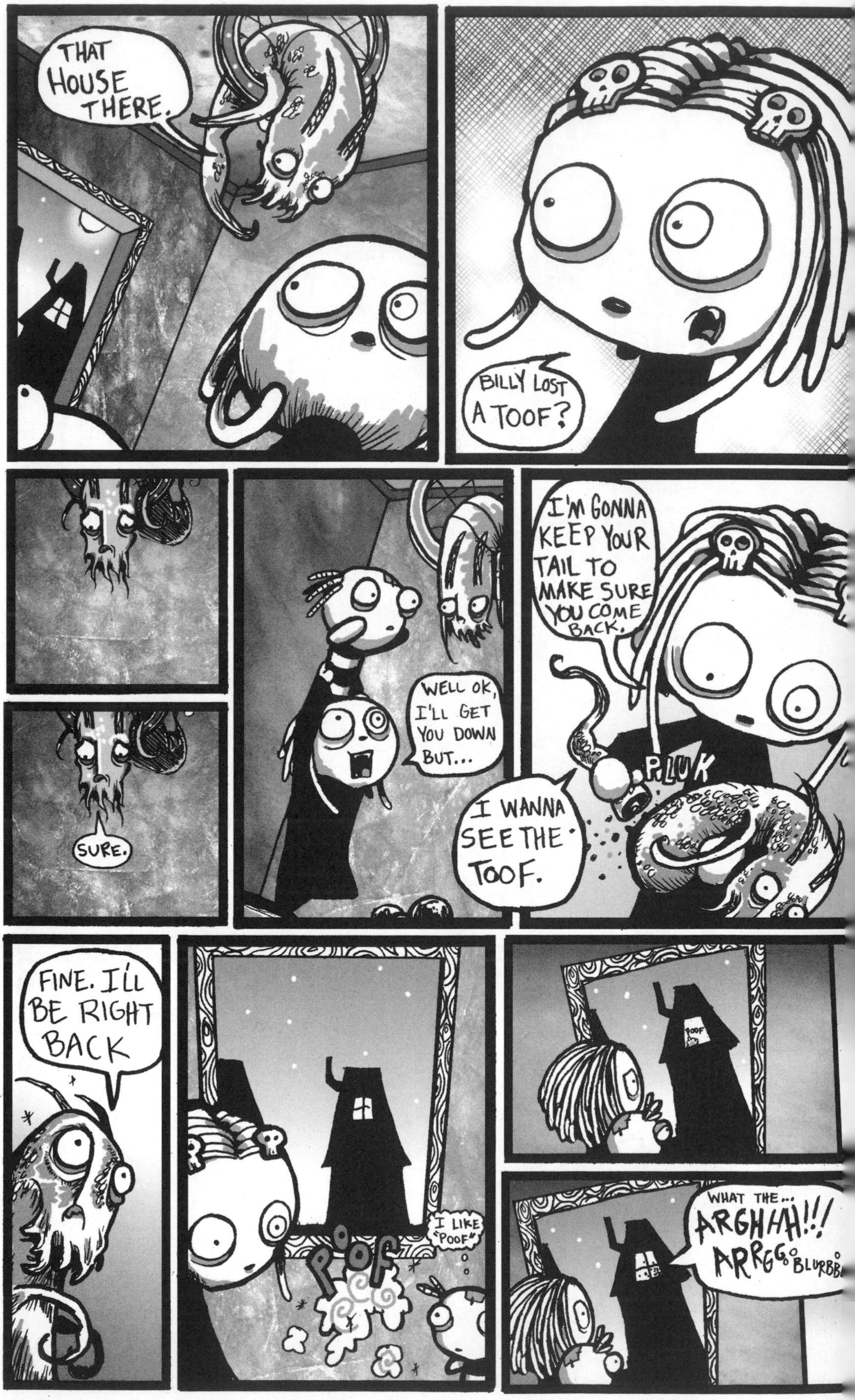
THAT HOUSE THERE.
BILLY LOST A TOOF?
SURE.
WELL OK, I'LL GET YOU DOWN BUT...
I'M GONNA KEEP YOUR TAIL TO MAKE SURE YOU COME BACK.
PLUK
I WANNA SEE THE TOOF.
FINE. I'LL BE RIGHT BACK
POOF
I LIKE "POOF"
POOF
WHAT THE... ARGHHH!!! ARRGG BLURBB

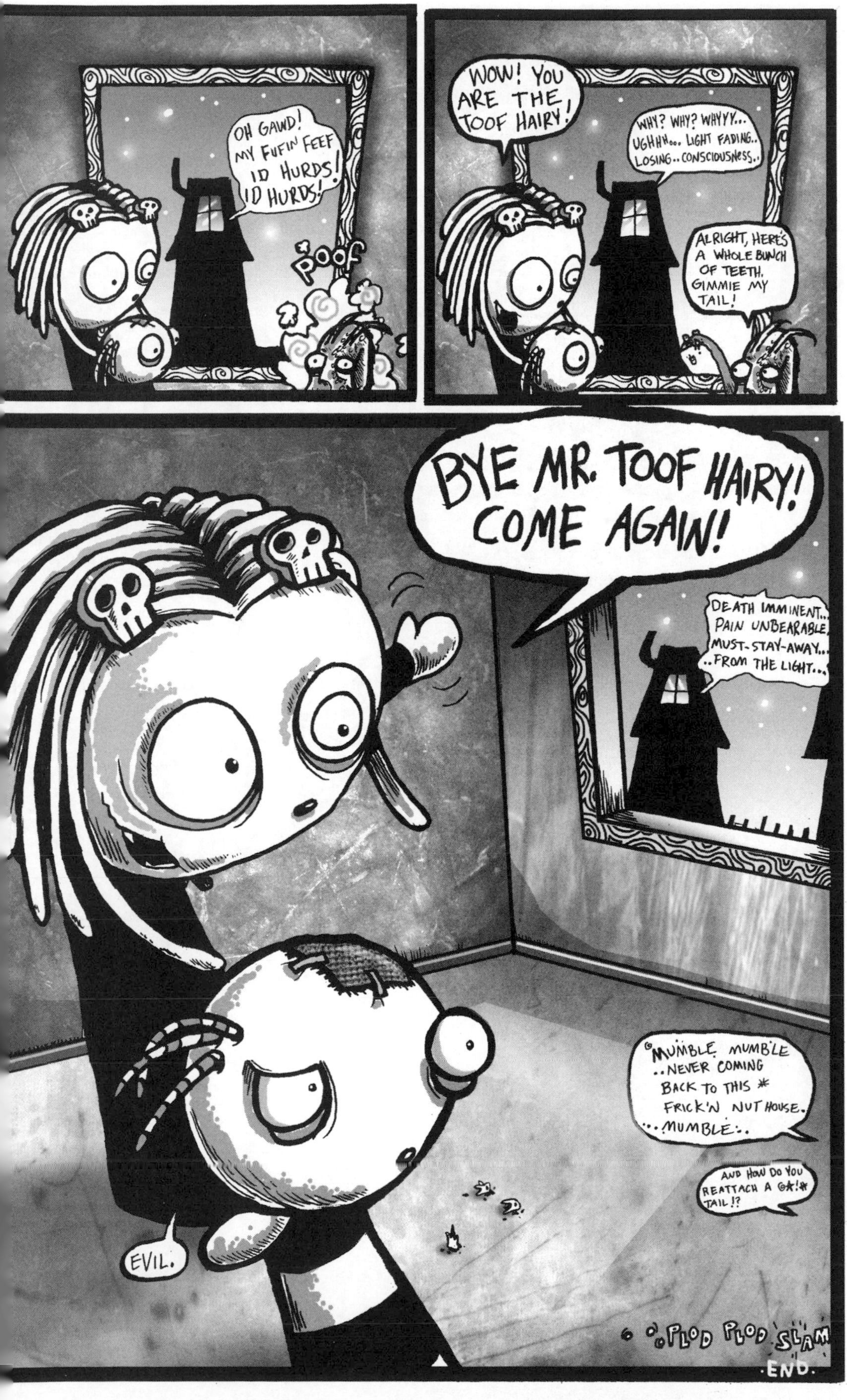
OH GAWD! MY FUFIN' FEEF ID HURDS! ID HURDS!
POOF
WOW! YOU ARE THE TOOF HAIRY!
WHY? WHY? WHYYY... UGHHH... LIGHT FADING.. LOSING.. CONSCIOUSNESS..
ALRIGHT, HERE'S A WHOLE BUNCH OF TEETH. GIMMIE MY TAIL!
BYE MR. TOOF HAIRY! COME AGAIN!
DEATH IMMINENT... PAIN UNBEARABLE, MUST-STAY-AWAY... ..FROM THE LIGHT...
MUMBLE MUMBLE ..NEVER COMING BACK TO THIS * FRICK'N NUT HOUSE. ...MUMBLE..
AND HOW DO YOU REATTACH A @★!* TAIL!?
EVIL.
PLOD PLOD SLAM
·END·

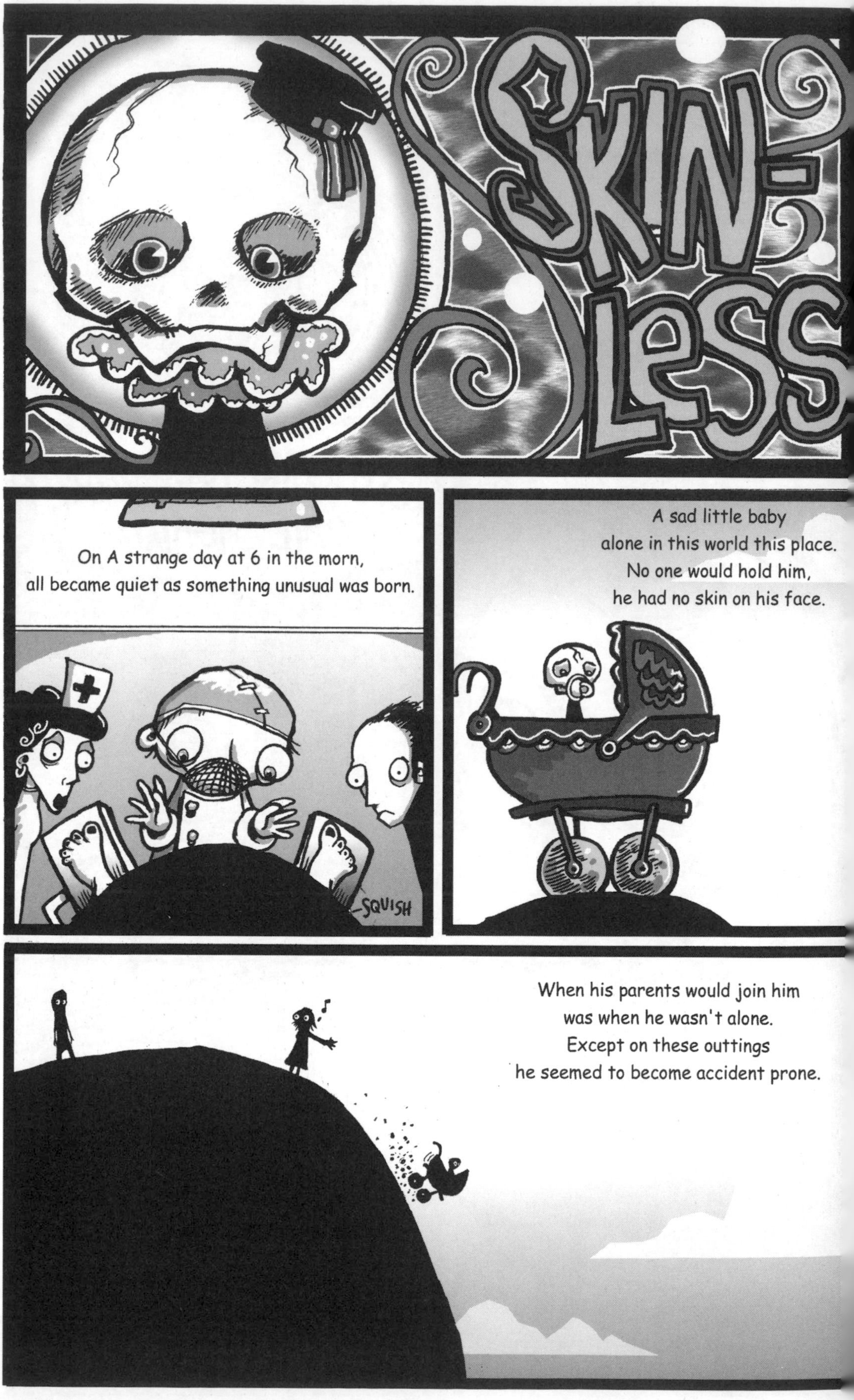
SKIN-LESS
On A strange day at 6 in the morn,
all became quiet as something unusual was born.
SQUISH
A sad little baby
alone in this world this place.
No one would hold him,
he had no skin on his face.
When his parents would join him
was when he wasn't alone.
Except on these outtings
he seemed to become accident prone.

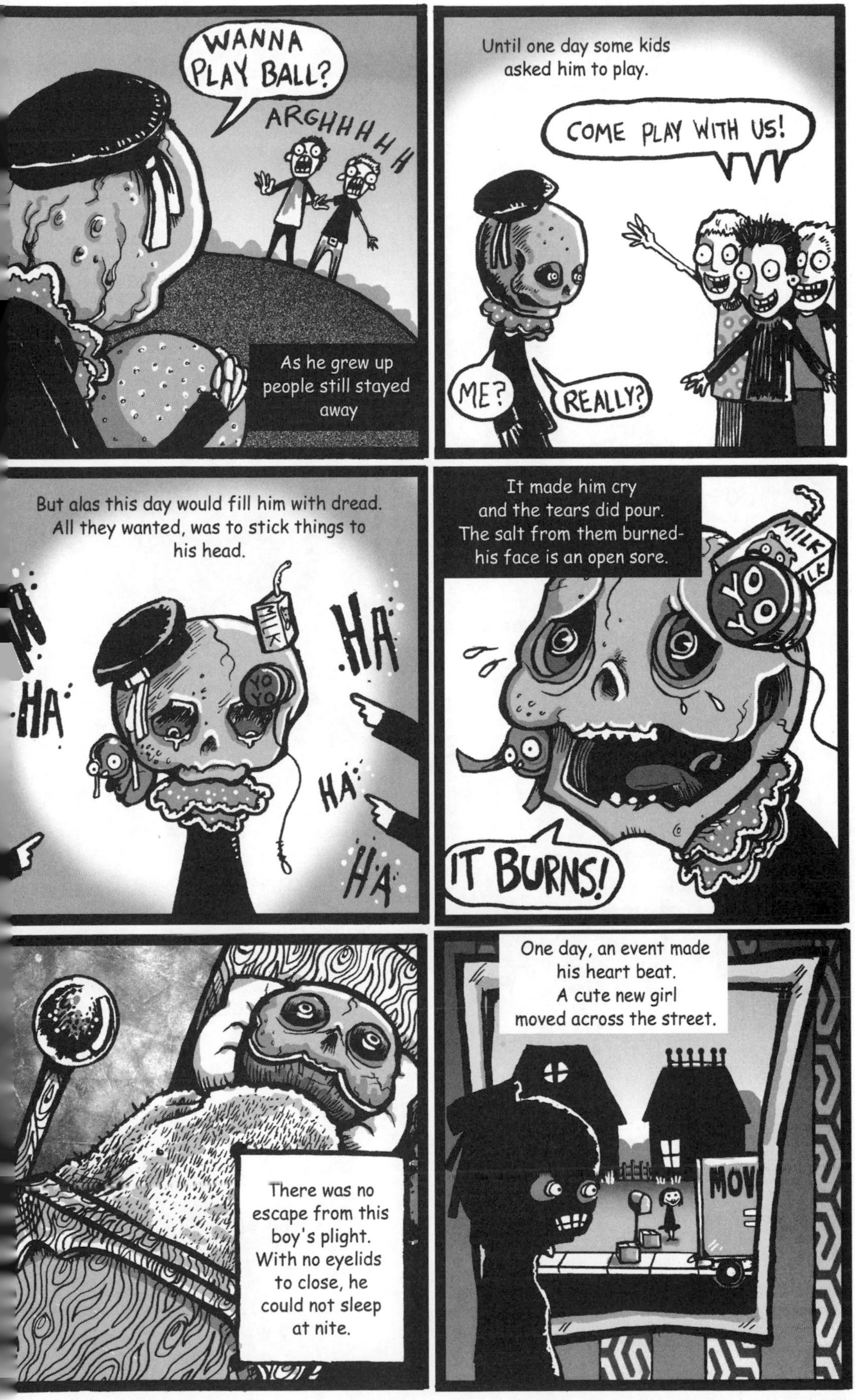
WANNA PLAY BALL?
ARGHHHHHH
As he grew up people still stayed away
Until one day some kids asked him to play.
COME PLAY WITH US!
ME?
REALLY?
But alas this day would fill him with dread. All they wanted, was to stick things to his head.
MILK
YO YO
HA
HA
HA
HA
It made him cry and the tears did pour. The salt from them burned- his face is an open sore.
MILK
YO YO
IT BURNS!
There was no escape from this boy's plight. With no eyelids to close, he could not sleep at nite.
One day, an event made his heart beat. A cute new girl moved across the street.
MOV

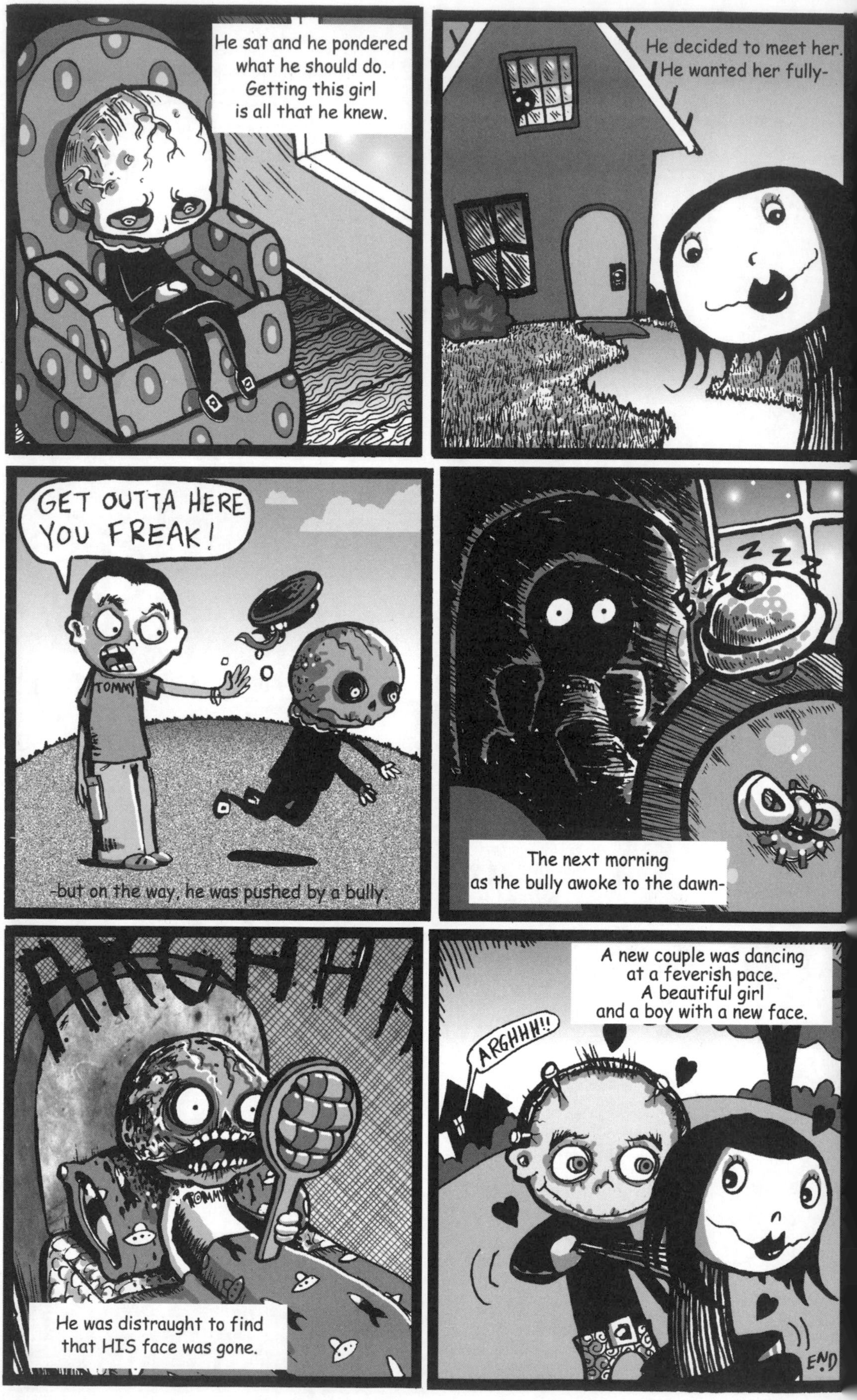

He sat and he pondered
what he should do.
Getting this girl
is all that he knew.
He decided to meet her.
He wanted her fully-
GET OUTTA HERE
YOU FREAK!
TOMMY
-but on the way, he was pushed by a bully.
The next morning
as the bully awoke to the dawn-
ARGHHH
TOMMY
He was distraught to find
that HIS face was gone.
A new couple was dancing
at a feverish pace.
A beautiful girl
and a boy with a new face.
ARGHHH!!
END

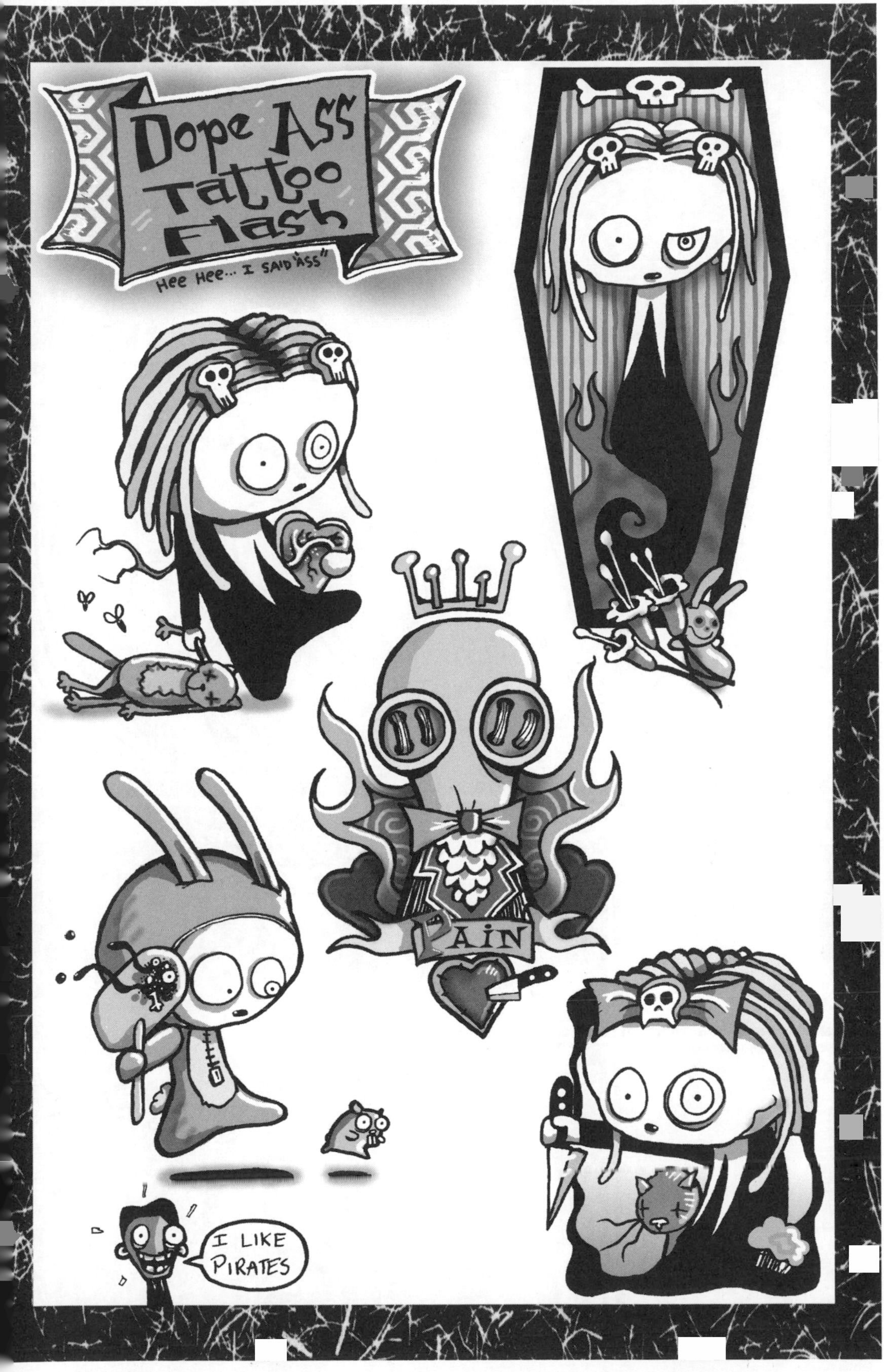
Dope Ass Tattoo Flash
Hee Hee... I said "Ass"
Pain
I LIKE PIRATES

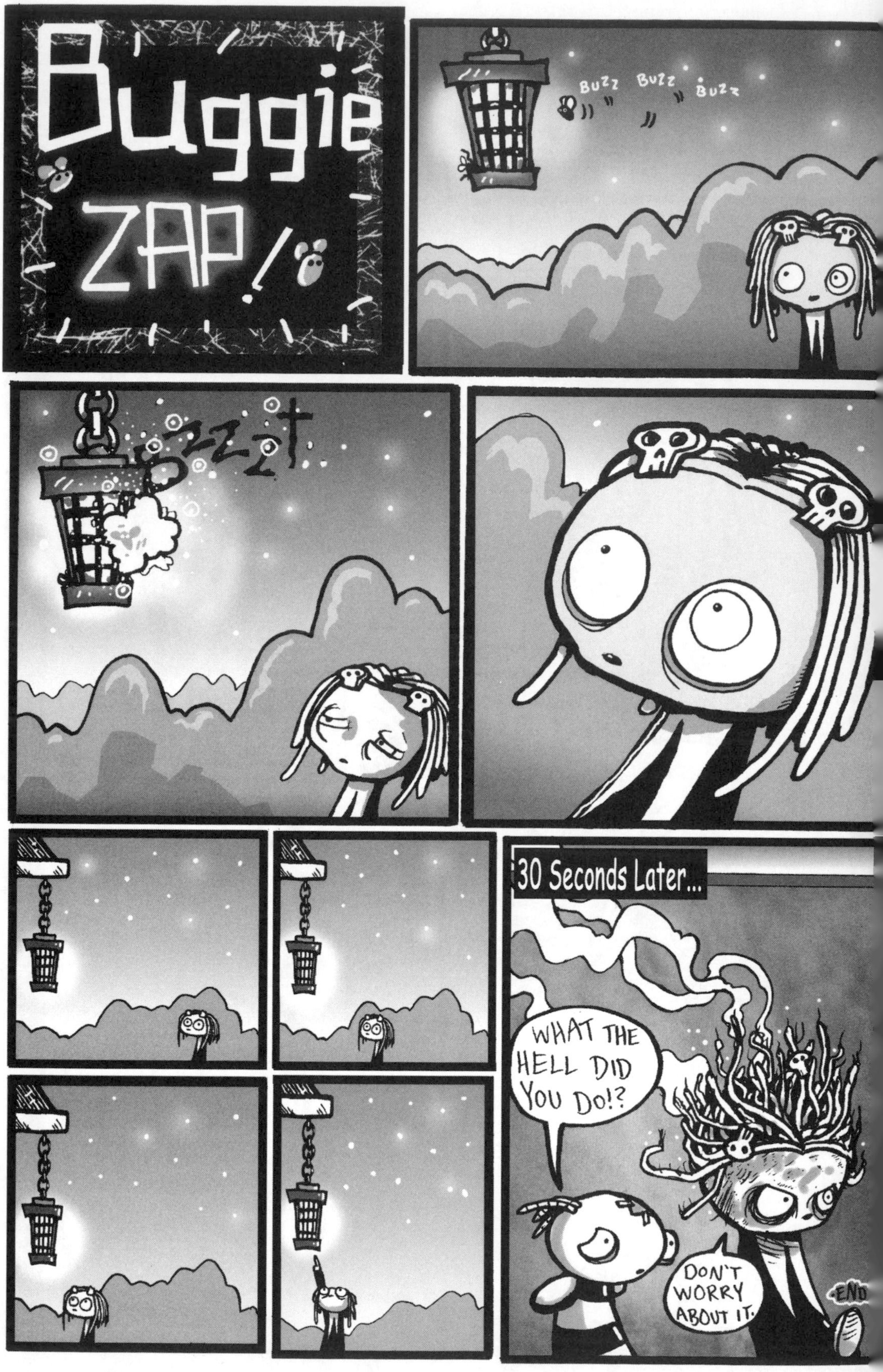
Buggie ZAP!
BUZZ BUZZ BUZZ
ZZZZT
30 Seconds Later...
WHAT THE HELL DID YOU DO!?
DON'T WORRY ABOUT IT.
END

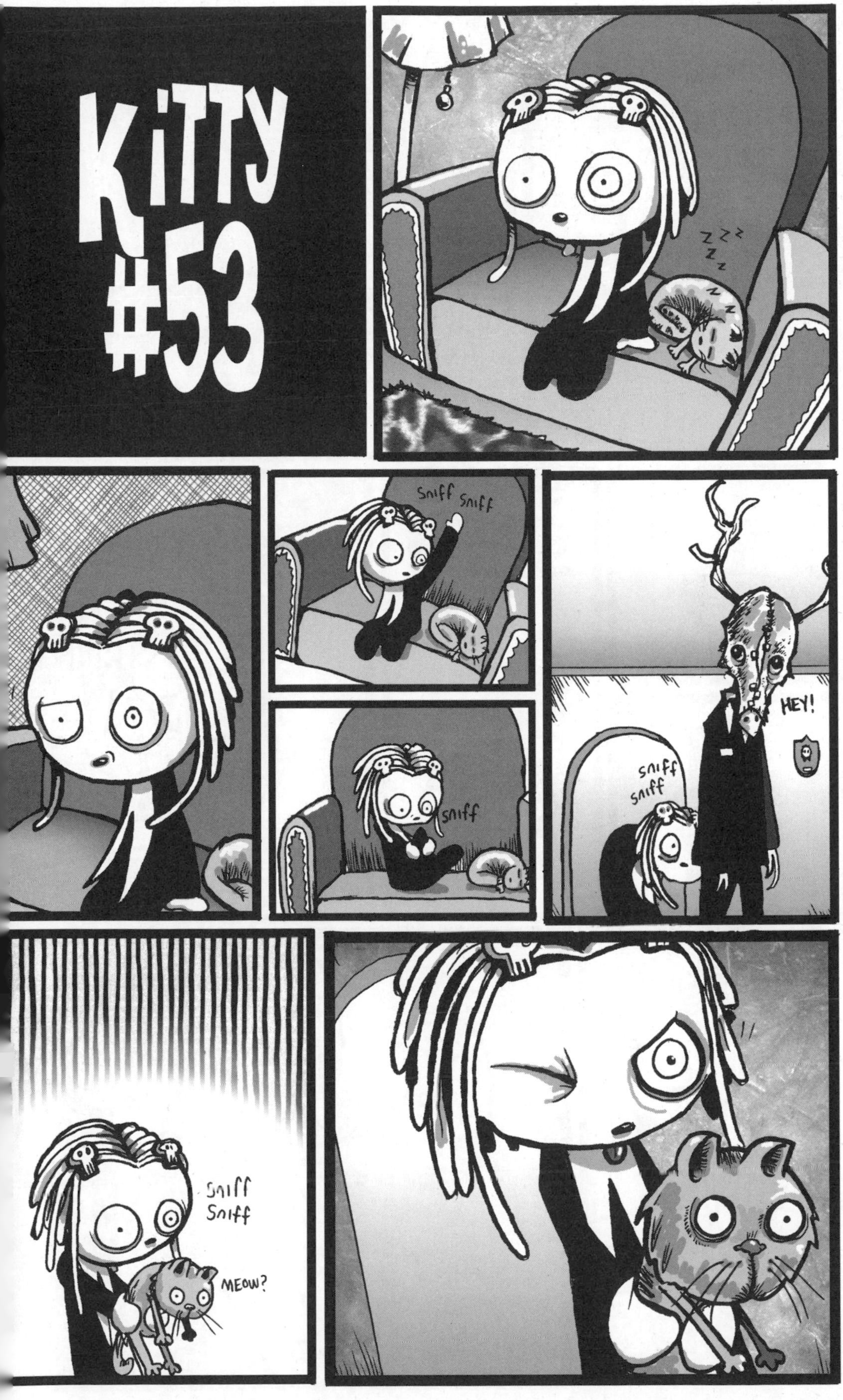
KITTY
#53
Z Z Z
Z
Z
Z
Z
Sniff Sniff
Sniff
Sniff
Sniff
HEY!
Sniff
Sniff
MEOW?

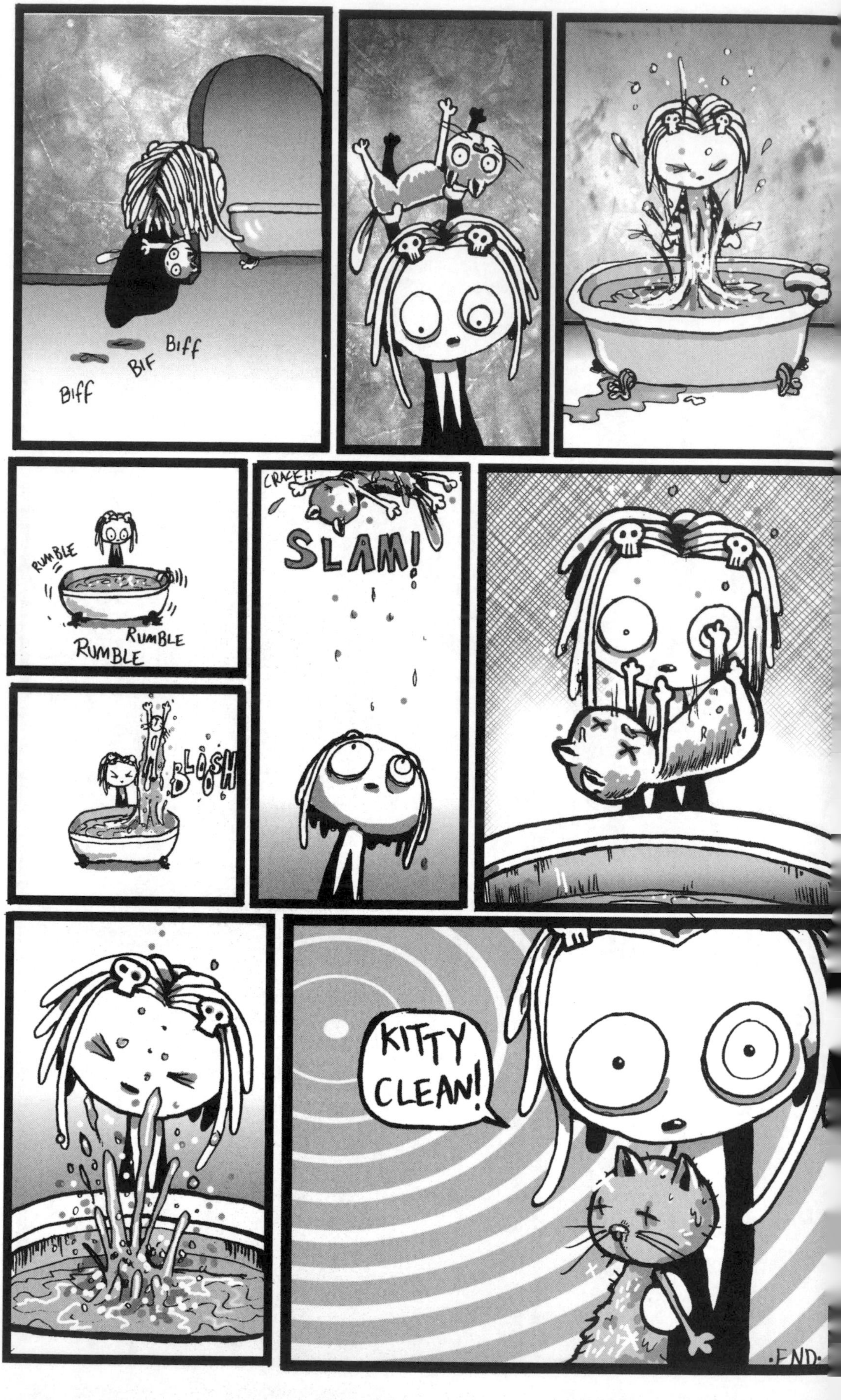
BIFF
BIF
BIFF
RUMBLE
RUMBLE
RUMBLE
BLOSH
CRACK!
SLAM!
KITTY CLEAN!
·END·

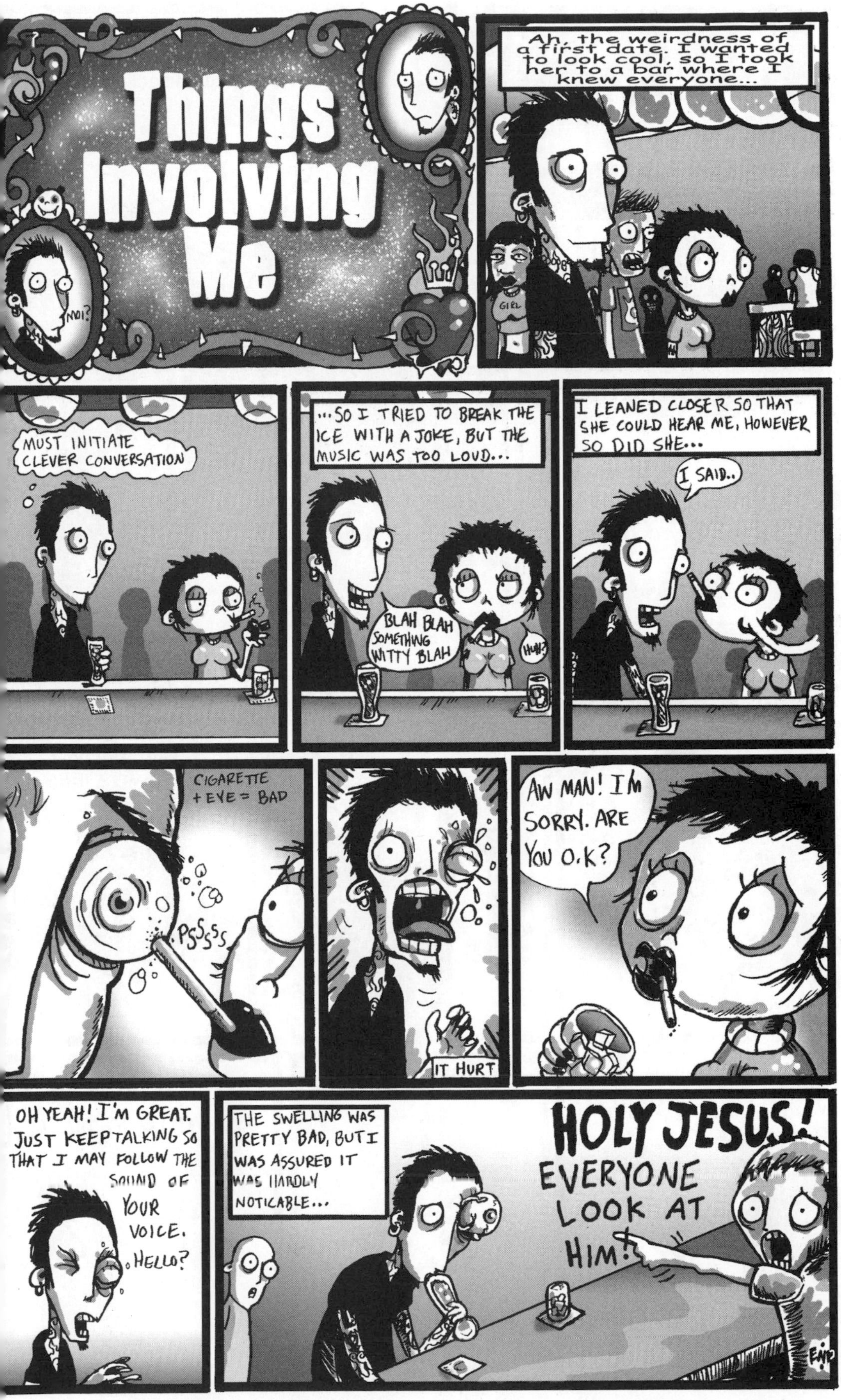

Things Involving Me
MOI?
Ah, the weirdness of a first date. I wanted to look cool, so I took her to a bar where I knew everyone...
GIRL
MUST INITIATE CLEVER CONVERSATION
...SO I TRIED TO BREAK THE ICE WITH A JOKE, BUT THE MUSIC WAS TOO LOUD...
BLAH BLAH SOMETHING WITTY BLAH
HUH?
I LEANED CLOSER SO THAT SHE COULD HEAR ME, HOWEVER SO DID SHE...
I SAID..
CIGARETTE + EYE = BAD
PSSSSS
IT HURT
AW MAN! I'M SORRY. ARE YOU O.K?
OH YEAH! I'M GREAT. JUST KEEP TALKING SO THAT I MAY FOLLOW THE SOUND OF YOUR VOICE. HELLO?
THE SWELLING WAS PRETTY BAD, BUT I WAS ASSURED IT WAS HARDLY NOTICABLE...
HOLY JESUS! EVERYONE LOOK AT HIM!
END

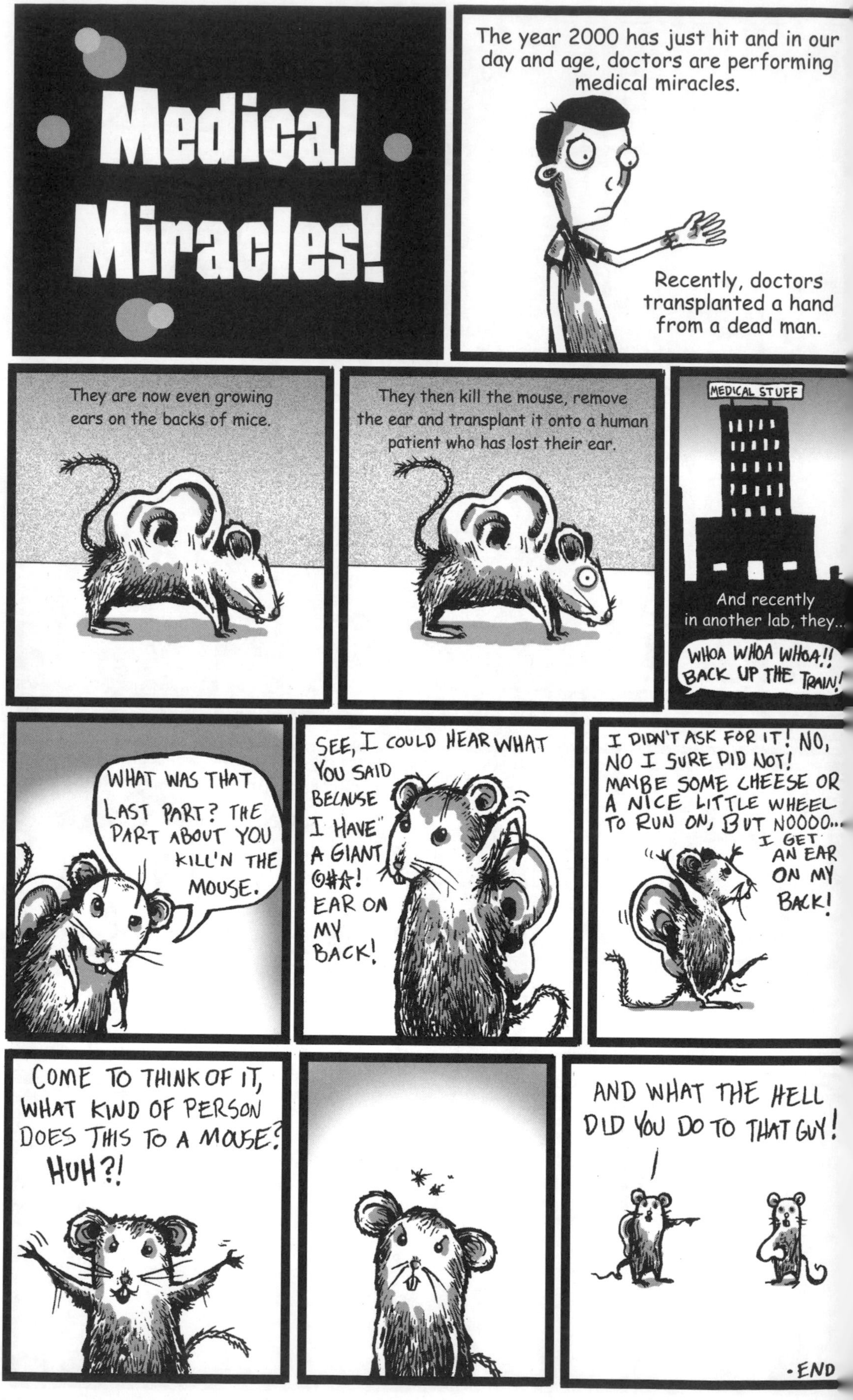
Medical Miracles!
The year 2000 has just hit and in our day and age, doctors are performing medical miracles.
Recently, doctors transplanted a hand from a dead man.
They are now even growing ears on the backs of mice.
They then kill the mouse, remove the ear and transplant it onto a human patient who has lost their ear.
MEDICAL STUFF
And recently in another lab, they...
WHOA WHOA WHOA!! BACK UP THE TRAIN!
WHAT WAS THAT LAST PART? THE PART ABOUT YOU KILL'N THE MOUSE.
SEE, I COULD HEAR WHAT YOU SAID BECAUSE I HAVE A GIANT @#*! EAR ON MY BACK!
I DIDN'T ASK FOR IT! NO, NO I SURE DID NOT! MAYBE SOME CHEESE OR A NICE LITTLE WHEEL TO RUN ON, BUT NOOOO... I GET AN EAR ON MY BACK!
COME TO THINK OF IT, WHAT KIND OF PERSON DOES THIS TO A MOUSE? HUH?!
AND WHAT THE HELL DID YOU DO TO THAT GUY!
-END

国

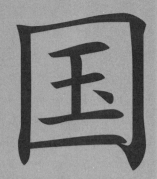

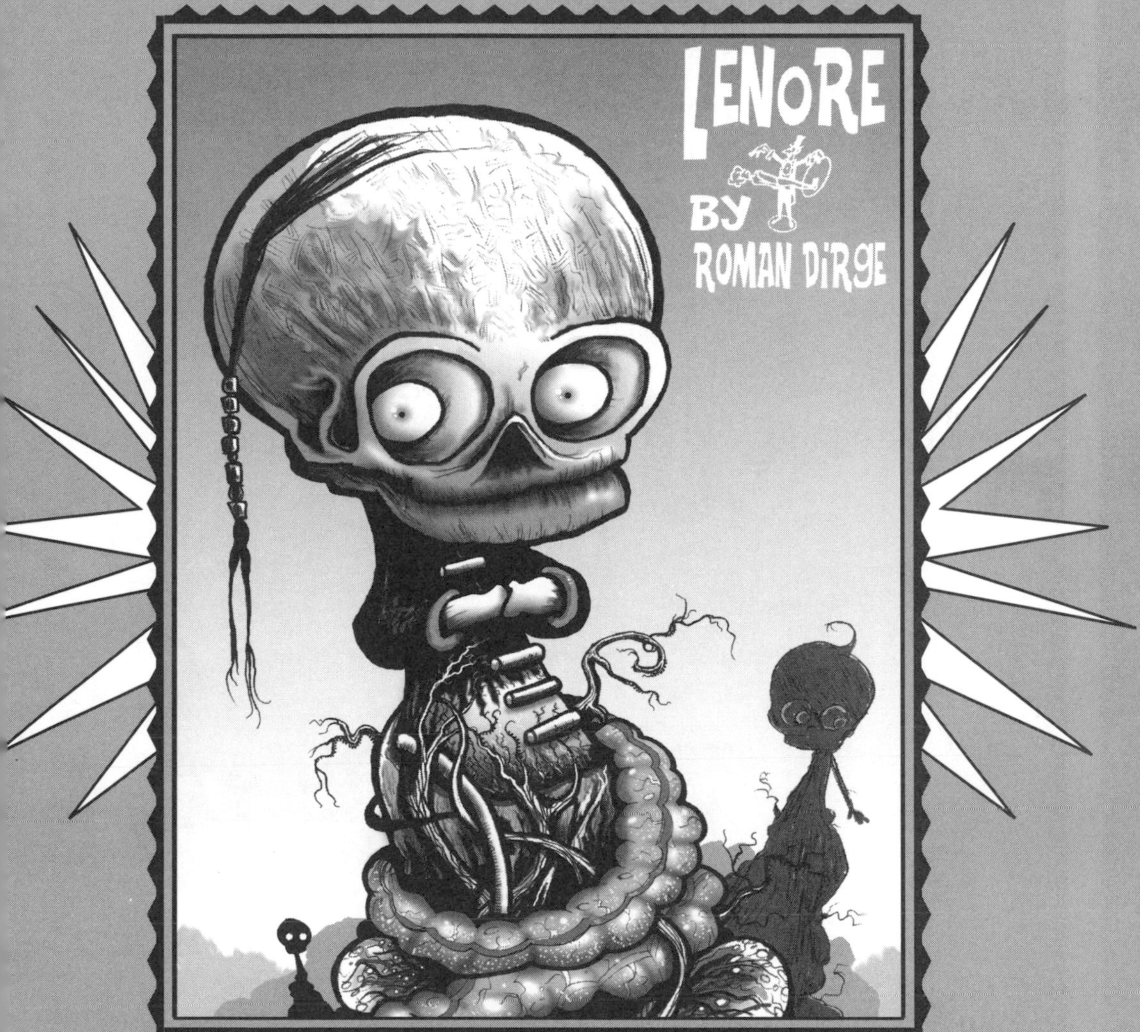
LENORE
BY
ROMAN DIRGE

issue eight

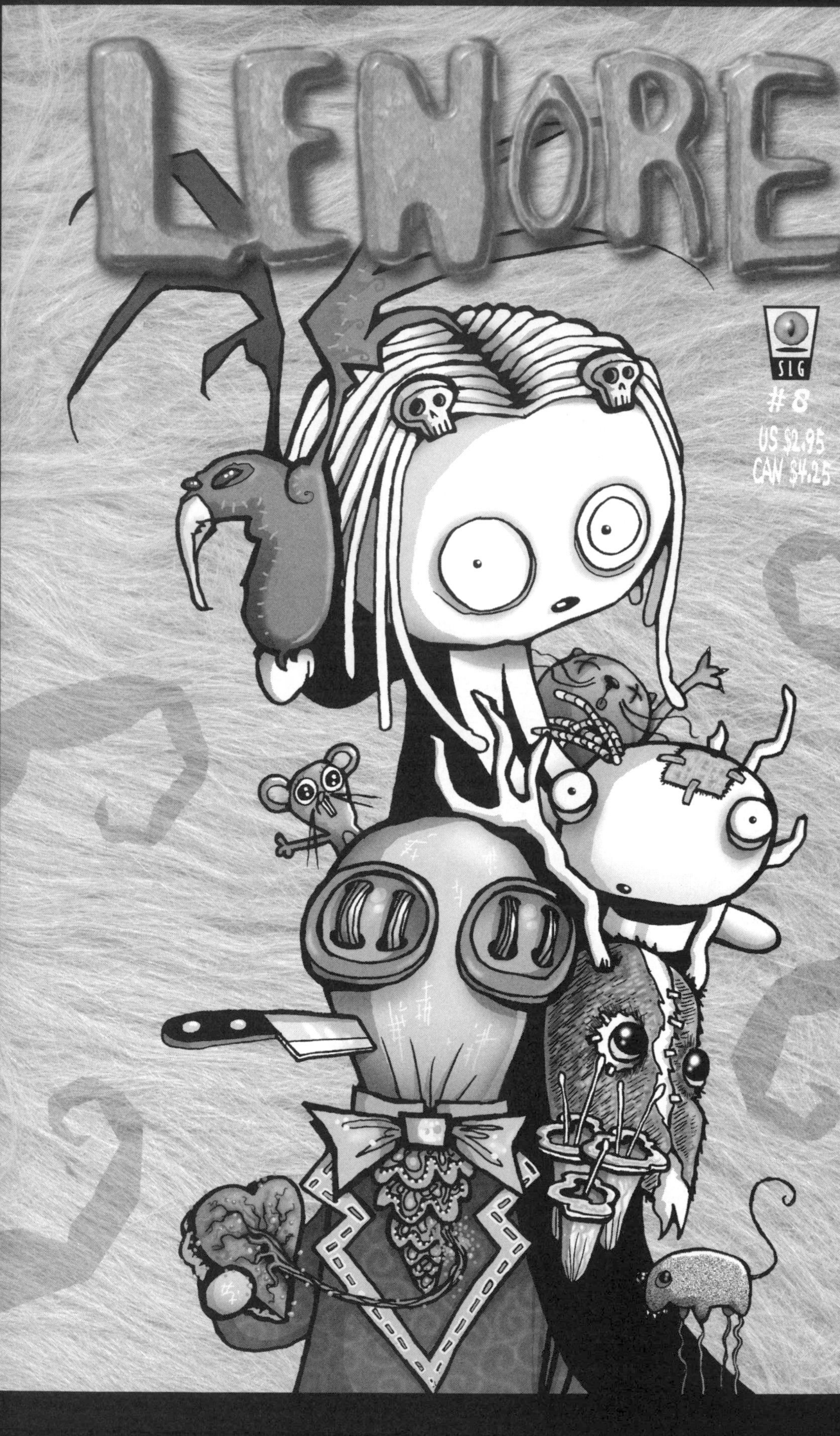
LENORE
SIG
#8
US $2.95
CAN $4.25

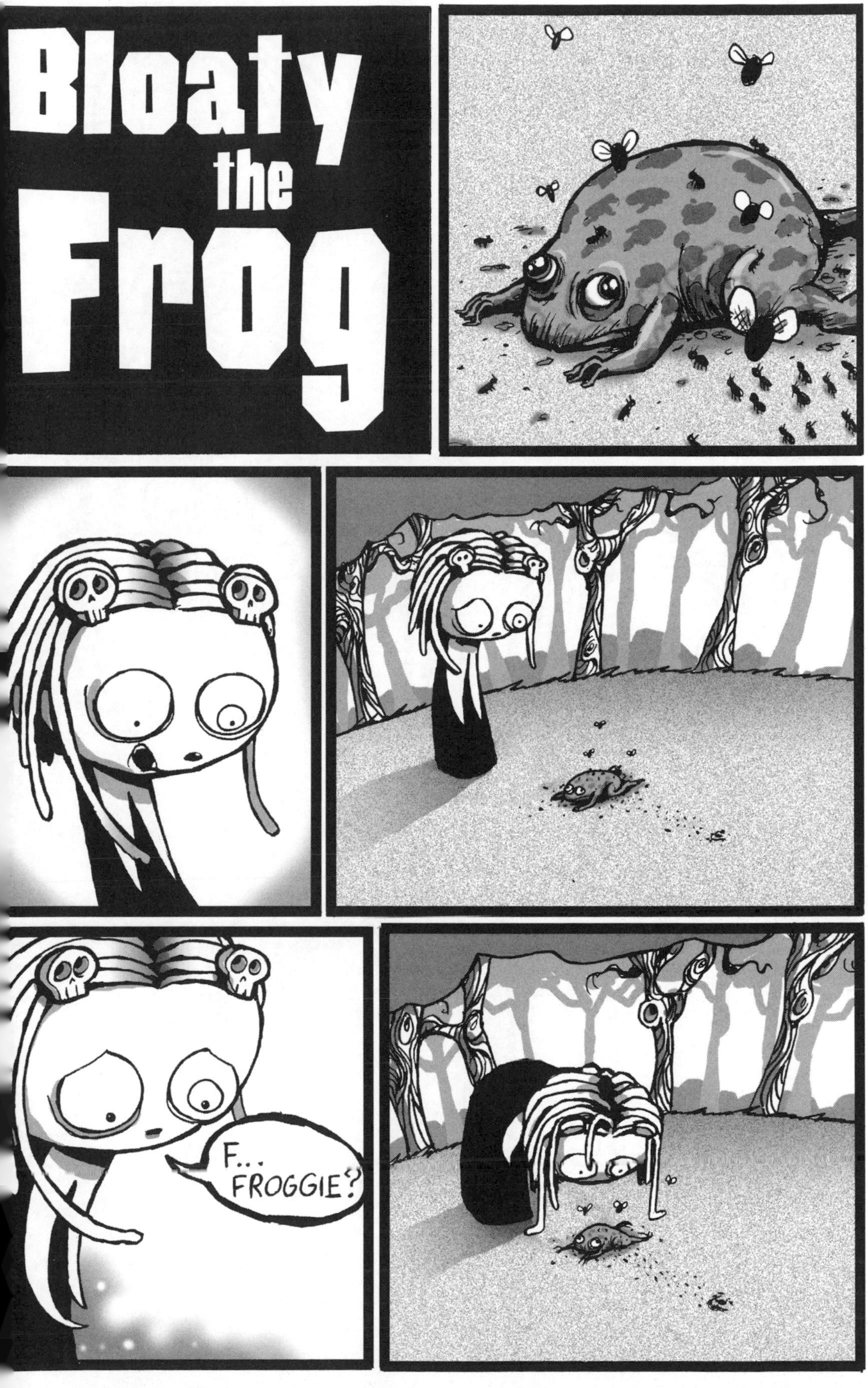
Bloaty the Frog
F... FROGGIE?

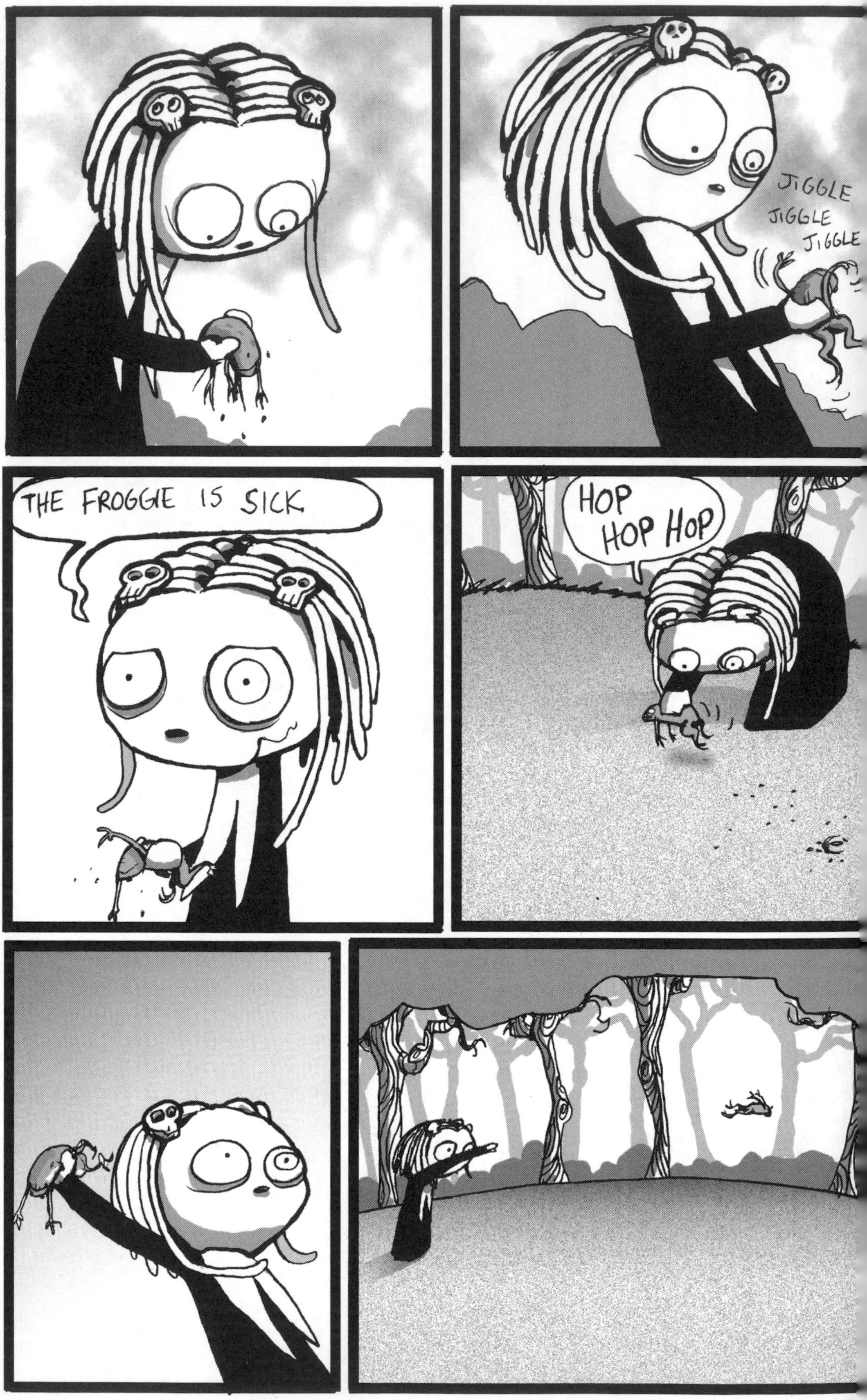
JIGGLE
JIGGLE
JIGGLE
THE FROGGIE IS SICK
HOP
HOP HOP

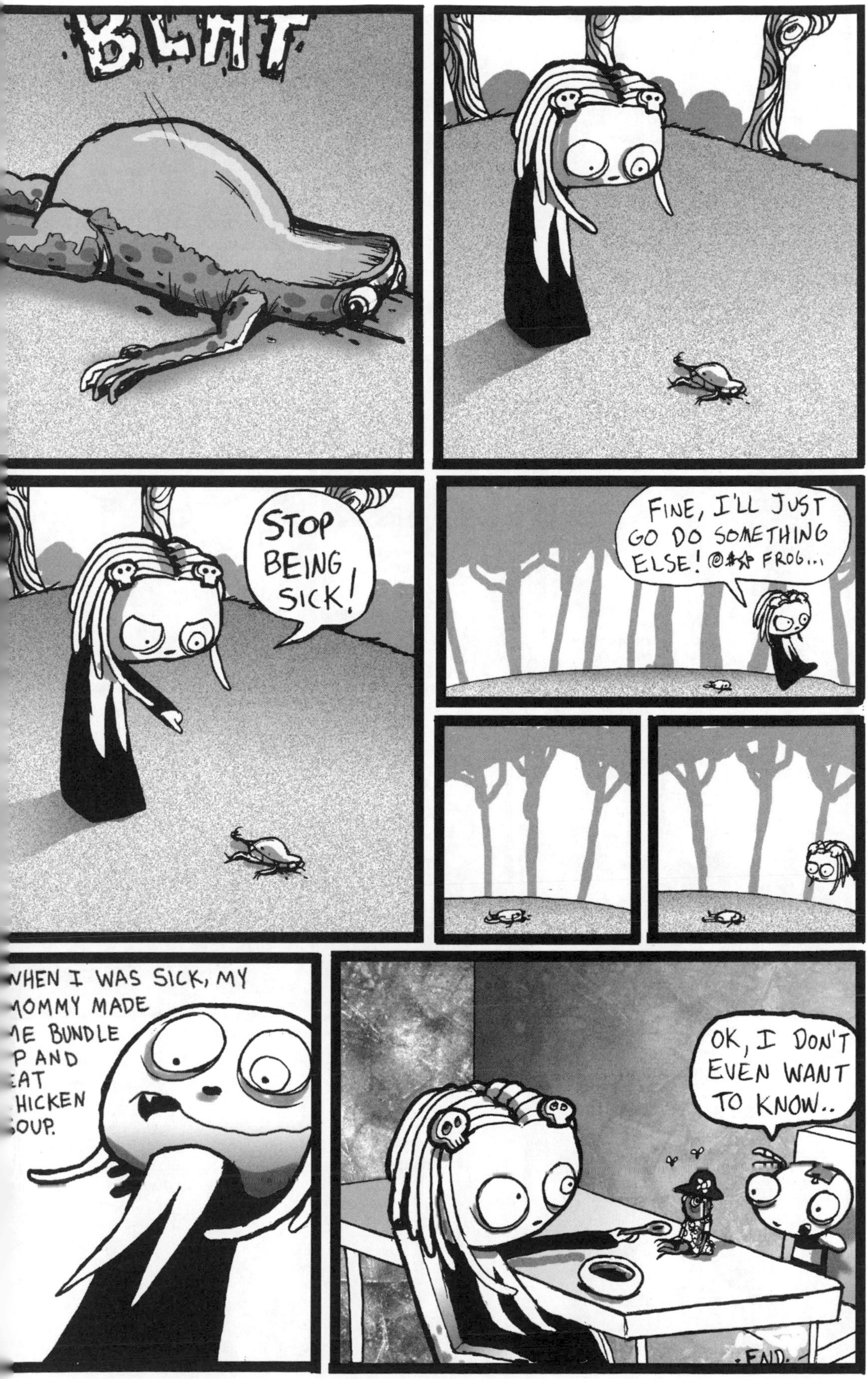
BLAT
STOP BEING SICK!
FINE, I'LL JUST GO DO SOMETHING ELSE! @#☆ FROG...
WHEN I WAS SICK, MY MOMMY MADE ME BUNDLE UP AND EAT CHICKEN SOUP.
OK, I DON'T EVEN WANT TO KNOW..
END.

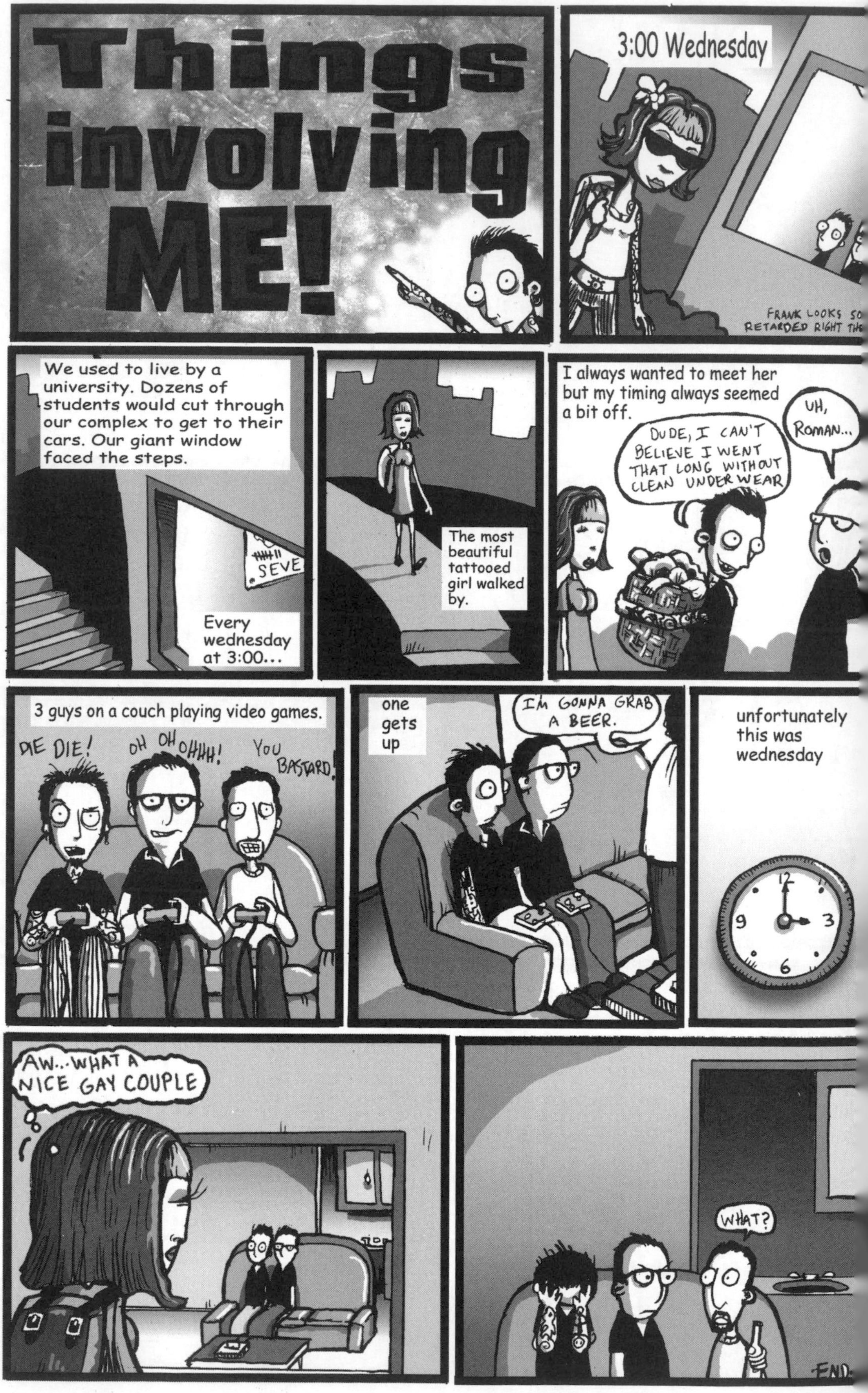

Things involving ME!
3:00 Wednesday
FRANK LOOKS SO
RETARDED RIGHT
We used to live by a university. Dozens of students would cut through our complex to get to their cars. Our giant window faced the steps.
SEVE
Every wednesday at 3:00...
The most beautiful tattooed girl walked by.
I always wanted to meet her but my timing always seemed a bit off.
DUDE, I CAN'T BELIEVE I WENT THAT LONG WITHOUT CLEAN UNDERWEAR
UH, ROMAN...
3 guys on a couch playing video games.
DIE DIE!
OH OH OHHH!
YOU BASTARD!
one gets up
I'M GONNA GRAB A BEER.
unfortunately this was wednesday
AW...WHAT A NICE GAY COUPLE
WHAT?
END

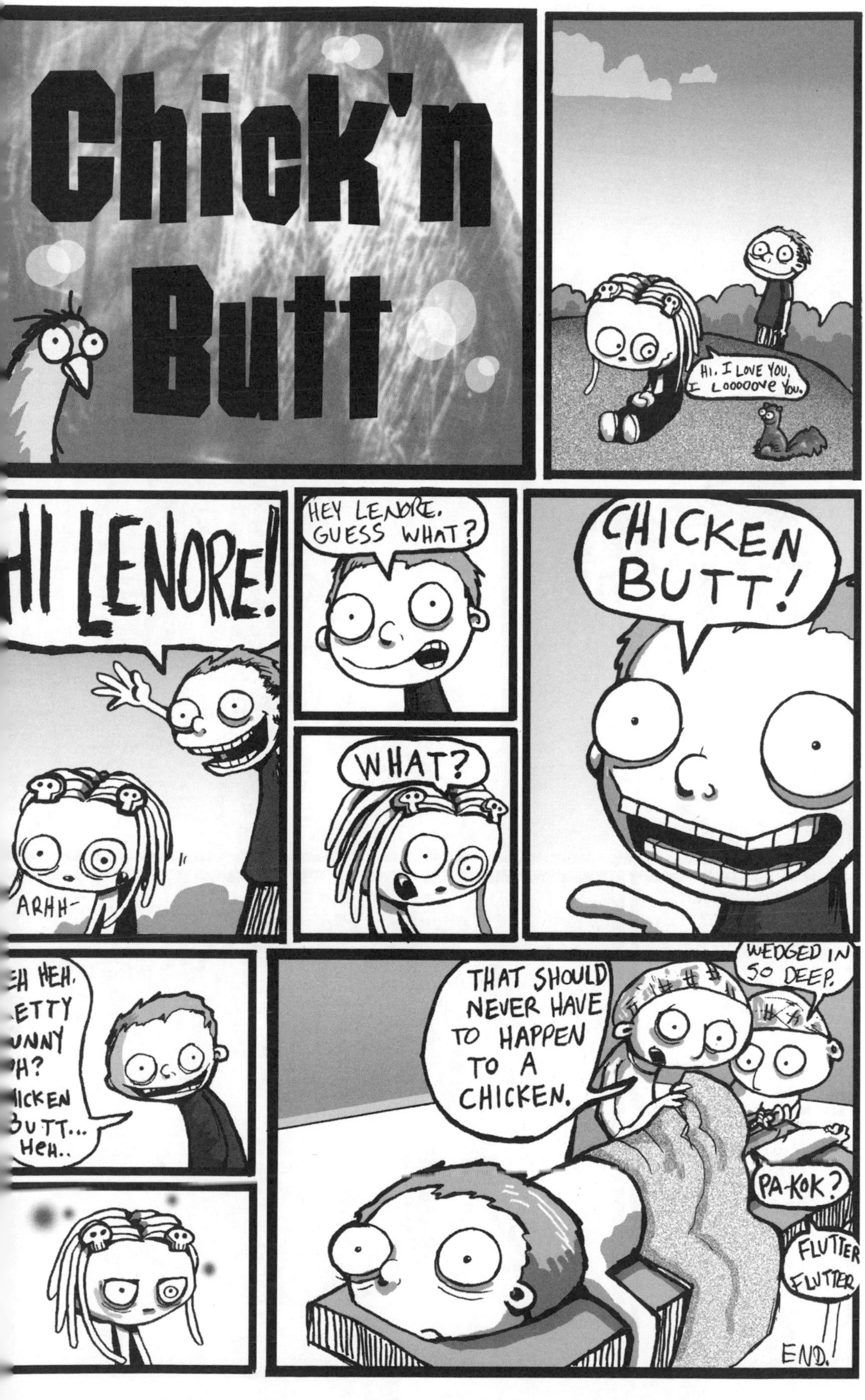
Chick'n Butt
HI. I LOVE YOU, I LOOOOOVE YOU.
HI LENORE!
ARHH-
HEY LENORE, GUESS WHAT?
WHAT?
CHICKEN BUTT!
EH HEH. ETTY UNNY H? ICKEN BUTT... HEH..
WEDGED IN SO DEEP.
THAT SHOULD NEVER HAVE TO HAPPEN TO A CHICKEN.
PA-KOK?
FLUTTER FLUTTER
END.

THE LAST DANCE OF THE LADYBUG

FUB
FUBB
FUB

There once was a ladybug
so happy and devine

:·AHEM·:

WIGGLE
WIGGLE

who needed
a moment
of silence-

but hey,
that's fine

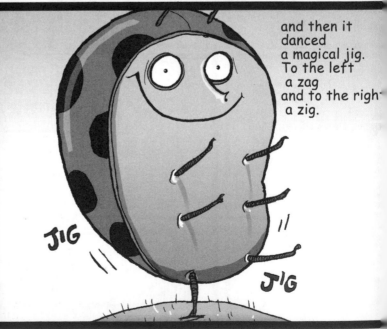

and then it
danced
a magical jig.
To the left
a zag
and to the right
a zig.

JIG

JIG

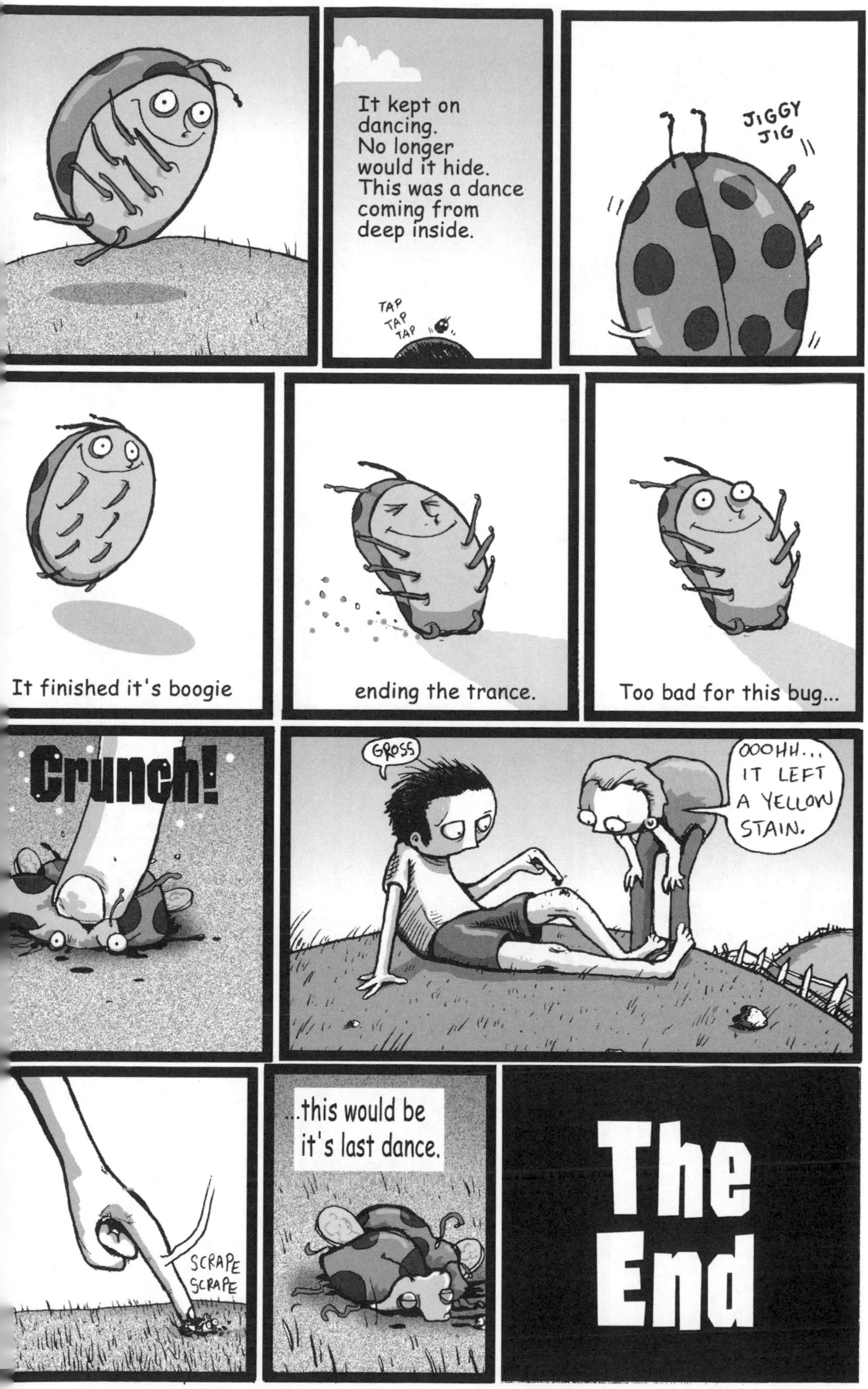
It kept on dancing. No longer would it hide. This was a dance coming from deep inside.
TAP TAP TAP
JIGGY JIG
It finished it's boogie
ending the trance.
Too bad for this bug...
Crunch!
GROSS
OOOHH... IT LEFT A YELLOW STAIN.
SCRAPE SCRAPE
...this would be it's last dance.
The End

The End
HELLO?
The End
HELLO? CAN YOU HEAR ME?
I THINK HE'S COMING TO
WH... WHERE AM I?
TRY NOT TO MOVE. YOU'VE EXPERIENCED SEVERE TRAUMA.
BEEP
BEEP
I.... HURT.
MY FACE... LET ME SEE MY... ..FACE.
NOOOOoo!! I'M A FREAK! A FREEEEAK!
horribly disfigured and told it would never walk again, a terrible emptiness consumed the lady bug.
...but vengeance is strong medicine.
SQUISH
SQUISH
SQUISH

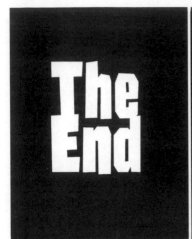

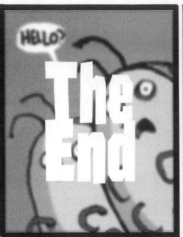

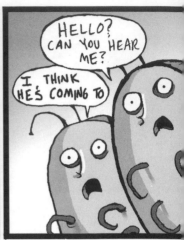

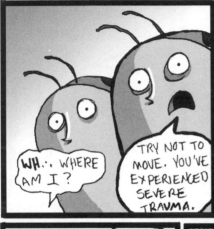

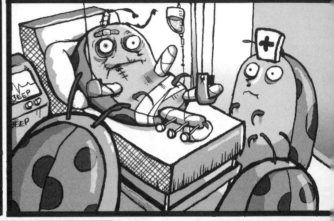

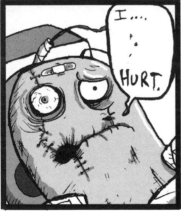

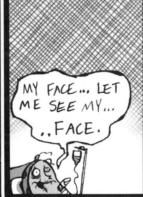

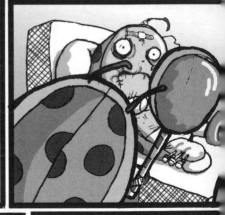

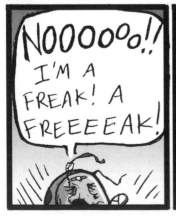

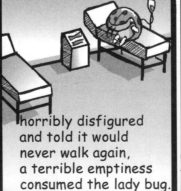

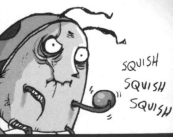

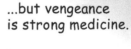

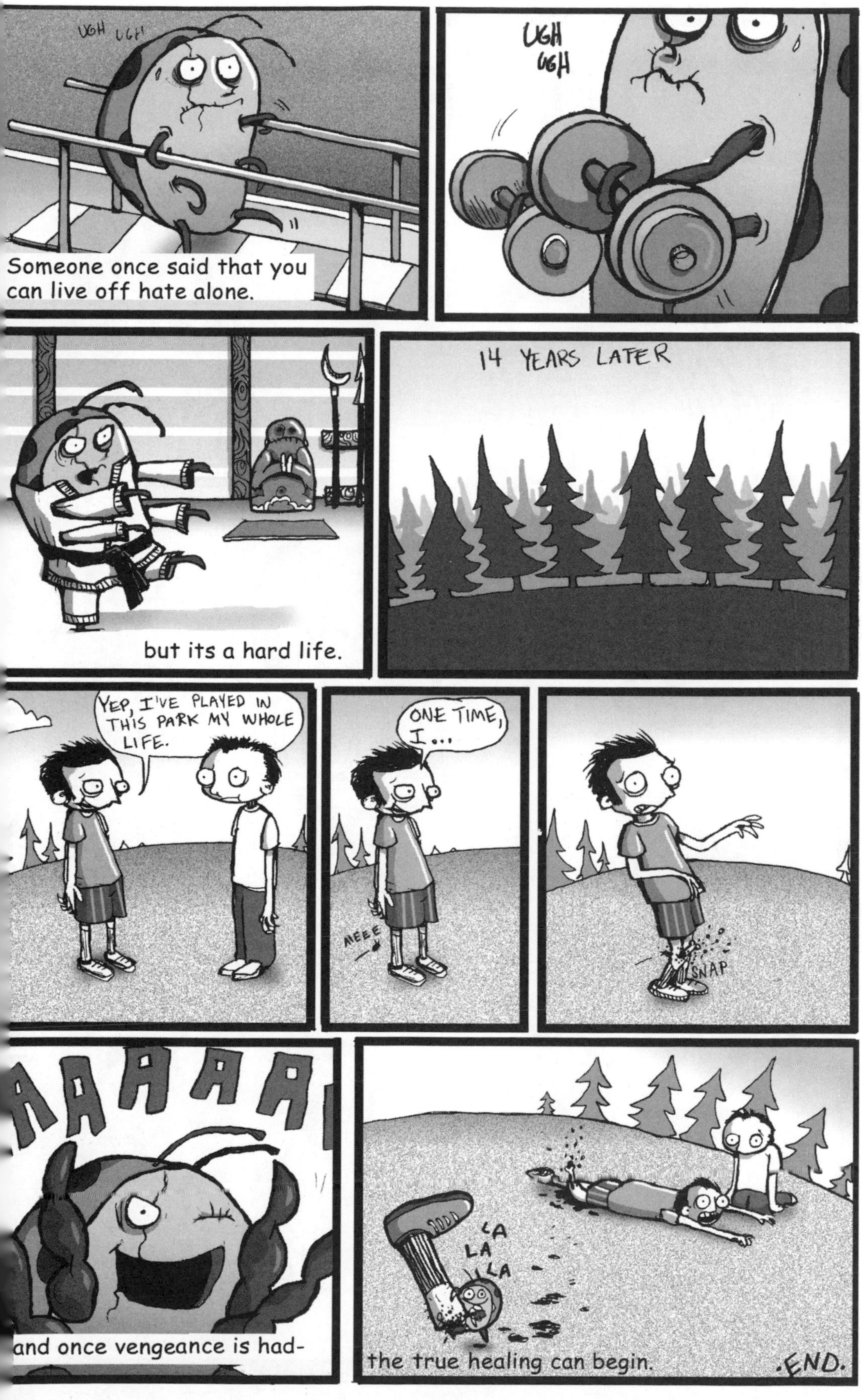
UGH UGH
Someone once said that you can live off hate alone.
UGH UGH
but its a hard life.
14 YEARS LATER
YEP, I'VE PLAYED IN THIS PARK MY WHOLE LIFE.
ONE TIME, I...
MEEE
SNAP
AAAAAA
and once vengeance is had-
LA LA LA
the true healing can begin.
.END.

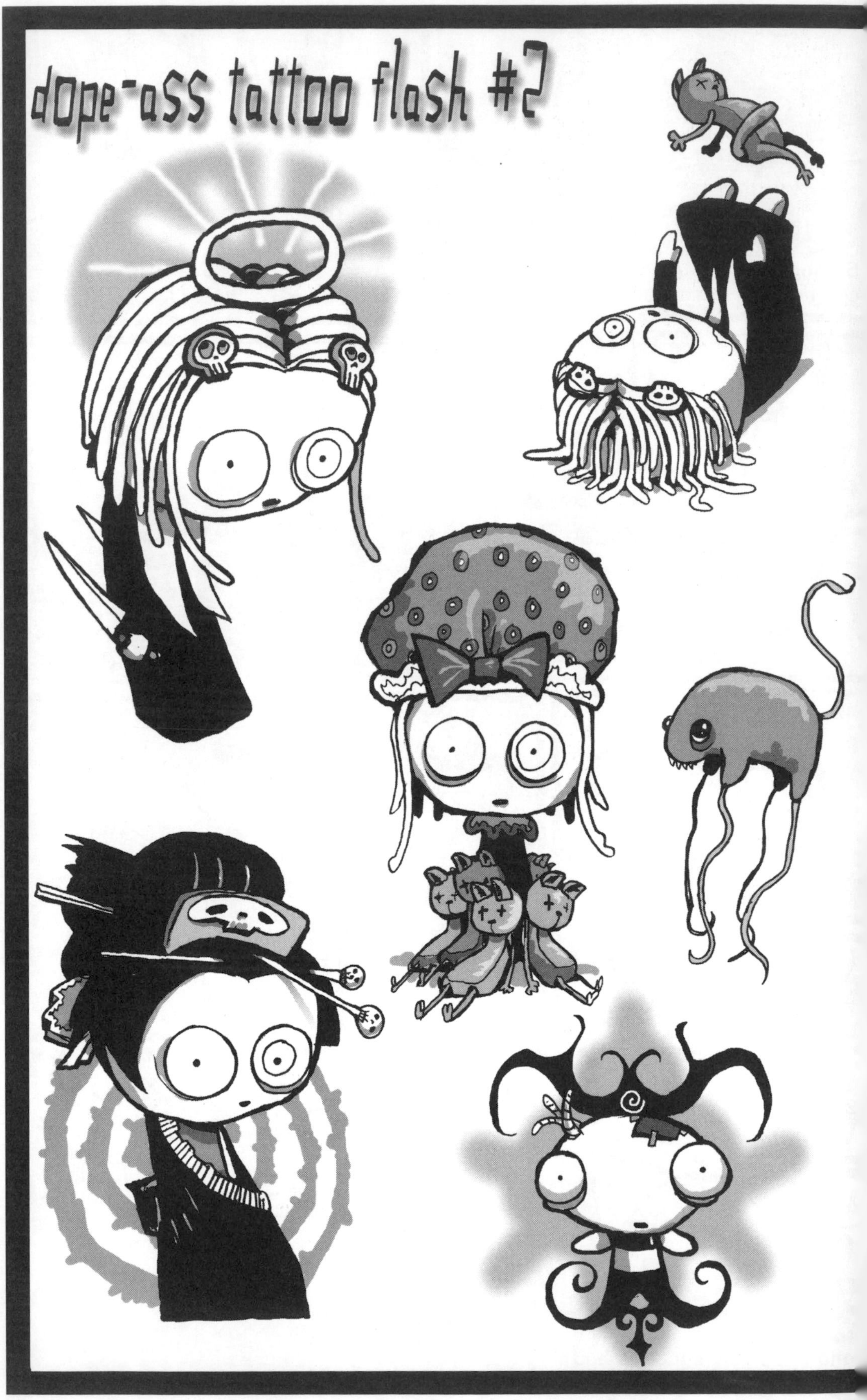
dope-ass tattoo flash #2

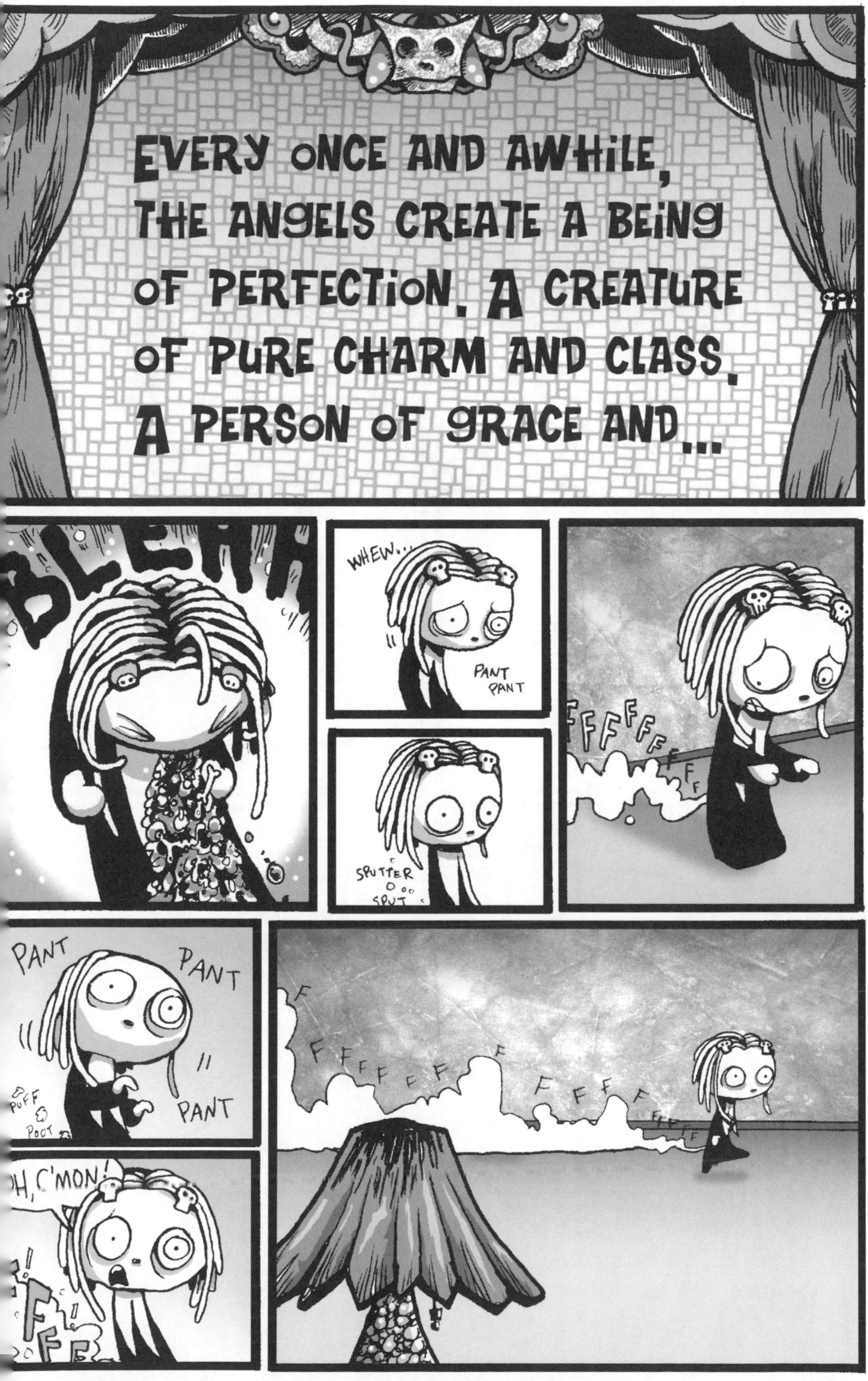
EVERY ONCE AND AWHILE, THE ANGELS CREATE A BEING OF PERFECTION. A CREATURE OF PURE CHARM AND CLASS. A PERSON OF GRACE AND...
BLEAH
WHEW...
PANT PANT
SPUTTER SPUT
PANT
PANT
PANT
PUFF
POOT
OH, C'MON!

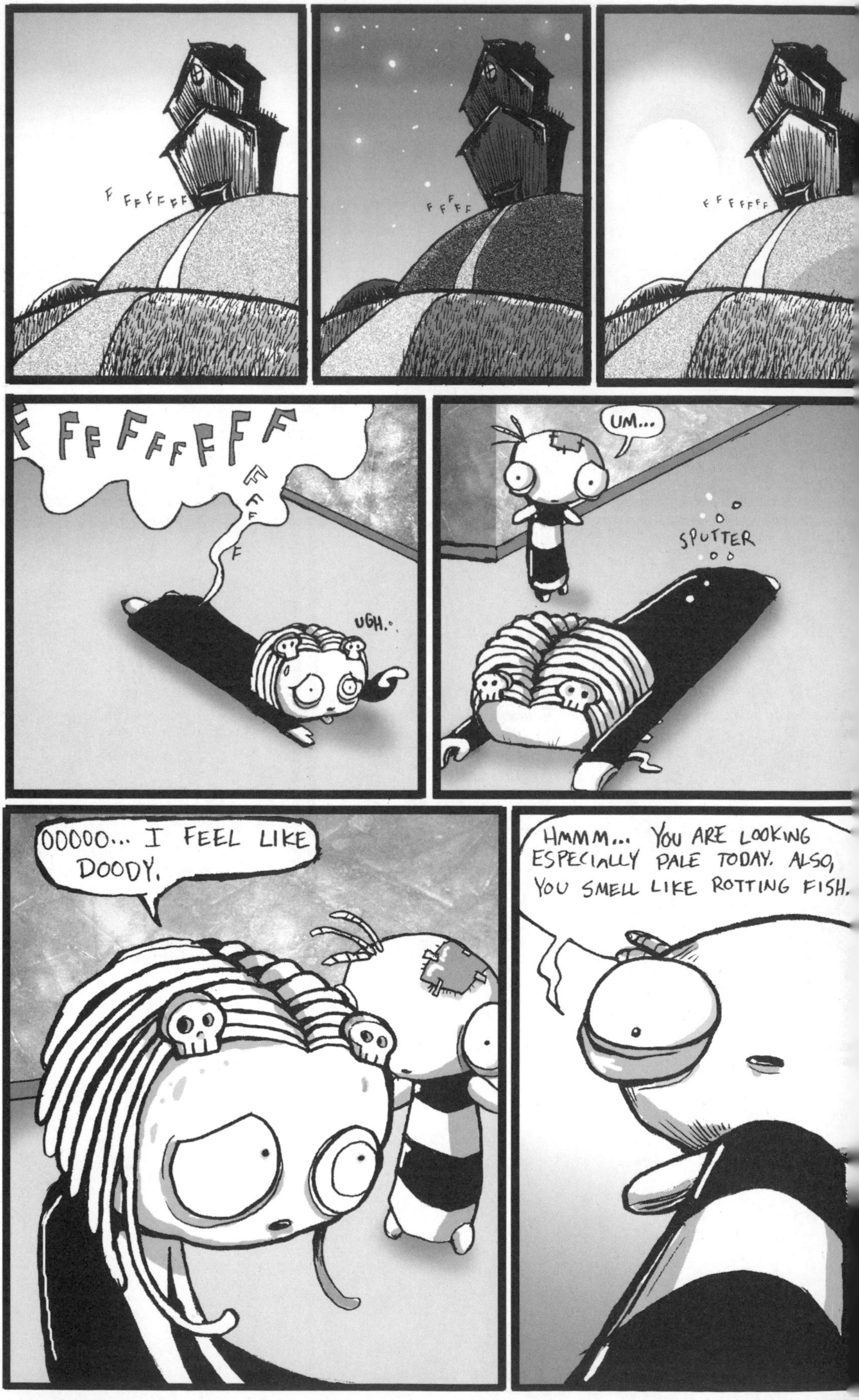
FFFFFFF
FFFF
FFFFFFF
FFFFFFFFFF
FFF
UGH.
UM...
SPUTTER
OOOOO... I FEEL LIKE DOODY.
HMMM... YOU ARE LOOKING ESPECIALLY PALE TODAY. ALSO, YOU SMELL LIKE ROTTING FISH.

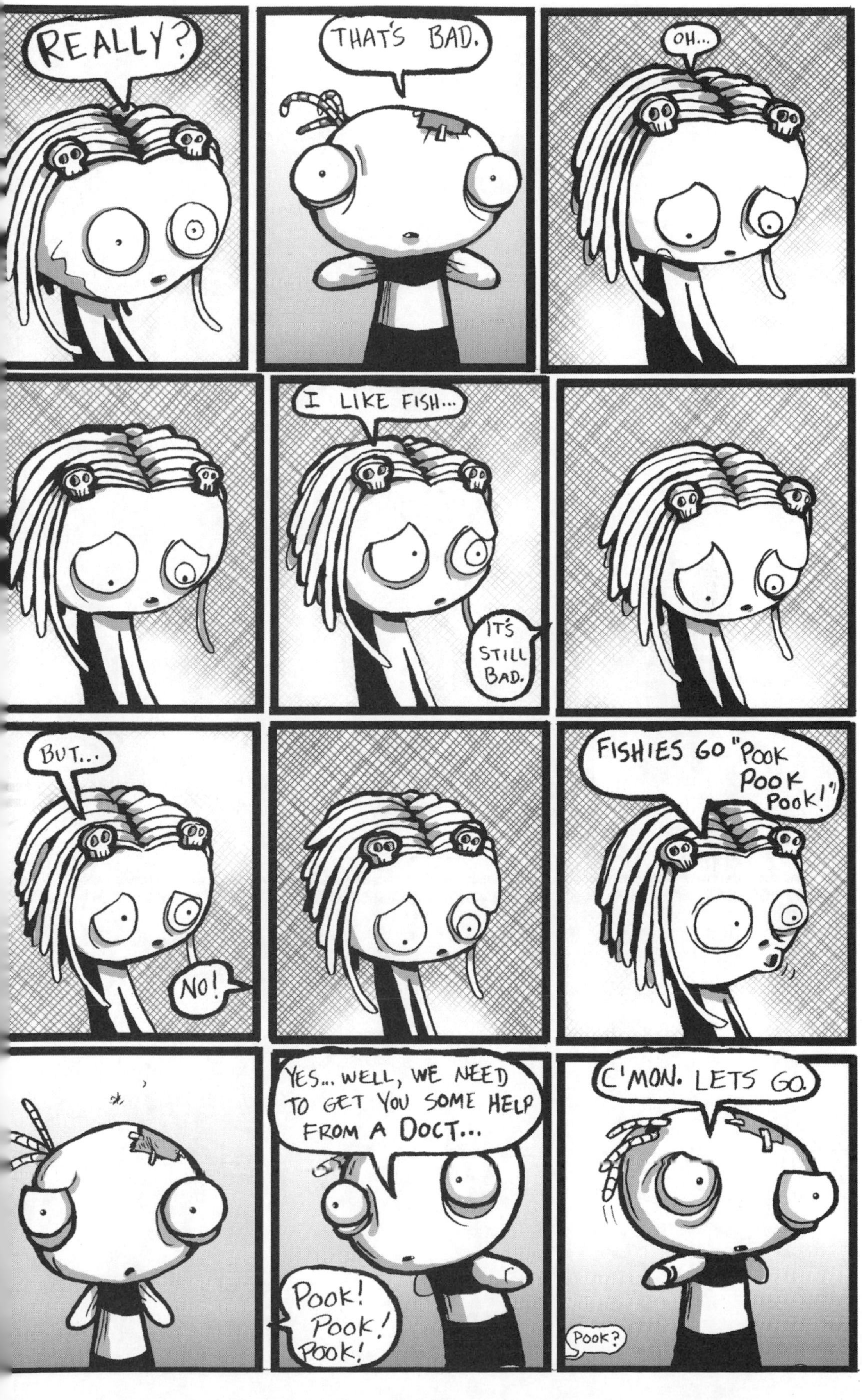
REALLY?
THAT'S BAD.
OH...
I LIKE FISH...
IT'S STILL BAD.
BUT...
NO!
FISHIES GO "POOK POOK POOK!"
YES... WELL, WE NEED TO GET YOU SOME HELP FROM A DOCT...
POOK! POOK! POOK!
C'MON. LETS GO.
POOK?

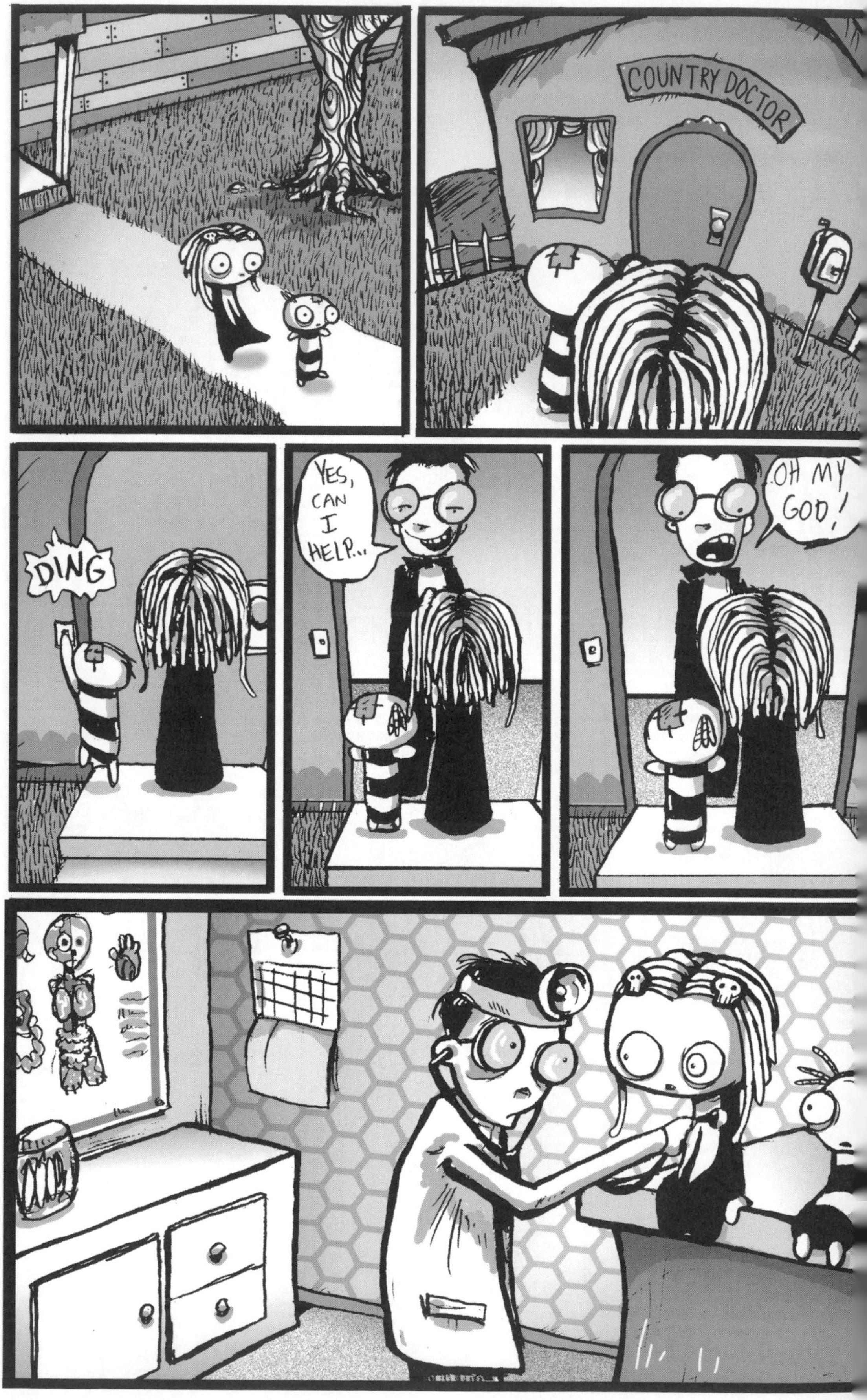

COUNTRY DOCTOR
DING
YES, CAN I HELP...
OH MY GOD!

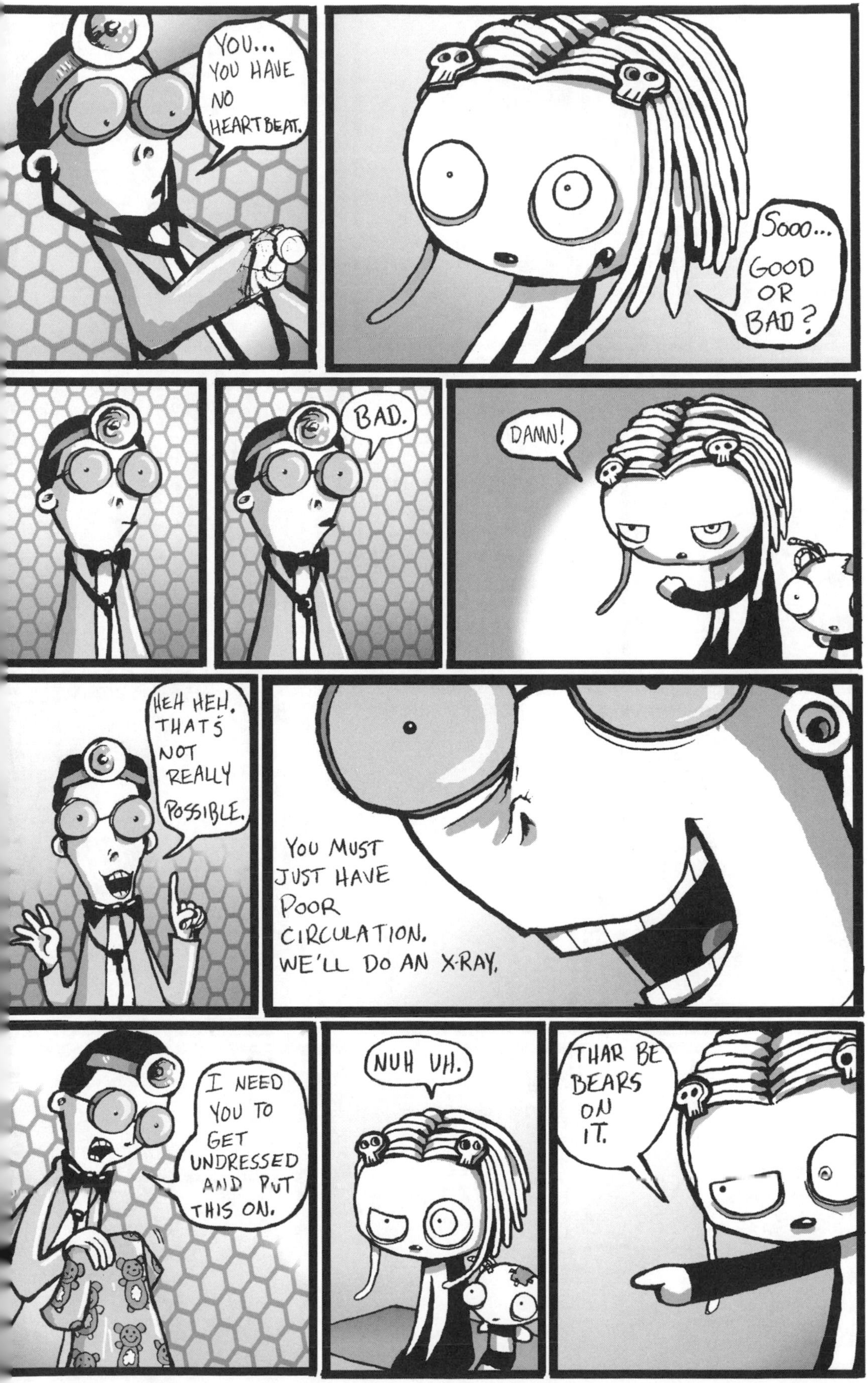
YOU... YOU HAVE NO HEARTBEAT.
SOOO... GOOD OR BAD?
BAD.
DAMN!
HEH HEH. THAT'S NOT REALLY POSSIBLE.
YOU MUST JUST HAVE POOR CIRCULATION. WE'LL DO AN X-RAY.
I NEED YOU TO GET UNDRESSED AND PUT THIS ON.
NUH UH.
THAR BE BEARS ON IT.

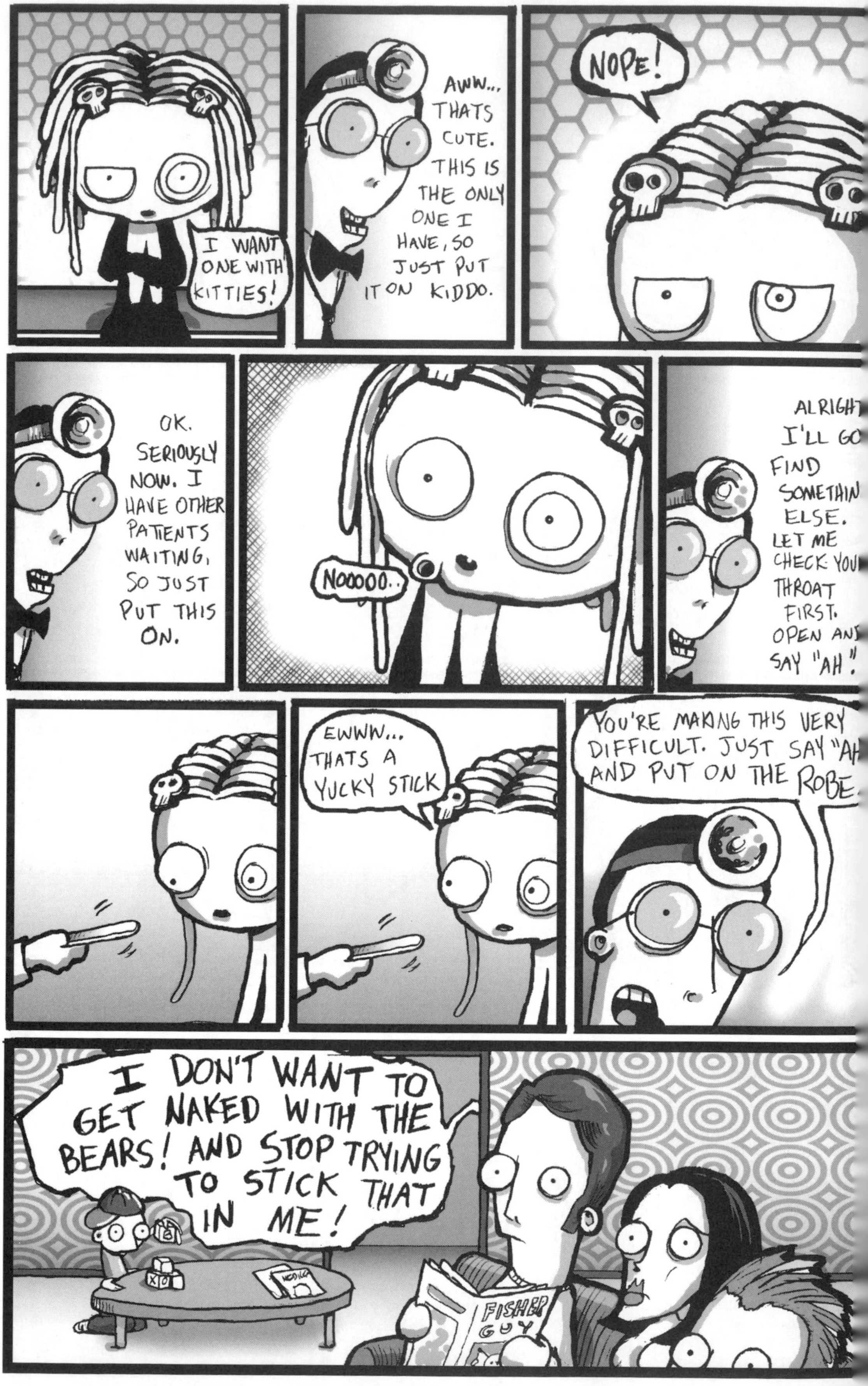

I WANT ONE WITH KITTIES!
AWW... THATS CUTE. THIS IS THE ONLY ONE I HAVE, SO JUST PUT IT ON KIDDO.
NOPE!
OK. SERIOUSLY NOW. I HAVE OTHER PATIENTS WAITING, SO JUST PUT THIS ON.
NOOOOO..
ALRIGHT I'LL GO FIND SOMETHIN ELSE. LET ME CHECK YOU THROAT FIRST. OPEN AN SAY "AH".
EWWW... THATS A YUCKY STICK
YOU'RE MAKING THIS VERY DIFFICULT. JUST SAY "AH AND PUT ON THE ROBE.
I DON'T WANT TO GET NAKED WITH THE BEARS! AND STOP TRYING TO STICK THAT IN ME!
FISHER GUY

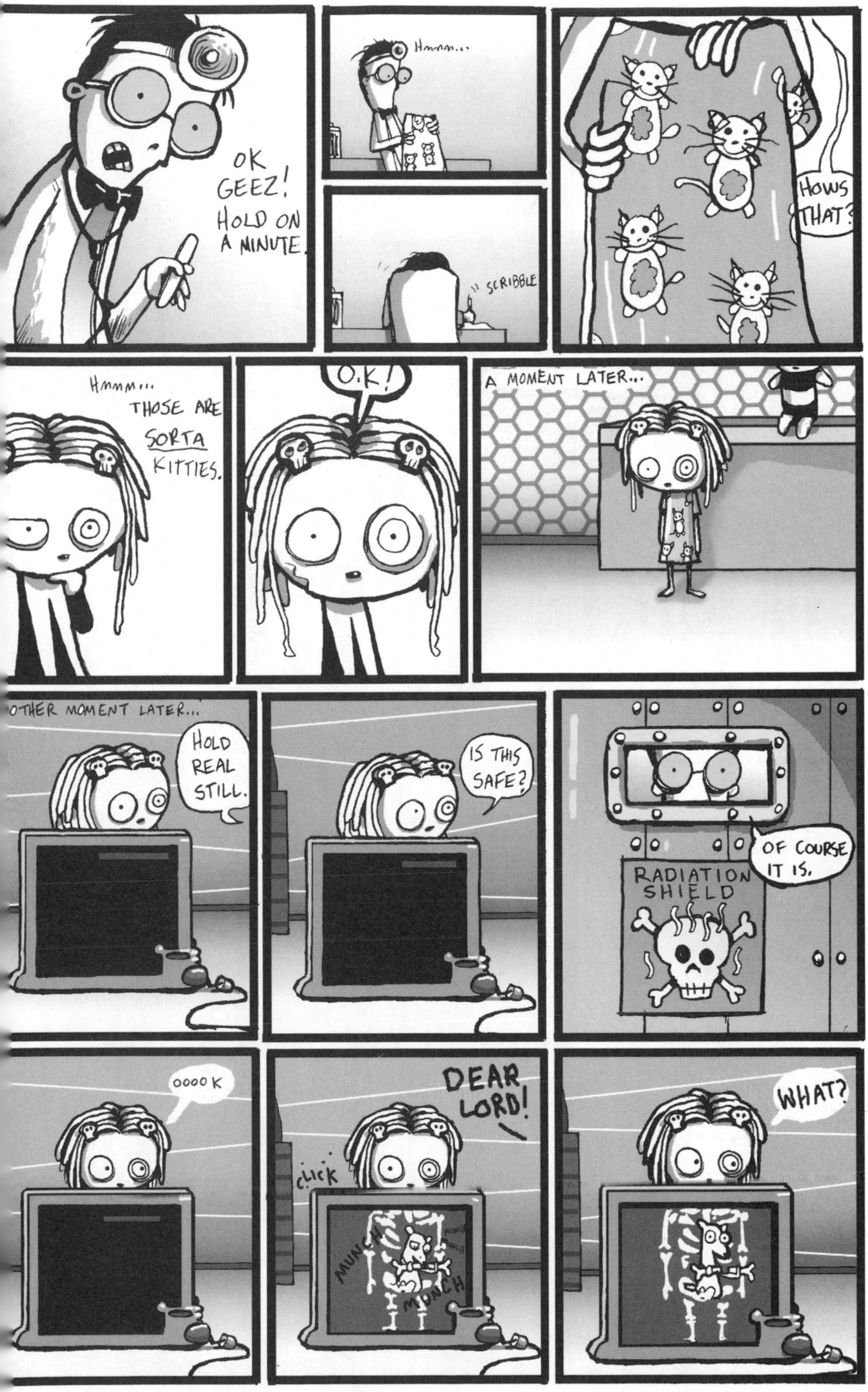
OK GEEZ! HOLD ON A MINUTE.
Hmmm...
SCRIBBLE
HOWS THAT?
Hmmm... THOSE ARE SORTA KITTIES.
O.K!
A MOMENT LATER...
OTHER MOMENT LATER...
HOLD REAL STILL.
IS THIS SAFE?
RADIATION SHIELD
OF COURSE IT IS.
OOOO K
DEAR LORD!
CLICK
MUNCH
MUNCH
WHAT?

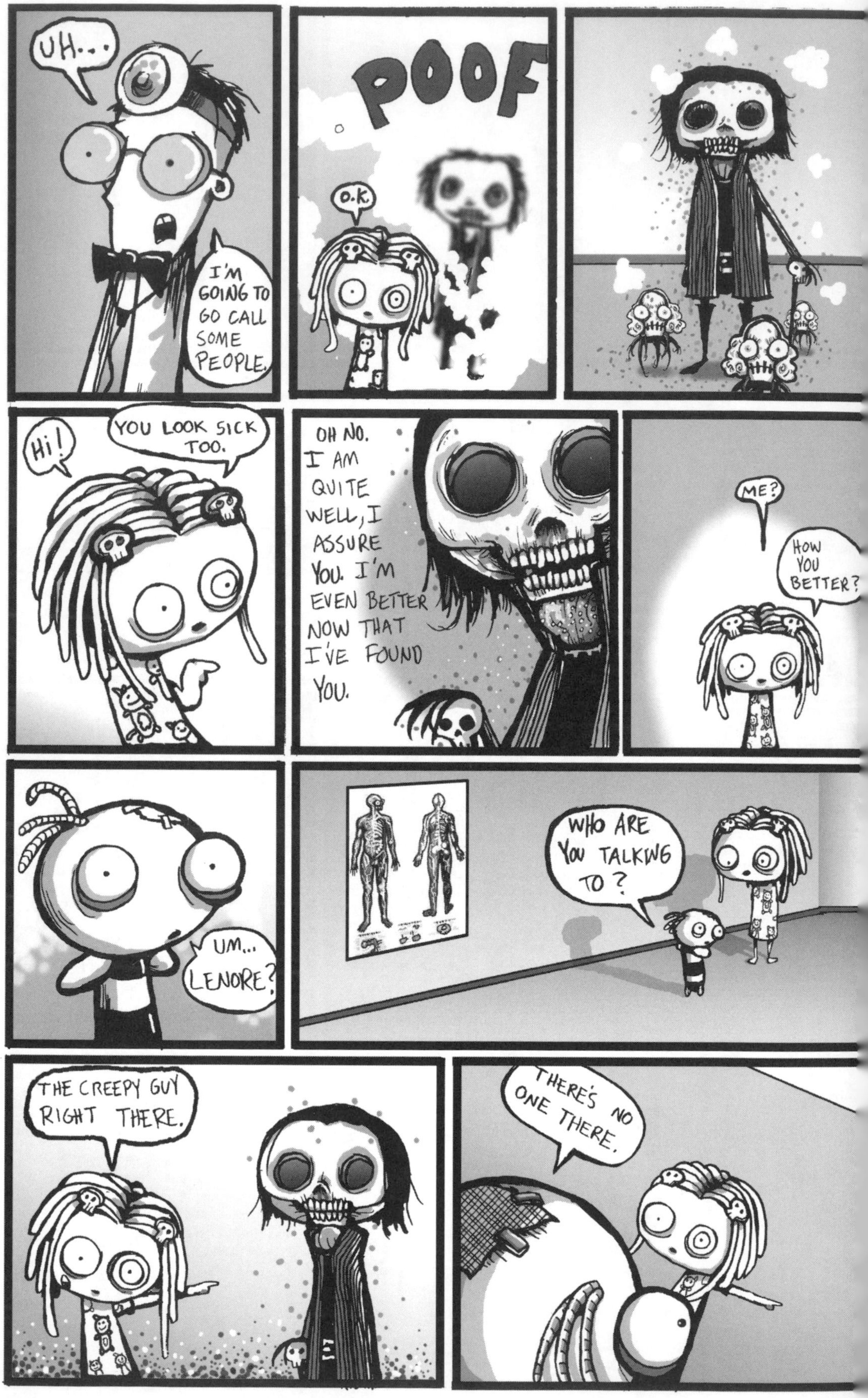
UH...
I'M GOING TO GO CALL SOME PEOPLE.
POOF
O.K.
Hi!
YOU LOOK SICK TOO.
OH NO. I AM QUITE WELL, I ASSURE YOU. I'M EVEN BETTER NOW THAT I'VE FOUND YOU.
ME?
HOW YOU BETTER?
UM... LENORE?
WHO ARE YOU TALKING TO?
THE CREEPY GUY RIGHT THERE.
THERE'S NO ONE THERE.

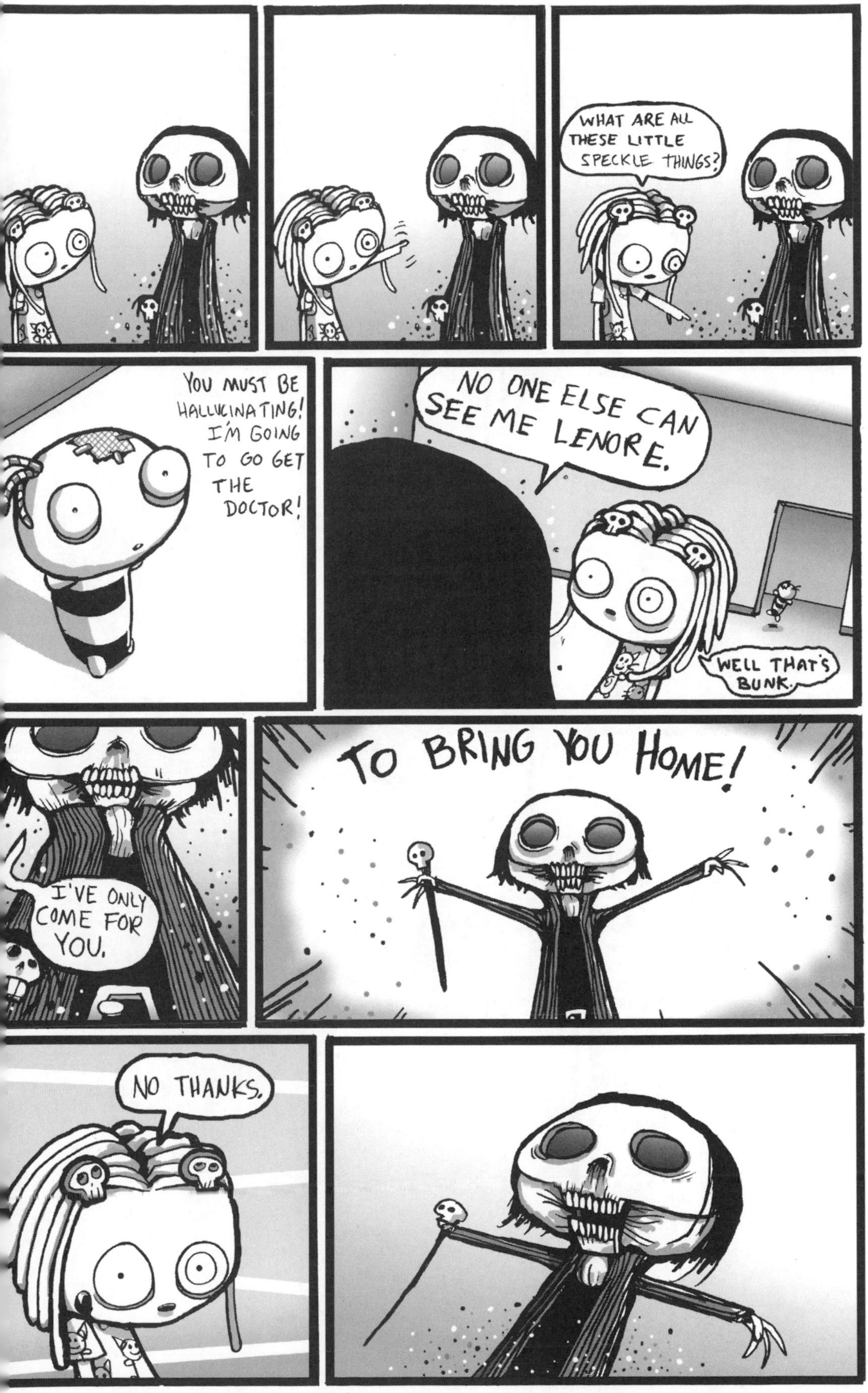
WHAT ARE ALL THESE LITTLE SPECKLE THINGS?
YOU MUST BE HALLUCINATING! I'M GOING TO GO GET THE DOCTOR!
NO ONE ELSE CAN SEE ME LENORE.
WELL THAT'S BUNK.
I'VE ONLY COME FOR YOU.
TO BRING YOU HOME!
NO THANKS.

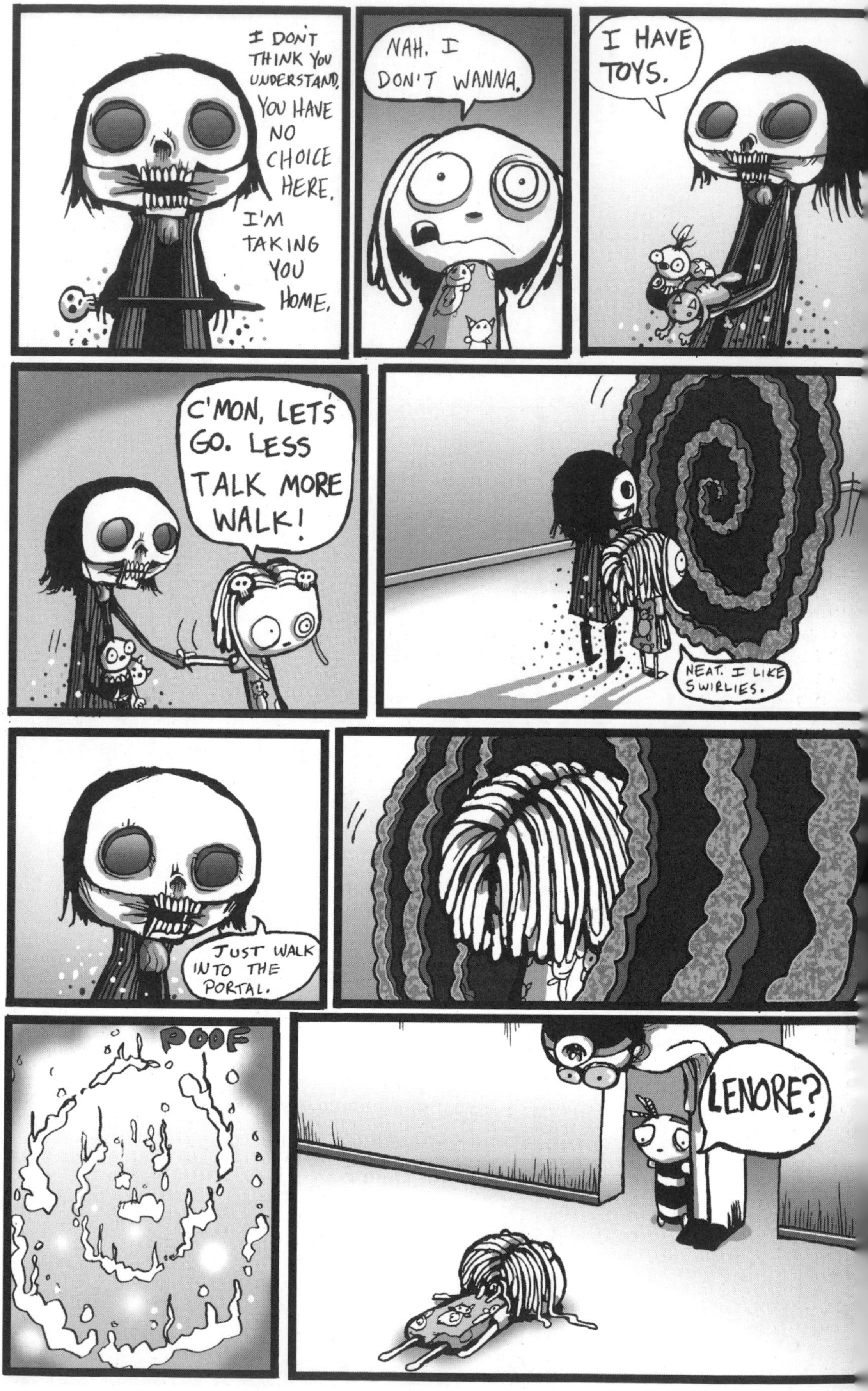
I DON'T THINK YOU UNDERSTAND, YOU HAVE NO CHOICE HERE. I'M TAKING YOU HOME.
NAH. I DON'T WANNA.
I HAVE TOYS.
C'MON, LET'S GO. LESS TALK MORE WALK!
NEAT. I LIKE SWIRLIES.
JUST WALK INTO THE PORTAL.
POOF
LENORE?

LENORE! PLEASE DON'T DIE! I'LL BE ALL ALONE! PLUS, LOOK WHAT YOU'RE WEARING.

NOOOOOOOOO

The next day

...she has shuffled off this mortal coil....

...again.

YOU ARE HOME.

Welcome Home!

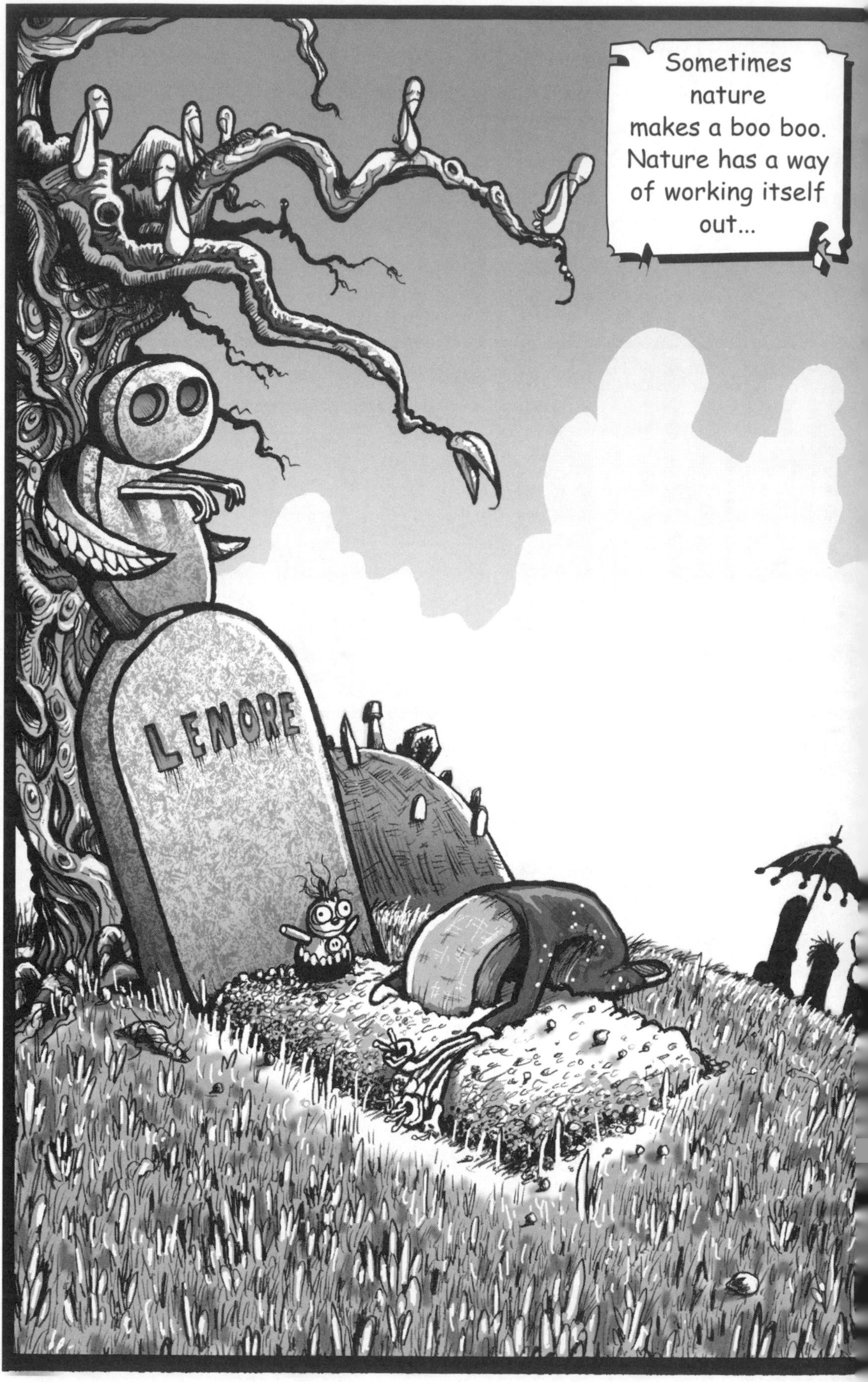
Sometimes nature makes a boo boo. Nature has a way of working itself out...
LENORE

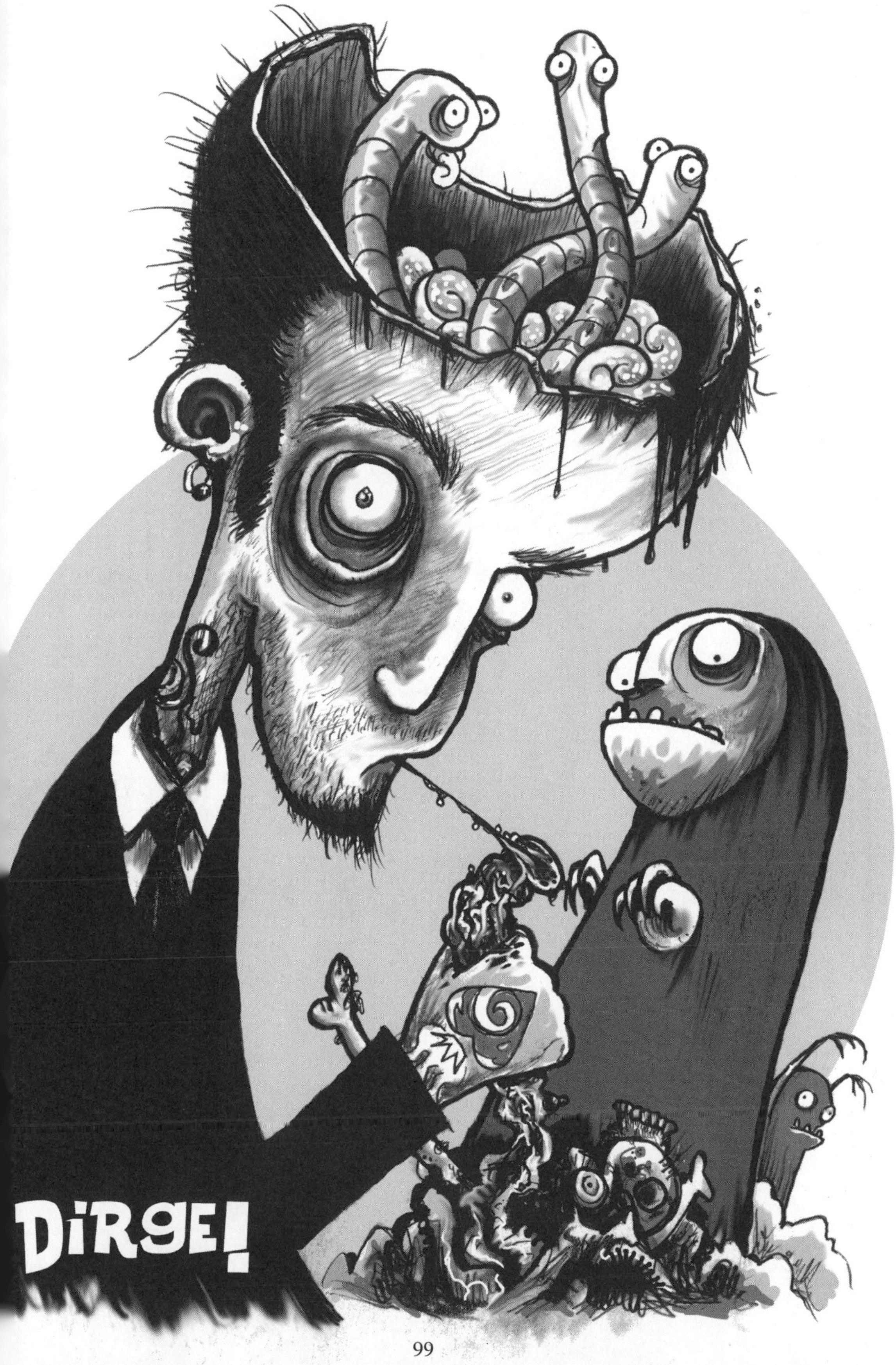
DIRGE!

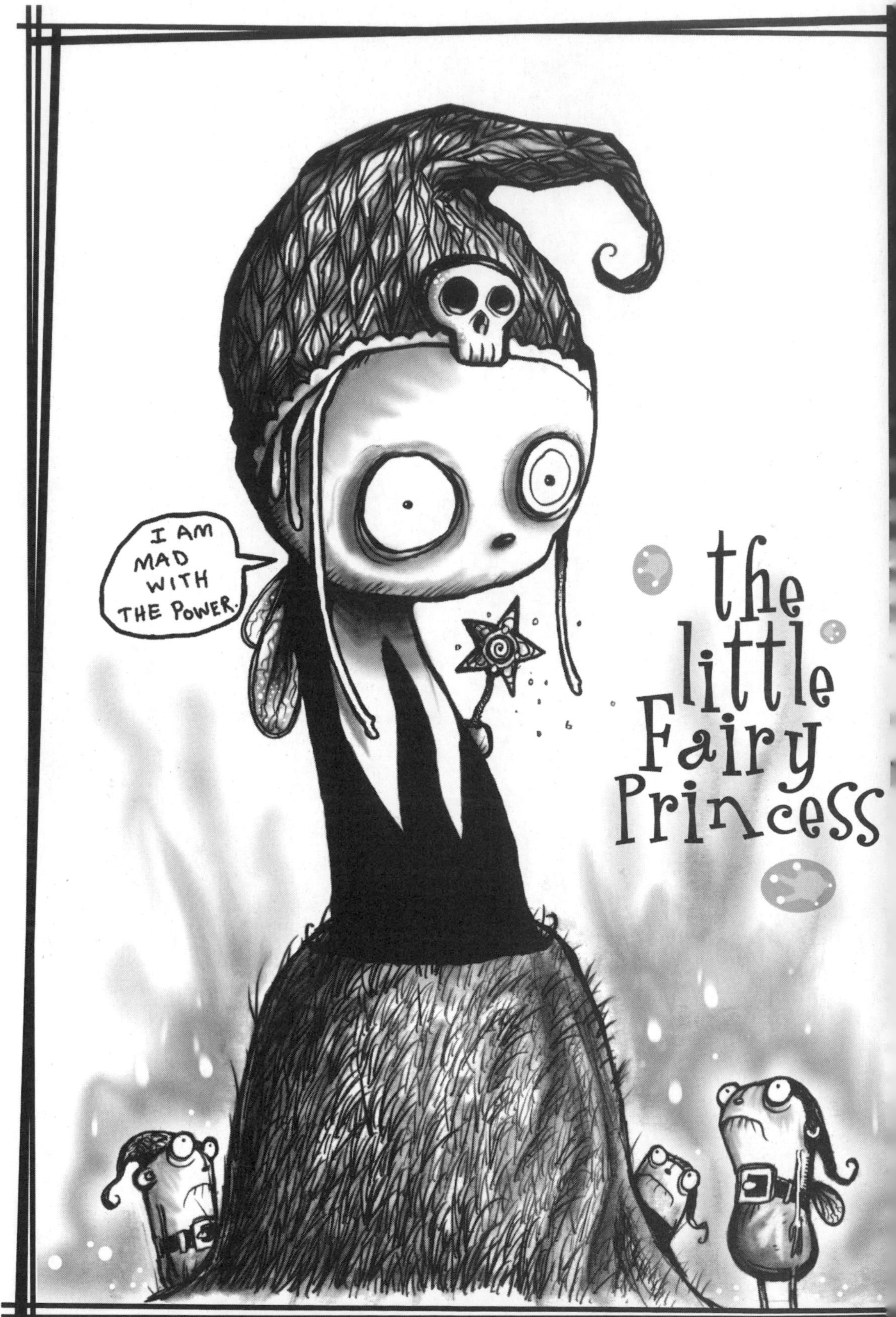
I AM MAD WITH THE POWER.
the little Fairy Princess

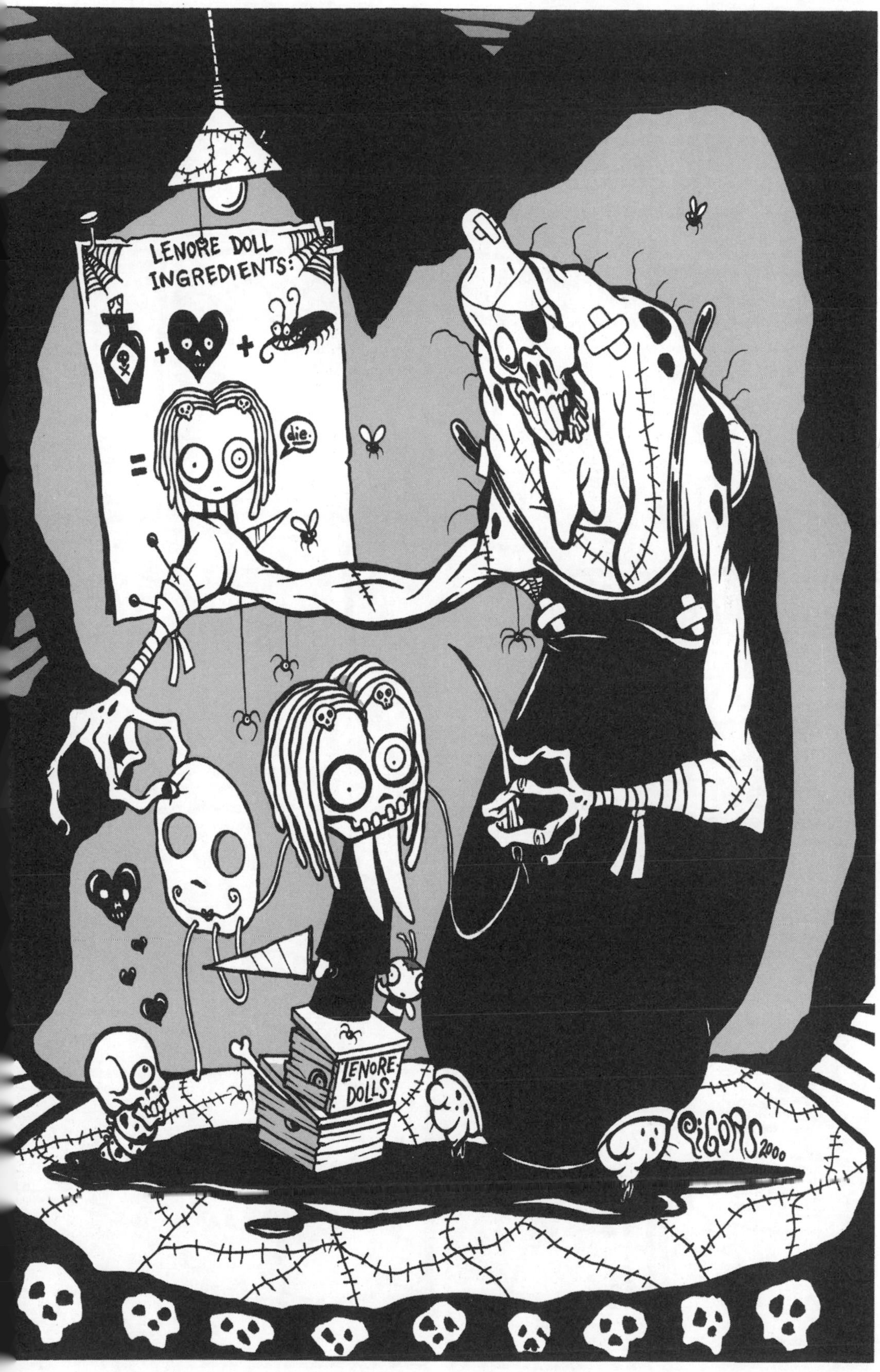

LENORE DOLL INGREDIENTS:
die.
LENORE DOLLS

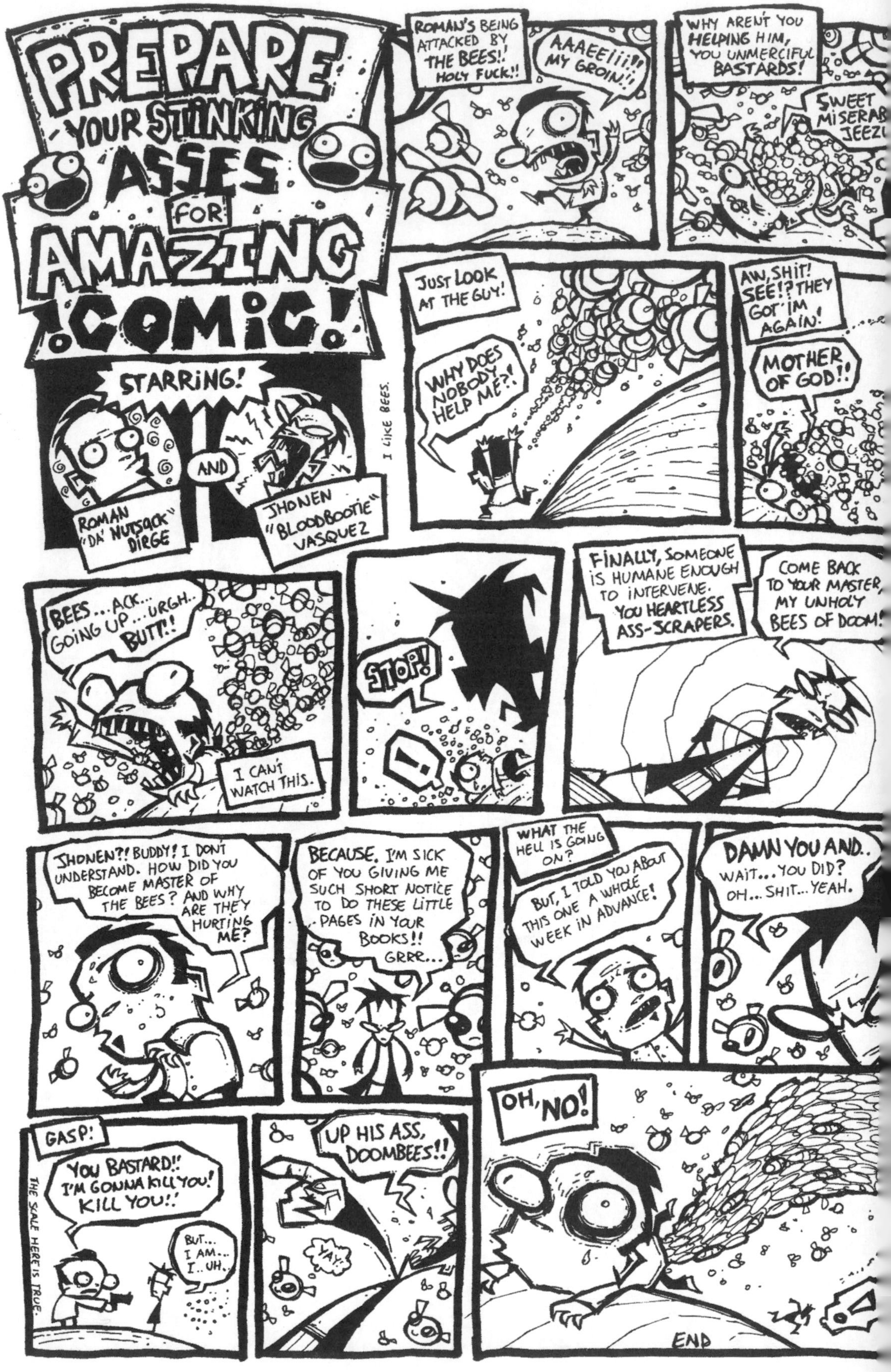
PREPARE YOUR STINKING ASSES FOR AMAZING COMIC!
STARRING!
AND
ROMAN "DA' NUTSACK" DIRGE
JHONEN "BLOODBOOTIE" VASQUEZ
I LIKE BEES.
ROMAN'S BEING ATTACKED BY THE BEES!! HOLY FUCK!!
AAAEE¡¡¡!!! MY GROIN!!
WHY AREN'T YOU HELPING HIM, YOU UNMERCIFUL BASTARDS!
SWEET MISERAB JEEZ
JUST LOOK AT THE GUY!
WHY DOES NOBODY HELP ME?!
AW, SHIT! SEE!? THEY GOT 'IM AGAIN!
MOTHER OF GOD!!
BEES...ACK... GOING UP...URGH.. BUTT!!
I CAN'T WATCH THIS.
STOP!
!
FINALLY, SOMEONE IS HUMANE ENOUGH TO INTERVENE. YOU HEARTLESS ASS-SCRAPERS.
COME BACK TO YOUR MASTER, MY UNHOLY BEES OF DOOM!
JHONEN?! BUDDY! I DON'T UNDERSTAND. HOW DID YOU BECOME MASTER OF THE BEES? AND WHY ARE THEY HURTING ME?
BECAUSE. I'M SICK OF YOU GIVING ME SUCH SHORT NOTICE TO DO THESE LITTLE PAGES IN YOUR BOOKS!! GRRR...
WHAT THE HELL IS GOING ON?
BUT, I TOLD YOU ABOUT THIS ONE A WHOLE WEEK IN ADVANCE!
DAMN YOU AND.. WAIT... YOU DID? OH... SHIT... YEAH.
GASP!
YOU BASTARD!! I'M GONNA KILL YOU! KILL YOU!!
BUT... I AM... I..UH..
THE SCALE HERE IS TRUE.
UP HIS ASS, DOOMBEES!!
YAY!
OH, NO!
END

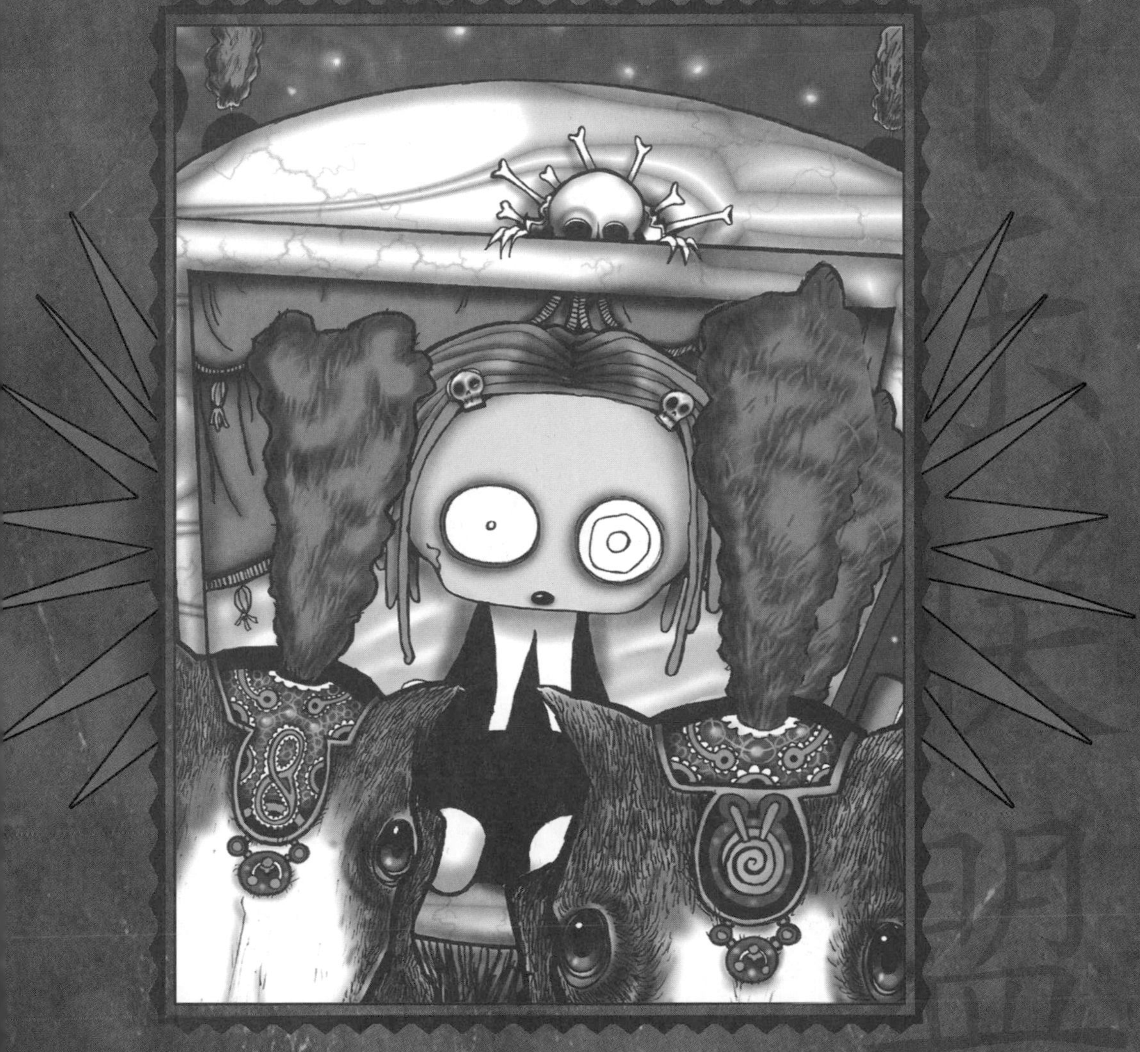

bonus section

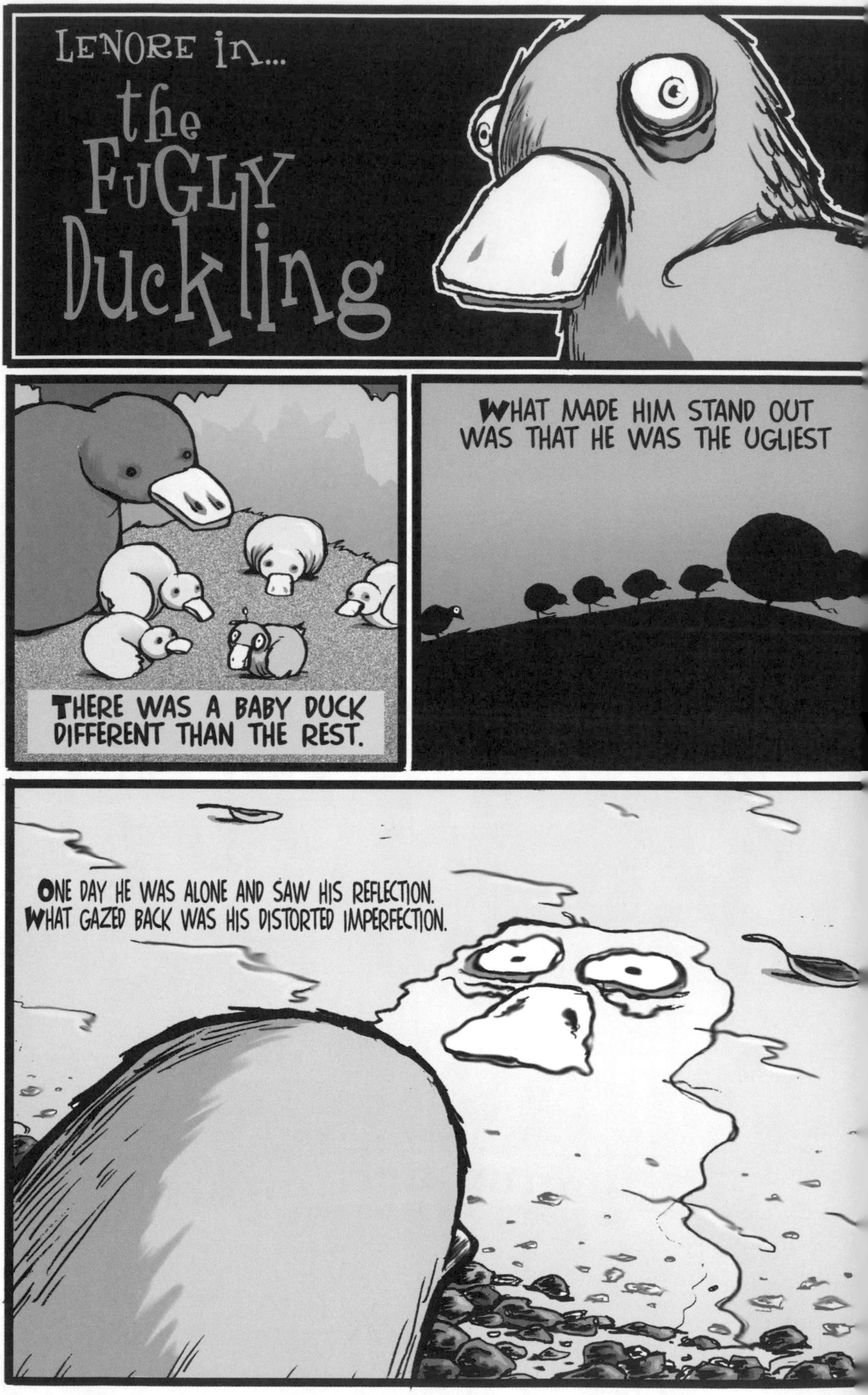
LENORE in...
the FUGLY Duckling
THERE WAS A BABY DUCK DIFFERENT THAN THE REST.
WHAT MADE HIM STAND OUT WAS THAT HE WAS THE UGLIEST
ONE DAY HE WAS ALONE AND SAW HIS REFLECTION. WHAT GAZED BACK WAS HIS DISTORTED IMPERFECTION.

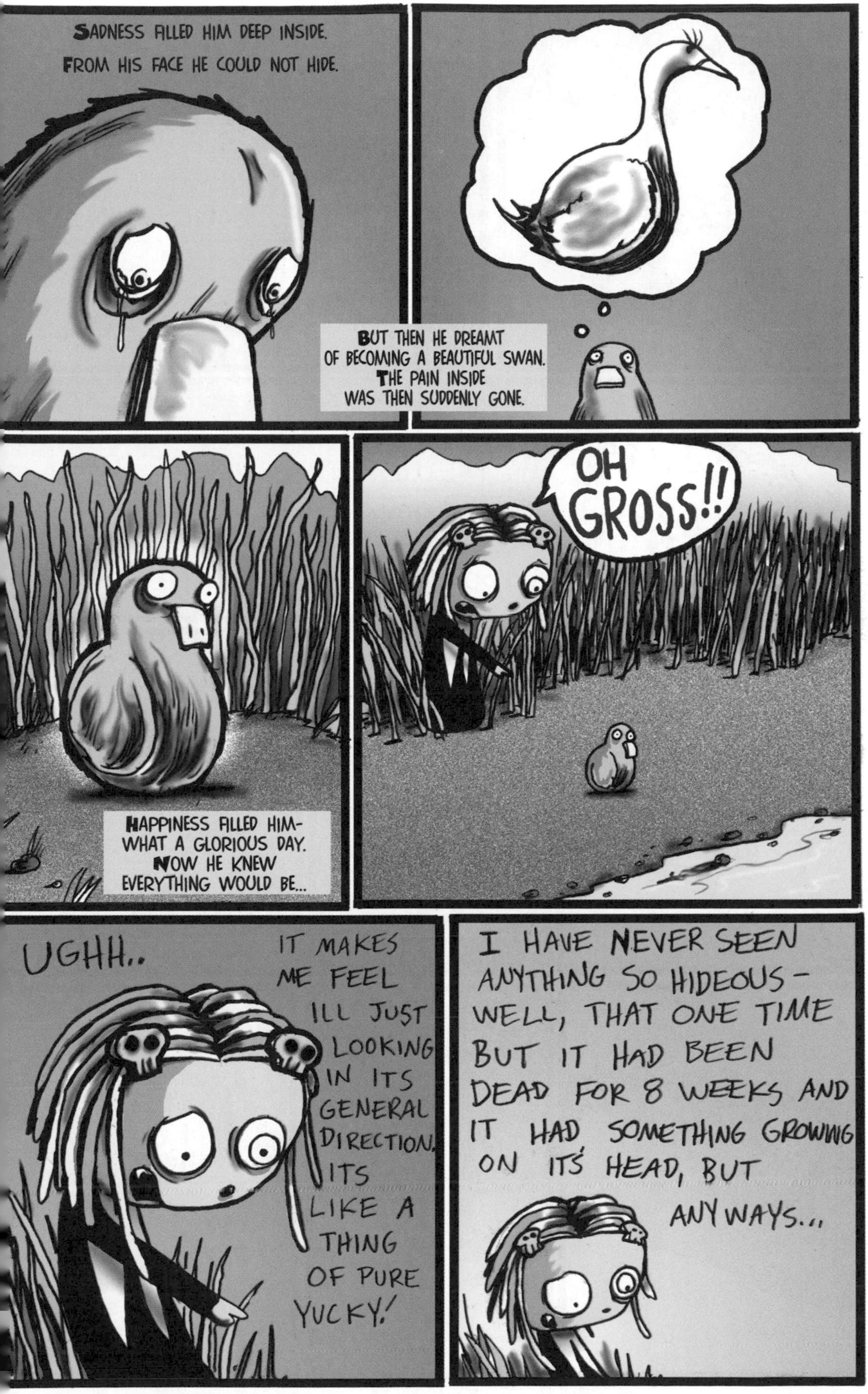
SADNESS FILLED HIM DEEP INSIDE.
FROM HIS FACE HE COULD NOT HIDE.
BUT THEN HE DREAMT OF BECOMING A BEAUTIFUL SWAN. THE PAIN INSIDE WAS THEN SUDDENLY GONE.
HAPPINESS FILLED HIM- WHAT A GLORIOUS DAY. NOW HE KNEW EVERYTHING WOULD BE...
OH GROSS!!
UGHH..
IT MAKES ME FEEL ILL JUST LOOKING IN ITS GENERAL DIRECTION. ITS LIKE A THING OF PURE YUCKY!
I HAVE NEVER SEEN ANYTHING SO HIDEOUS - WELL, THAT ONE TIME BUT IT HAD BEEN DEAD FOR 8 WEEKS AND IT HAD SOMETHING GROWING ON IT'S HEAD, BUT ANYWAYS...

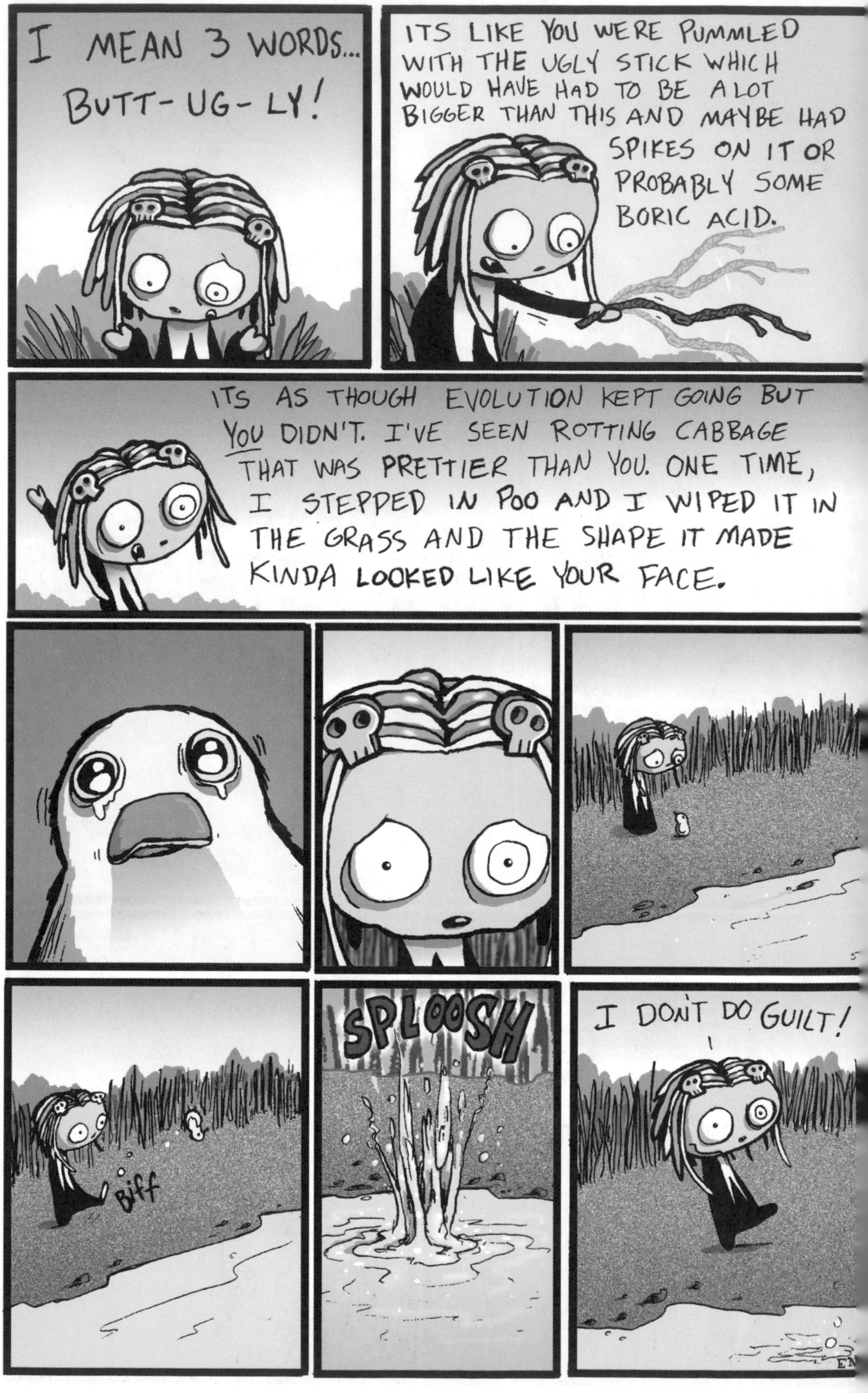
I MEAN 3 WORDS...
BUTT-UG-LY!
ITS LIKE YOU WERE PUMMLED WITH THE UGLY STICK WHICH WOULD HAVE HAD TO BE A LOT BIGGER THAN THIS AND MAYBE HAD SPIKES ON IT OR PROBABLY SOME BORIC ACID.
ITS AS THOUGH EVOLUTION KEPT GOING BUT YOU DIDN'T. I'VE SEEN ROTTING CABBAGE THAT WAS PRETTIER THAN YOU. ONE TIME, I STEPPED IN POO AND I WIPED IT IN THE GRASS AND THE SHAPE IT MADE KINDA LOOKED LIKE YOUR FACE.
Biff
SPLOOSH
I DON'T DO GUILT!

LENORE IN...
There Was An OLD WOMAN

THEEEEEEEEEEEEEEEEE....

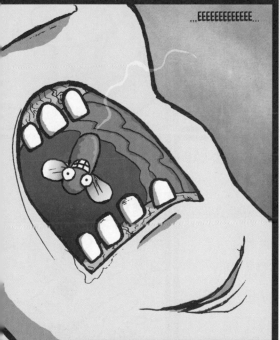

...EEEEEEEEEEEEE...

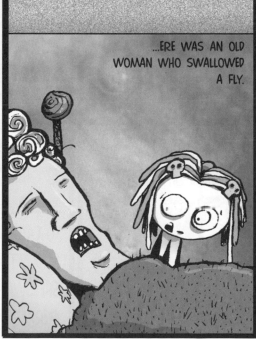

...ERE WAS AN OLD WOMAN WHO SWALLOWED A FLY.

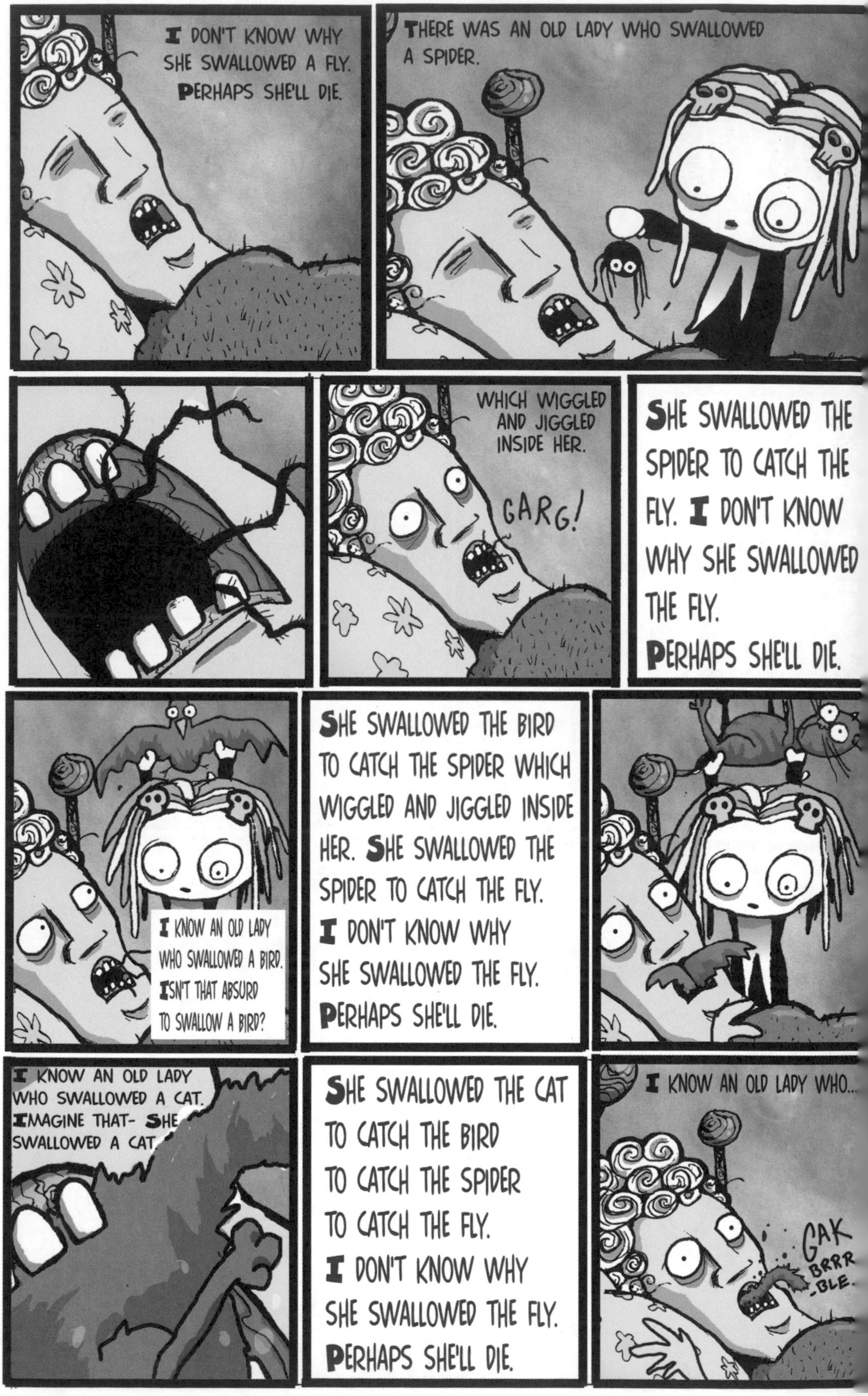
I DON'T KNOW WHY SHE SWALLOWED A FLY. PERHAPS SHE'LL DIE.
THERE WAS AN OLD LADY WHO SWALLOWED A SPIDER.
WHICH WIGGLED AND JIGGLED INSIDE HER.
GARG!
SHE SWALLOWED THE SPIDER TO CATCH THE FLY. I DON'T KNOW WHY SHE SWALLOWED THE FLY. PERHAPS SHE'LL DIE.
I KNOW AN OLD LADY WHO SWALLOWED A BIRD. ISN'T THAT ABSURD TO SWALLOW A BIRD?
SHE SWALLOWED THE BIRD TO CATCH THE SPIDER WHICH WIGGLED AND JIGGLED INSIDE HER. SHE SWALLOWED THE SPIDER TO CATCH THE FLY. I DON'T KNOW WHY SHE SWALLOWED THE FLY. PERHAPS SHE'LL DIE.
I KNOW AN OLD LADY WHO SWALLOWED A CAT. IMAGINE THAT- SHE SWALLOWED A CAT.
SHE SWALLOWED THE CAT TO CATCH THE BIRD TO CATCH THE SPIDER TO CATCH THE FLY. I DON'T KNOW WHY SHE SWALLOWED THE FLY. PERHAPS SHE'LL DIE.
I KNOW AN OLD LADY WHO...
GAK
BRRR
_BLE.

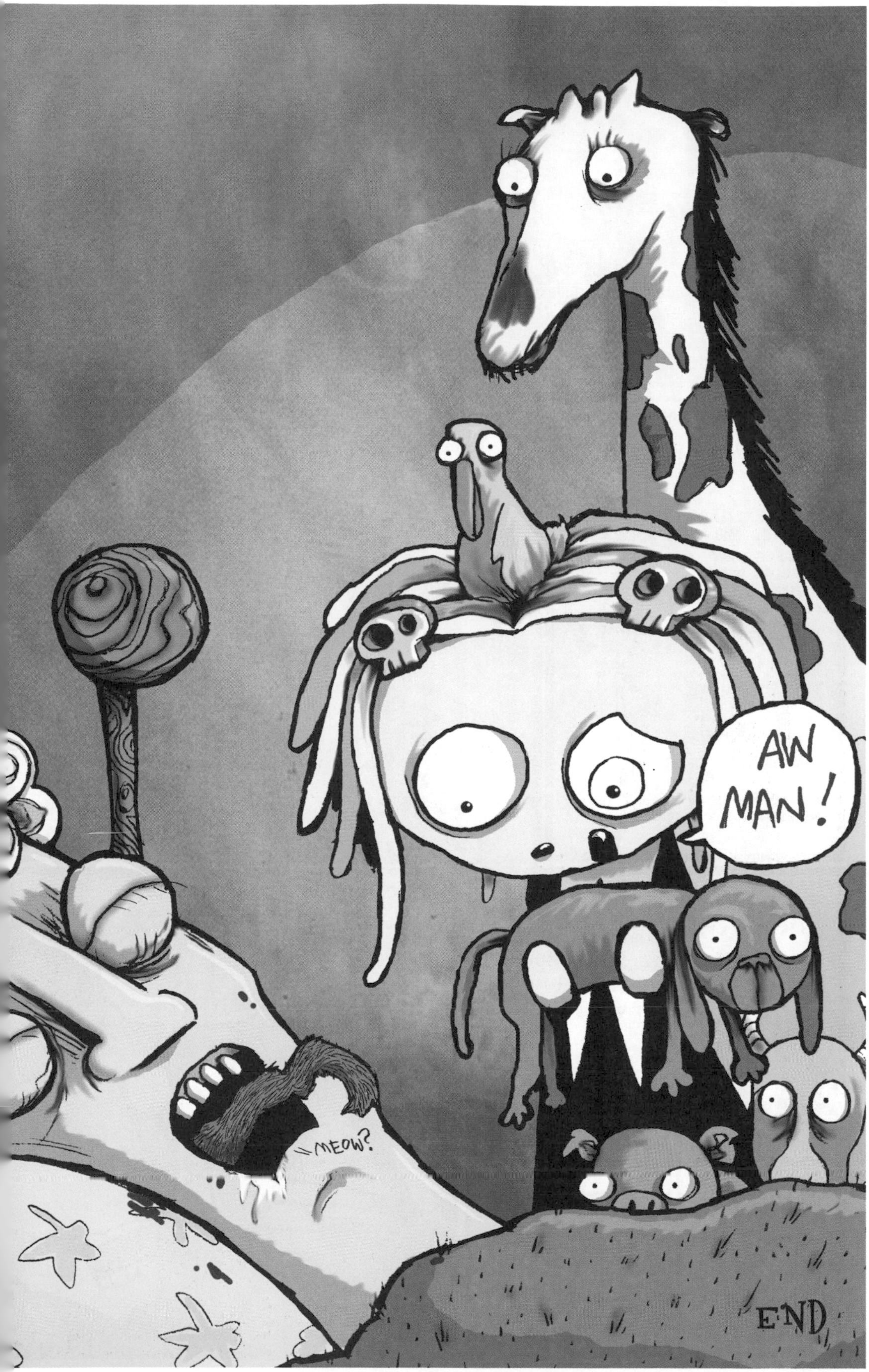
AW MAN!
MEOW?
END

Things Involving Me

MY WIFE AND I WENT TO A REPTILE STORE TO JUST LOOK AROUND WHEN SOMETHING CAUGHT MY EYE...

OOOO.... SNAKES.

LISA DOESN'T LIKE SNAKES, SO I DID WHAT ANY TOUGH GUY WOULD DO...

OH PLEEEEEASE! I NEED THAT SNAKE. PRETTY PLEASE? HUH? HAVE I TOLD YOU TODAY HOW MUCH I LOVE YOU? HAVE YOU BEEN DIETING? YOUR BUTT LOOKS SMALLER.

SO, I GOT A SNAKE. THE GUY WHO WORKED THERE PUT HIM IN A LITTLE SACK.

HEH... SNAKE.

WE'RE DRIVING HOME AND THE SNAKE IN THE BAG ON MY LAP STARTS GOING CRAZY.

HEY, STOP SQUIRMING AROUND DOWN THERE. I'LL TAKE YOU OUT AND PLAY WITH YOU WHEN WE GET HOME. MAN, THIS THING IS SO STRONG AND HARD TO HOLD ON TO.

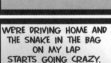

I HOPE IT DOESN'T RIP THROUGH THE SACK!

UH ROMAN...

UNFORTUNATELY, THE PEOPLE THAT PULLED UP NEXT TO US DID NOT KNOW THERE WAS A SNAKE.

AWW... WOOK AT IT WIGGLE!

THOSE PEOPLE DROVE AWAY SO FAST.